P9-ECY-980

The American Novel
Through Henry James

GOLDENTREE BIBLIOGRAPHIES
In Language and Literature
under the series editorship of
O. B. Hardison, Jr.

The American Novel Through Henry James

SECOND EDITION

compiled by

C. Hugh Holman

The University of North Carolina

with the assistance of
Janis Richardi

AHM Publishing Corporation
Arlington Heights, Illinois 60004

Copyright © 1979

AHM PUBLISHING CORPORATION

All rights reserved

This book, or parts thereof, must not be
used or reproduced in any manner without
written permission. For information ad-
dress the publisher, AHM PUBLISHING
CORPORATION, 3110 North Arlington
Heights Road, Arlington Heights, Illinois
60004.

ISBN: 0-88295-577-2, paper
ISBN: 0-88295-576-4, cloth

Library of Congress Card Number:
79-84212

CAMROSE LUTHERAN COLLEGE
Library

REF.
Z
1231
.F4
H64/24,800
1979

PRINTED IN THE UNITED STATES OF AMERICA
729

Contents

CONTENTS

CONTENTS

CONTENTS

Preface

The following bibliography is intended for graduate and advanced undergraduate students in courses on the American novel and related subjects who desire a convenient guide to scholarship in the field. The listings are necessarily selective, but a serious effort has been made to provide ample coverage of the major works and topics, with emphasis on work published in the twentieth century.

In order to keep this bibliography to a practical size, it has been necessary to omit a number of kinds of references: unpublished dissertations, literary histories (except for a very few), most bibliographies of bibliography, short notes and explications (except in instances where they contain important data), and older biographical studies that have been superseded by later work.

In general the compiler has attempted to steer a middle course between the brief list of references included in the average textbook and the long, professional bibliography in which significant items are often lost in the sheer number of references given. This bibliography is designed to aid the student in his efforts to survey a topic, write reports and term papers, prepare for examinations, and do independent study.

Attention is called to the following features intended to enhance the book's utility:

1. All items are numbered consecutively throughout the book. Thus, each title can be readily identified by its own number, both in the cross-reference and in the index.
2. Wide margins on each page provide for listing the call numbers of frequently used references.
3. Extra space at the bottom of each page can be used for additional references and pertinent notes.
4. More space is provided for personal annotations and comments on the blank pages headed "NOTES" following the index.
5. Works that are available in paperback editions are indicated by a dagger (†).

Abbreviations identifying journals follow the forms given in the "Master List and Table of Abbreviations" of the June, 1975, *PMLA* bibliography.

This revision represents a complete re-examination of the original edition. A number of items in that edition which have lost much of their usefulness have been dropped. Other items have been re-assessed in terms of their comparative value when considered against the enormous amount of material on the nineteenth century American novel published between 1966 and 1976 and the desire to hold the bibliography to a practical and manageable size. The bibliography proper contains entries for material published through 1974. The supplement, which has the same arrangement as the bibliography proper, adds material published through most of 1976.

The compiler of this bibliography would like to acknowledge the indispensable, intelligent, and enthusiastic assistance given him by Janis Richardi in the preparation of this revision. Miss Richardi pursued the tasks of checking references, preparing manuscript, and making indexes with commitment, enthusiasm, and fine good humor, and the compiler is deeply in her debt, a debt inadequately discharged by the notice of assistance on the title page. The compiler remains, however, responsible for all decisions regarding the inclusion and exclusion of items and, of course, for all errors of fact or judgment.

C. Hugh Holman

Abbreviations

Symbols for journals, reviews, and quarterlies follow the standard forms used in the PMLA *bibliographies.*

ABC	American Book Collector
AH	American Heritage
AI	American Imago
AL	American Literature
AlaR	Alabama Review
ALR	American Literary Realism, 1870–1910
AmerS	American Studies
AQ	American Quarterly
AR	Antioch Review
Archiv	Archiv für das Studium der Neueren Sprachen und Literaturen
ArlQ	Arlington Quarterly
ArQ	Arizona Quarterly
AS	American Speech
ASch	American Scholar
Atl	Atlantic Monthly
ATQ	American Transcendental Quarterly
BB	Bulletin of Bibliography
BNYPL	Bulletin of the New York Public Library
BPLQ	Boston Public Library Quarterly
BRMMLA	Bulletin of the Rocky Mountain Modern Language Association
BSUF	Ball State University Forum
BuR	Bucknell Review
BUSE	Boston University Studies in English
CE	College English
CEA	CEA Critic
CentR	The Centennial Review (Michigan State University) Christian Scholar
CHSQ	California Historical Society Quarterly (Now California History Quarterly: Journal of the California Historical Society)
CimR	Cimarron Review (Oklahoma State University)
CL	Comparative Literature
CLAJ	College Language Association Journal (Morgan State College, Baltimore)
ClioW	An Interdisciplinary Journal of Literature, History, and the Philosophy of History (University of Wisconsin)
CLQ	Colby Library Quarterly
CLS	Comparative Literature Studies (University of Illinois)

ABBREVIATIONS

CollL	College Literature
ColQ	Colorado Quarterly
ConL	Contemporary Literature
ConnR	Connecticut Review
CR	The Critical Review (Melbourne; Sydney)
CRCL	Canadian Review of Comparative Literature
CRevAS	Canadian Review of American Studies
CritI	Critical Inquiry: A Voice for Reasoned Inquiry into Significant Creations of the Human Spirit
Criticism	(Wayne State)
CritQ	Critical Quarterly
CUF	Columbia University Forum
DeltaES	(Montpellier)
DR	Dalhousie Review
EA	Études Anglaises
EAL	Early American Literature
ECS	Eighteenth-Century Studies (University of California, Davis)
EIC	Essays in Criticism (Oxford)
EIHC	Essex Institute Historical Collections
EJ	English Journal
ELH	Journal of English Literary History
ELN	English Language Notes (University of Colorado)
ELT	English Literature in Transition (1880–1920)
ELUD	Essays in Literature (University of Denver)
ELWIU	Essays in Literature (Western Illinois University)
EngR	English Record
ES	English Studies
ESA	English Studies in Africa (Johannesburg)
ESQ	Emerson Society Quarterly
EvQ	Evergreen Quarterly
Folklore	(London)
ForumH	Forum (Houston)
GaR	Georgia Review
GyS	Gypsy Scholar
HLB	Harvard Library Bulletin
HLQ	Huntington Library Quarterly
HR	Hudson Review
HSL	Hartford Studies in Literature
IASOP	Institute of African Studies, Occasional Publishings (Ibadan)
IMH	Indiana Magazine of History
JA	Jahrbuch für Amerikastudien
JAF	Journal of American Folklore
JAmS	Journal of American Studies
JEGP	Journal of English and Germanic Philology
JGE	Journal of General Education
JML	Journal of Modern Literature
JNH	Journal of Negro History
JNT	Journal of Narrative Technique
JPC	Journal of Popular Culture (Bowling Green University)

JQ	Journalism Quarterly
JRUL	Journal of the Rutgers University Library
JSH	Journal of Southern History
KAL	Kyushu American Literature (Fukuoka, Japan)
KanQ	Kansas Quarterly (formerly *KM*)
KFQ	Keystone Folklore Quarterly
KM	Kansas Magazine
KR	Kenyon Review
KyR	Kentucky Review (University of Kentucky)
L&P	Literature and Psychology (Fairleigh Dickinson University)
Lang&L	Language and Literature
Lang&S	Language and Style
LaS	Louisiana Studies
LC	Library Chronicle (University of Pennsylvania)
LCrit	Literary Criterion (University of Mysore, India)
LFQ	Literature/Film Quarterly
LHR	Lock Haven Review
LitR	Literary Review (Fairleigh Dickinson University)
LMonog	Literary Monographs
MarkhamR	Markham Review
MD	Modern Drama
MFS	Modern Fiction Studies
MH	Minnesota History
MHM	Maryland Historical Magazine
MichA	Michigan Academician (supersedes PMASAL)
MinnR	Minnesota Review
MissQ	Mississippi Quarterly
MLN	Modern Language Notes
MLQ	Modern Language Quarterly
MLS	Modern Language Studies
MP	Modern Philology
MQ	Midwest Quarterly (Pittsburg, Kansas)
MQR	Michigan Quarterly Review
MR	Massachusetts Review (University of Massachusetts)
MSE	Massachusetts Studies in English
MSpr	Moderna Sprak (Stockholm)
MTJ	Mark Twain Journal
MVHR	Mississippi Valley Historical Review
MWF	Midwest Folklore
NALF	Negro American Literature Forum
NCF	Nineteenth-Century Fiction
NConL	Notes on Contemporary Literature
NDQ	North Dakota Quarterly
NEQ	New England Quarterly
NHJ	Nathaniel Hawthorne Journal
NLauR	New Laurel Review (The Pennington School, Pennington, New Jersey)
NM	Neuphilologische Mitteilungen
NMQ	New Mexico Quarterly

NOQ	Northwest Ohio Quarterly
NR	New Republic
NS	Die Neueren Sprachen
NY	New Yorker
NYFQ	New York Folklore Quarterly
NYH	New York History
OR	Ohio Review
PBA	Proceedings of the British Academy
PBSA	Papers of the Bibliographical Society of America
PCP	Pacific Coast Philology
Per	Perspective
Person	The Personalist
PhR	Philosophical Review
PLL	Papers on Language and Literature
PMLA	Publications of the Modern Language Association of America
PQ	Philological Quarterly (Iowa City)
PR	Partisan Review
PrS	Prairie Schooner
PsyR	Psychoanalytical Review
PW	Publishers Weekly
QQ	Queen's Quarterly
RALS	Resources for American Literary Studies
ReAL	Re: Arts and Letters
REL	Review of English Literature (Leeds)
RIP	Revue Internationale de Philosophie (Bruxelles)
RLC	Revue de Littérature Comparée
RMS	Renaissance & Modern Studies (University of Nottingham)
RS	Research Studies (Washington State University)
RUO	Revue de l'Université d'Ottawa
RUS	Rice University Studies
SA	Studi Americani (Rome)
SAB	South Atlantic Bulletin
SAF	Studies in American Fiction
SAQ	South Atlantic Quarterly
SB	Studies in Bibliography: Papers of the Bibliographical Society of the University of Virginia
SCB	South Central Bulletin
SCR	South Carolina Review
SDR	South Dakota Review
SEL	Studies in English Literature, 1500–1900
SELit	Studies in English Literature (English Literary Society of Japan)
SFQ	Southern Folklore Quarterly
SHR	Southern Humanities Review
SIR	Studies in Romanticism (Boston University)
SLitI	Studies in the Literary Imagination (Georgia State College)
SLJ	Southern Literary Journal
SNNTS	Studies in the Novel (North Texas State University)
SoQ	The Southern Quarterly (University of Southern Mississippi)

ABBREVIATIONS

SoR	Southern Review (Louisiana State University)
SP	Studies in Philology
SR	Sewanee Review
SRAZ	Studia Romanica et Anglica Zagrabiensia
SRL	Saturday Review of Literature
SSF	Studies in Short Fiction (Newberry College, South Carolina)
SWF	Southwest Review
TCL	Twentieth-Century Literature
TexSE	Texas Studies in English
TriQ	Tri-Quarterly (Evanston, Illinois)
TSE	Tulane Studies in English
TSL	Tennessee Studies in Literature
TSLL	Texas Studies in Literature and Language
TWA	Transactions of the Wisconsin Academy of Sciences, Arts, and Letters
UKCR	University of Kansas City Review
UMSE	University of Mississippi Studies in English
UR	University Review (Kansas City, Missouri)
UTQ	University of Toronto Quarterly
VC	Virginia Cavalcade
VMHB	Virginia Magazine of History and Biography
VQR	Virginia Quarterly Review
WAL	Western American Literature
WGCR	West Georgia College Review
WHR	Western Humanities Review
WMH	Wisconsin Magazine of History
WMQ	William and Mary Quarterly
WR	Western Review
WVUPP	West Virginia University Philological Papers
WWR	Walt Whitman Review
XUS	Xavier University Studies
YR	Yale Review
YULG	Yale University Library Gazette
ZAA	Zeitschrift für Anglistik und Amerikanistik (East Berlin)

NOTE: The publisher and compiler invite suggestions for additions to future editions of this bibliography.

Bibliographies

1 *American Literary Scholarship:* An Annual/1963. Durham, N.C.: Duke Univ. Press, 1965, and annually since. [Each volume has essays by various authors on individual authors and topics, including Hawthorne, Melville, Twain, James, 19th Century Fiction, and Fiction: 1900–1930.]†

2 *American Literature.* Periodical, published quarterly since 1929. Durham, N.C.: Duke Univ. Press. [Each issue contains "Articles on American Literature Appearing in Current Periodicals," prepared by the Bibliography Committee of the American Literature Section of the Modern Language Association.]

3 BLANCK, Jacob. *Bibliography of American Literature.* 10 vols. New Haven: Yale Univ. Press, 1955–, [6 vols. published; through "Parsons."]

4 BRYER, Jackson R., ed. *Sixteen Modern American Authors: A Survey of Research and Criticism.* Durham, N.C.: Duke Univ. Press, 1973.†

5 COAN, Otis W., and LILLARD, Richard G. *America in Fiction: An Annotated List of Novels That Interpret Aspects of Life in the United States.* 5th ed. Palo Alto: Pacific Books, 1967.

6 DOBIE, J. Frank. *Guide to Life and Literature of the Southwest.* Rev. ed. Dallas: So. Methodist Univ. Press, 1952.†

7 EICHELBERGER, Clayton L. *A Guide to Critical Reviews of United States Fiction.* Scarecrow Press, 1971.

8 GERSTENBERGER, Donna, and HENDRICK, George. *The American Novel 1789–1959: A Checklist of Twentieth-Century Criticism.* Denver: Alan Swallow, 1961.†

9 GERSTENBERGER, Donna, and HENDRICK, George. *The American Novel 1960–1968: A Checklist of Twentieth-Century Criticism.* Vol. II. Denver: Alan Swallow, 1970.†

10 GOHDES, Clarence. *Bibliographical Guide to the Study of the Literature of the U.S.A.* 2d ed. Durham, N.C.: Duke Univ. Press, 1964.

11 GOHDES, Clarence. *Literature and Theater in the States and Regions of the U.S.A.: An Historical Bibliography.* Durham, N.C.: Duke Univ. Press, 1967.

12 HAGEN, Ordean A. *Who Done It? An Encyclopedic Guide to Detective, Mystery, and Suspense Fiction.* New York: Bowker, 1969.

13 JONES, Howard Mumford, and LUDWIG, Richard M. *Guide to American Literature and Its Backgrounds Since 1890.* 4th ed. Cambridge: Harvard Univ. Press, 1972.†

14 LEARY, Lewis G. *Articles on American Literature 1900–1950.* Durham, N.C.: Duke Univ. Press, 1954.

15 LEARY, Lewis G. *Articles on American Literature 1950–1967.* Durham, N.C.: Duke Univ. Press, 1970.

16 *MLA International Bibliography,* under various eds., published annually as a supplement to *PMLA.* [Each issue lists scholarly and critical works of the preceding year.]

1

17 NILON, Charles H. *Bibliography of Bibliographies in American Literature.* New York: Bowker, 1971.

18 SPILLER, Robert E.; THORP, Willard; JOHNSON, Thomas H.; CANBY, Henry S.; and LUDWIG, Richard M.; eds. *Literary History of the United States: Bibliography.* 4th ed. New York: Macmillan, 1974. [Indispensable.]

19 VANDERHOOF, Jack. *A Bibliography of Novels Related to American Frontier and Colonial History.* Troy, N.Y.: Whitston, 1971.

20 WEGELIN, Oscar. *Early American Fiction, 1774–1830: A Compilation of the Titles of Works of Fiction.* Rev. ed. New York: Peter Smith, 1929.

21 WHITEMAN, Maxwell. *A Century of Fiction by American Negroes, 1853–1952: A Descriptive Bibliography.* Philadelphia: [the author], 1955.

22 WOODRESS, James, ed. *Eight American Authors: A Review of Research and Criticism.* Rev. ed. Durham, N.C.: Duke Univ. Press, 1972. [Includes Poe, Hawthorne, Melville, Twain, and James.]†

23 WRIGHT, Lyle H. *American Fiction, 1774–1850: A Contribution Toward a Bibliography.* 2d rev. ed. San Marino, Calif.: Huntington Library, 1969.

24 WRIGHT, Lyle H. *American Fiction, 1851–1875: A Contribution Toward a Bibliography.* San Marino, Calif.: Huntington Library, 1965.

25 WRIGHT, Lyle H. *American Fiction, 1876–1900: A Contribution Toward a Bibliography.* San Marino, Calif.: Huntington Library, 1966.

Reference Works

26 BRADBURY, Malcolm; MOTTRAM, Eric; and FRANCO, Jean. *Penguin Companion to USA and Latin American Literature.* New York: McGraw-Hill, 1971.†

27 BURKE, W. I., and HOWE, Will D. *American Books and Authors: 1640 to the Present Day [1971].* 3d rev. ed. by Irving and Anne Weiss. New York: Crown, 1972.

28 *Dictionary of American Biography.* Ed. Allen Jackson, Dumas Malone, and others. 20 vols. New York: Charles Scribner's Sons. 1928–1937, 1946, 1958, 1973. [Brief, accurate biographies of most deceased American novelists. Includes index, plus 3 supplements.]

29 HART, James D. *The Oxford Companion to American Literature.* 4th ed. New York: Oxford Univ. Press, 1965.

30 HERZBERG, Max, Jr., ed. *The Reader's Encyclopedia of American Literature.* New York: Crowell, 1962.

31 HOLMAN, C. Hugh. *A Handbook to Literature.* 3d ed. based on the original by W. F. Thrall and Addison Hibbard. New York and Indianapolis: The Odyssey Press, 1972. 4th ed. forthcoming. [The most comprehensive of the compact general literary handbooks.]†

32 KUNITZ, Stanley J., and HAYCRAFT, Howard, eds. *American Authors, 1600–1900.* New York: H. W. Wilson Co., 1942. [Useful short sketches.]

33 MAGILL, Frank N., ed. *Masterplots: American Fiction Series.* New York: Salem Press, 1964.

American Literary History

34 BLAIR, Walter; HORNBERGER, Theodore; and STEWART, Randall. *American Literature: A Brief History.* Chicago: Scott, Foresman, 1973.

35 BROOKS, Van Wyck. *Makers and Finders: A History of the Writers in America, 1800–1915.* New York: E. P. Dutton Co., 1936–1952. [Detailed treatments of most novelists and practitioners of other genres with emphasis on their times and professional careers. Includes:
The Flowering of New England 1815–1865 (1936).†
New England: Indian Summer, 1865–1915 (1940).†
The World of Washington Irving (1944).
The Times of Melville and Whitman (1947).
The Confident Years: 1885–1915 (1952).]

36 COMMAGER, Henry Steele. *The American Mind: An Interpretation of American Thought and Character Since the 1880s.* New Haven: Yale Univ. Press, 1950.†

37 CUNLIFFE, Marcus. *The Literature of the United States.* Rev. ed. Penguin, 1967. [British view.]†

38 HORTON, Rod W., and EDWARDS, Herbert W. *Backgrounds of American Literary Thought.* 3d ed. New York: Appleton-Century-Crofts, 1974.†

39 HOWARD, Leon. *Literature and the American Tradition.* Garden City, New York: Doubleday & Co., 1960.†

40 JONES, Howard Mumford. *O Strange New World: American Culture: The Formative Years.* New York: Viking, 1964.†

41 JONES, Howard Mumford. *The Age of Energy: Varieties of American Experience, 1865–1915.* New York: Viking, 1971.†

42 MARTIN, Jay. *Harvests of Change: American Literature 1865–1914.* New York: Prentice-Hall, 1967.†

43 MATTHIESSEN, F. O. *American Renaissance: Art and Expression in the Age of Emerson and Whitman.* New York: Oxford Univ. Press, 1941. [Excellent on Hawthorne, Melville, and James.]†

44 PARRINGTON, Vernon Louis. *Main Currents in American Thought.* 3 vols. New York: Harcourt, Brace and Co., 1927, 1930, 1955.†

45 QUINN, Arthur Hobson, ed. *The Literature of the American People.* New York: Appleton-Century-Crofts, 1951. [Sections by Kenneth B. Murdock, A. H. Quinn, Clarence Gohdes, and George F. Whicher.]

46 SPILLER, Robert E. *The Cycle of American Literature.* New York: Macmillan, 1955. [Good treatment of fiction in brief general history.]†

47 SPILLER, Robert E., et al., eds. *Literary History of the United States.* 4th ed. New York: Macmillan, 1974. [58 authors, many subjects.]

48 TAYLOR, Walter F. *The Story of American Letters.* Chicago: Henry Regnery Co., 1956. [A revision of *A History of American Letters* (1936).]

American Publishing and Bookselling

49 BARNES, James J. *Authors, Publishers and Politicians: The Quest for an Anglo-American Copyright Agreement 1815–1854.* London: Routledge & Kegan Paul, 1974.

50 BOYNTON, Henry W. *Annuals of American Bookselling: 1638–1850.* New York: John Wiley and Sons, 1932.

51 BRADSHER, Earl L. *Mathew Carey: Editor, Author, and Publisher.* New York: Columbia Univ. Press, 1912.

52 BURLINGAME, Roger. *Of Making Many Books: A Hundred Years of Reading, Writing and Publishing.* New York: Scribner's, 1946.

53 CHARVAT, William. *Literary Publishing in America: 1790–1850.* Philadelphia: Univ. of Pennsylvania Press, 1959.

54 CHARVAT, William. *The Profession of Authorship in America 1800–1870: The Papers of William Charvat.* Ed. Matthew J. Bruccoli. Columbus: Ohio State Univ. Press, 1968.

55 EXMAN, Eugene. *The Brothers Harper: A Unique Publishing Partnership and Its Impact on the Cultural Life of America From 1817 to 1853.* New York: Harper & Row, 1965.

56 EXMAN, Eugene. *The House of Harper: One Hundred and Fifty Years of Publishing.* New York: Harper, 1967.

57 HACKETT, Alice P. *Seventy Years of Best Sellers, 1895–1965.* New York: R. R. Bowker, 1968.

58 HART, James D. *The Popular Book: A History of America's Literary Taste.* New York: Oxford Univ. Press, 1950.†

59 LEHMANN-HAUPT, Hellmut, et al. *The Book in America: A History of the Making and Selling of Books in the U.S.* 2d ed. New York: R. R. Bowker & Co., 1952.

60 MADISON, Charles A. *Book Publishing in America.* New York: McGraw-Hill, 1966.

61 MADISON, Charles A. *Irving to Irving: Author-Publisher Relations, 1800–1974.* New York: Bowker, 1974. [Includes Cooper, Hawthorne, James, Twain, and Wharton.]

62 MOTT, Frank Luther. *Golden Multitudes: The Story of Best Sellers in the United States.* New York: Macmillan, 1947.

63 PATTERSON, Lyman Ray. *Copyright in Historical Perspective.* Nashville: Vanderbilt Univ. Press, 1968.

64 SCHICK, Frank L. *The Paperbound Book in America: The History of Paperbacks and Their European Backgrounds.* New York: R. R. Bowker, 1958.

65 SHEEAN, Donald. *This Was Publishing: A Chronicle of the Book Trade in the Gilded Age.* Bloomington: Indiana Univ. Press, 1952.

66 SHOVE, Raymond H. *Cheap Book Production in the U. S., 1870–1891.* Urbana: Univ. of Illinois Press, 1937. [Various popular "series" and "libraries."]

67 TEBBEL, John. *A History of Book Publishing in the United States.* New York: Bowker. Vol. I (1630–1865), 1972. Vol. II (1865–1919), 1974.

68 Tichnor and Fields Firm. *The Cost Books of Tichnor and Fields.* New York: Bibliographical Society of America, 1949.

The Novel as a Form

69 BEACH, Joseph Warren. *The Twentieth Century Novel: Studies in Technique.* New York: Appleton-Century-Crofts, 1932.

70 BOOTH, Wayne. *The Rhetoric of Fiction.* Chicago: Univ. of Chicago Press, 1961.†

71 DEVOTO, Bernard. *The World of Fiction.* Boston: Houghton Mifflin Co., 1950.

72 FORSTER, E. M. *Aspects of the Novel.* New York: Harcourt, Brace and Co., 1927.†

73 FRYE, Northrop. "Rhetorical Criticism: Theory of Genres." *Anatomy of Criticism.* Princeton: Princeton Univ. Press, 1957, pp. 243–337.†

74 GOLDKNOPF, David. *The Life of the Novel.* Chicago: Univ. of Chicago Press, 1972.†

75 GROSSVOGEL, David I. *Limits of the Novel: Evolutions of a Form from Chaucer to Robbe-Grillet.* Ithaca: Cornell Univ. Press, 1968.†

76 HALPERIN, John, ed. *The Theory of the Novel: New Essays.* New York: Oxford Univ. Press, 1974.

77 HARVEY, W. J. *Character and the Novel.* Ithaca: Cornell Univ. Press, 1965.

78 KERMODE, Frank. *The Sense of An Ending: Studies in the Theory of Fiction.* New York: Oxford Univ. Press, 1967.†

79 LEVER, Katherine. *The Novel and the Reader.* New York: Appleton-Century-Crofts, n.d.†

80 LUBBOCK, Percy. *The Craft of Fiction.* New York: Charles Scribner's Sons, 1921.†

81 LUKÁCS, Georg. *The Historical Novel.* Trans. Hannah and Stanley Mitchell. New York: Beacon, 1965.†

82 LUKÁCS, Georg. *Realism in Our Time: Literature and the Class Struggle.* Trans. John and Necke Mauder. "World Perspectives, Vol. XXXIII." New York: Harper & Row, 1964. [Marxist criticism, chiefly of fiction—of high order.]†

83 LUKÁCS, Georg. *The Theory of the Novel: A Historico-Philosophical Essay on the Forms of Great Epic Literature.* Cambridge: M.I.T. Univ. Press, 1971.†

84 MUIR, Edwin. *The Structure of the Novel.* London: The Hogarth Press, 1928.†

85 NEMEROV, Howard. "Like Warp and Woof: Composition and Fate in the Short Novel." *Graduate Journal* (Univ. of Texas), V (1963), 375–391.

86 O'CONNOR, William Van, ed. *Forms of Modern Fiction.* Minneapolis: Univ. of Minnesota Press, 1948. [On novel as form—essays by various hands, including Schorer on "Technique as Discovery," Tate on "Techniques of Fiction," Trilling on "Manners, Morals, and the Novel."]†

87 RUBIN, Louis D., Jr. *The Teller in the Tale.* Seattle: Univ. of Washington Press, 1967.

88 SALE, Roger, ed. *Discussions of the Novel.* Boston: D. C. Heath, 1960.†

89 SCHOLES, Robert, ed. *Approaches to the Novel.* San Francisco: Chandler Publishing Co., 1961.†

90 SCHOLES, Robert, and KELLOGG, Robert. *The Nature of Narrative.* New York: Oxford Univ. Press, 1966. [A stimulating inquiry into the nature and qualities of narrative.]†

91 SCHOLES, Robert. *Structuralism in Literature.* New Haven: Yale Univ. Press, 1974.

92 STANZEL, Franz. *Narrative Situations in the Novel.* Trans. J. P. Pusack. Bloomington: Indiana Univ. Press, 1971.

93 STEVICK, Philip, comp. *The Theory of the Novel.* New York: Free Press, 1967.†

94 TOLIVER, Harold. *Animate Illusions: Explorations of Narrative Structure.* Lincoln: Univ. of Nebraska Press, 1974.

95 WARREN, Austin, and WELLEK, René. "The Nature and Modes of Fiction." *The Theory of Literature.* New York: Harcourt, Brace and Co., 1949.†

Histories of the American Novel

96 CHASE, Richard. *The American Novel and Its Tradition.* Garden City, N.Y.: Doubleday & Co., 1957. [Sees its "tradition" as that of the Romance.]†

97 COWIE, Alexander. *The Rise of the American Novel.* New York: American Book Co., 1948. [Detailed and scholarly treatment through James.]

98 QUINN, Arthur Hobson. *American Fiction: An Historical and Critical Survey.* New York: Appleton-Century-Crofts, 1936. [Includes short stories.]

99 SNELL, George J. *The Shapers of American Fiction, 1798–1947.* New York: E. P. Dutton & Co., 1947.

100 VAN DOREN, Carl. *The American Novel, 1789–1939.* New York: Macmillan, 1940.

101 WAGENKNECHT, Edward. *Calvalcade of the American Novel.* New York: Holt, 1952.

Special Studies of the American Novel

By Period

102 GEISMAR, Maxwell. *Rebels and Ancestors: The American Novel, 1890–1915.* Boston: Houghton Mifflin Co., 1953. [Norris, Crane, London, Glasgow, and Dreiser.]†

103 HARTWICK, Harry. *The Foreground of American Fiction.* New York: American Book Co., 1934. [Covers period 1890–1930.]

104 HIRSCH, David H. *Reality and Idea in the Early American Novel* [*SAmL* 9]. The Hague: Mouton, 1971.

105 KAZIN, Alfred. *On Native Grounds.* New York: Reynal and Hitchcock, 1942. [Prose writers, 1900–1940.]†

106 LOSHE, Lillie D. *The Early American Novel.* New York: Columbia Univ. Press, 1907. [1789–1830.]

107 MILLER, Perry. *The Raven and the Whale: The War of Words and Wits in the Era of Poe and Melville.* New York: Harcourt, Brace and Co., 1956.†

108 PETTER, Henri. *The Early American Novel.* Columbus: Ohio State Univ. Press, 1971. [To 1820.]

109 SCHNEIDER, Robert W. *Five Novelists of the Progressive Era.* New York: Columbia Univ. Press, 1965. [Howells, Crane, Dreiser, Norris, and Churchill.]

110 STAFFORD, John. *The Literary Criticism of "Young America": A Study in the Relationship of Politics and Literature, 1837–1850.* Berkeley: Univ. of California Press. 1952.

By Genre

The Sentimental–Domestic Novel

111 BROWN, Herbert Ross. *The Sentimental Novel in America 1789–1860.* Durham, N.C.: Duke Univ. Press, 1940.

112 PAPASHVILY, Helen Waite. *All the Happy Endings.* New York: Harpers, 1956.

113 WASSERSTROM, William. *Heiress of All the Ages: Sex and Sentiment in the Genteel Tradition.* Minneapolis: Univ. of Minnesota Press, 1959.

The Naturalistic Novel

114 ÅHNEBRINK, Lars. *The Beginnings of Naturalism in American Fiction: A Study of the Works of Hamlin Garland, Stephen Crane, and Frank Norris . . . 1891–1903.* New York: Russell & Russell, 1961. [Originally published in Uppsala, Sweden, in 1952.]

7

115 PIZER, Donald. *Realism and Naturalism in 19th Century American Literature.* Carbondale: So. Illinois Univ. Press, 1966. [Essays on Howells, Twain, James, Norris, and Dreiser.]

116 STONE, Edward, ed. *What Was Naturalism: Materials for an Answer.* New York: Appleton-Century-Crofts, 1959. [A "casebook" with essays by various hands and extracts from several novels.]†

117 WALCUTT, Charles Child. *American Literary Naturalism, A Divided Stream.* Minneapolis: Univ. of Minnesota Press, 1956. [Frederic, Garland, Crane, London, Norris, and Dreiser.]

The Popular Forms

118 ALDRISS, Brian. *Billion Year Spree: The True History of Science Fiction.* Garden City, N.Y.: Doubleday, 1973.†

119 AUSTIN, James C., and KOCH, Donald A., eds. *Popular Literature in America: A Symposium in Honor of Lyon N. Richardson.* Bowling Green, Ohio: Bowling Green Univ. Popular Press, 1972.

120 BAILEY, J. O. *Pilgrims Through Space and Time: Trends and Patterns in Scientific and Utopian Fiction.* New York: Argus Books, 1947.

121 BARZUN, Jacques, and TAYLOR, Wendell H. *A Catalogue of Crime.* New York: Harper & Row, 1974.

122 BODE, Carl. *Antebellum Culture.* Carbondale: So. Illinois Univ. Press, 1970.†

123 DAVENPORT, Basil, et al. *The Science Fiction Novel: Imagination and Social Criticism.* Chicago: Advent Publishers, 1959.†

124 DICK, Everett. *Tales of the Frontier: From Lewis and Clark to the Last Roundup.* Lincoln: Univ. of Nebraska Press, 1963.†

125 DICKINSON, A. T., Jr. *American Historical Fiction.* 3d ed. Metuchen, N.J.: Scarecrow, 1971.

126 FOLSOM, James K. *The American Western Novel.* New Haven: College & University Press, 1966.†

127 FRANKLIN, H. Bruce. *Future Perfect: American Science Fiction of the Nineteenth Century.* New York: Oxford Univ. Press, 1966.†

128 HAYCRAFT, Howard. *Murder for Pleasure: The Life and Times of the Detective Story.* New York: Appleton-Century-Crofts, 1941. [English and American, 1841–1940.]

129 LEISY, Ernest E. *The American Historical Novel.* Norman: Univ. of Oklahoma Press, 1950.

130 LIVELY, Robert A. *Fiction Fights the Civil War.* Chapel Hill: Univ. of North Carolina Press, 1957.

131 MURCH A. E. *The Development of the Detective Novel.* London: Peter Owen, 1958.

132 SYMONS, Julian. *Mortal Consequences: A History—from the Detective Story to the Crime Novel.* New York: Harper & Row, 1972.†

133 TINKER, E. L. *The Horsemen of the Americas and the Literature They Inspired.* Austin and London: Univ. of Texas Press, 1967.

The Realistic Novel

134 AUCHINCLOSS, Louis. *Reflections of a Jacobite.* Boston: Houghton Mifflin Co., 1961. [On the novel of manners.]

135 AUERBACH, Erich. *Mimesis: The Representation of Reality in Western Literature.* Trans. Willard Trask. Princeton: Princeton Univ. Press, 1953.†

136 BECKER, George J., ed. *Documents of Modern Literary Realism.* Princeton: Princeton Univ. Press, 1963.†

137 CADY, Edwin H. *The Light of Common Day: Realism in American Fiction.* Bloomington: Indiana Univ. Press, 1971.

138 CARTER, Everett. *Howells and the Age of Realism.* Philadelphia: Lippincott, 1954. [Analyzes characteristics of American realism in detail.]

139 EDEL, Leon. *The Psychological Novel.* London: Rupert Hart-Davis, 1955.†

140 FALK, Robert P. *The Victorian Mode in American Fiction, 1865–1885.* East Lansing: Michigan State Univ. Press, 1965. [James, Howells, De Forest, and Twain.]

141 KOLB, Harold H., Jr. *The Illusion of Life: American Realism as a Literary Form.* Charlottesville: Univ. Press of Virginia, 1969.

142 MILLGATE, Michael. *American Social Fiction: James to Cozzens.* New York: Barnes and Noble, 1964. [The Novel of Manners.]†

143 MIZENER, Arthur. *The Sense of Life in the Modern Novel.* Boston: Houghton Mifflin, 1964.

144 PIZER, Donald. *Realism and Naturalism in Nineteenth-Century American Literature.* Carbondale: So. Illinois Univ. Press, 1966.

145 WELLEK, René. "The Concept of Realism in Literary Scholarship." *Concepts of Criticism.* Ed. Stephen G. Nichols, Jr. New Haven: Yale Univ. Press, 1963, 222–255.†

The Social Novel

146 BLOTNER, Joseph L. *The Political Novel.* Garden City, N.Y.: Doubleday, 1955. [From 1852 to the present.]†

147 DIETRICHSON, Jan W. *The Image of Money in the American Novel of the Gilded Age.* Oslo: Universitetsforlaget; New York: Humanities, 1969.

148 MILNE, Gordon. *The American Political Novel.* Norman: Univ. of Oklahoma Press, 1966.†

149 PARRINGTON, Vernon L., Jr. *American Dreams: A Study of American Utopias.* Providence: Brown Univ. Press, 1947.

150 RANSOM, Ellene. *Utopus Discovers America or Critical Realism in American Utopian Fiction, 1798–1900.* Nashville, Tenn.: Joint Univ. Libraries, 1947.

151 ROSE, Lisle A. *A Survey of American Economic Fiction, 1902–1909.* Chicago: Univ. of Chicago Libraries, 1958.

152 SPEARE, Morris E. *The Political Novel: Its Development in England and America.* New York: Oxford Univ. Press, 1924.

153 TAYLOR, Walter F. *The Economic Novel in America.* Chapel Hill, N.C.: Univ. of North Carolina Press, 1942. [Covers period from 1865–1900.]

By Theme and Subject

154 BARNETT, James H. *Divorce and the American Divorce Novel, 1858–1937.* Philadelphia: [The Author], 1939.

155 BEWLEY, Marius. *The Complex Fate: Hawthorne, Henry James and Some Other American Writers.* London: Chatto and Windus, 1952.

156 BEWLEY, Marius. *The Eccentric Design: Form in the Classic American Novel.* London: Chatto and Windus, 1959.†

157 BLAKE, Fay M. *The Strike in the American Novel.* Metuchen, N.J.: Scarecrow, 1972.

158 BLUEFARB, Sam. *The Escape Motif in the American Novel: Mark Twain to Richard Wright.* Columbus: Ohio State Univ. Press, 1972.

159 BONE, Robert A. *The Negro Novel in America.* Rev. ed. New Haven: Yale Univ. Press, 1965. [From 1853 to present.]†

160 BOWDEN, Edwin T. *The Dungeon of the Heart: Human Isolation and the American Novel.* New York: Macmillan, 1961.†

161 BROOKS, Van Wyck. *The Dream of Arcadia: American Writers and Artists in Italy.* New York: E. P. Dutton & Co., 1958.

162 CADY, Edwin H. *The Gentleman in America: A Literary Study in American Culture.* Syracuse, N.Y.: Syracuse Univ. Press, 1949.

163 DAVIS, David Brion. *Homicide in American Fiction, 1789–1860: A Study in Social Values.* Ithaca, N.Y.: Cornell Univ. Press, 1957.†

164 DENNY, Margaret, and GILMAN, William H., eds. *The American Writer and the European Tradition.* Minneapolis: Univ. of Minnesota Press, 1950.†

165 DUNLAP, George Arthur. *The City in the American Novel, 1789–1900: A Study of American Novels Portraying Contemporary Conditions in New York, Philadelphia, and Boston.* New York: Russell and Russell, 1965. [A reprint of a study originally published in 1934.]

166 EARNEST, Ernest. *The American Eve in Fact and Fiction, 1775–1914.* Urbana: Univ. of Illinois Press, 1975.

167 FEIDELSON, Charles, Jr. *Symbolism and American Literature.* Chicago: Univ. of Chicago Press, 1953. [Some emphasis on Hawthorne and Melville.]

168 FIEDLER, Leslie A. *Love and Death in the American Novel.* New York: Criterion Books, 1960.†

169 FREDERICK, John T. *The Darkened Sky: Nineteenth-Century American Novelists and Religion.* Notre Dame: Univ. of Notre Dame Press, 1969.

170 FUSSELL, Edwin S. *Frontier: American Literature and the American West.* Princeton: Princeton Univ. Press, 1965. [Cooper, Hawthorne, Poe, and Melville.]†

171 GAINES, Francis Pendleton. *The Southern Plantation: A Study in the Development and Accuracy of a Tradition.* New York: Columbia Univ. Press, 1924.

172 GARDINER, Harold C., S. J., ed. *American Classics Reconsidered: A Christian Appraisal.* New York: Scribner's, 1958. [Catholic interpretation.]

SPECIAL STUDIES OF THE AMERICAN NOVEL

173 GASTON, Edwin W., Jr. *The Early Novel of the Southwest 1819–1918.* Albuquerque: Univ. of New Mexico Press, 1961.

174 GELFANT, Blanche H. *The American City Novel.* Norman: Univ. Of Oklahoma Press, 1954. [Mostly recent but includes Dreiser and Wharton.]

175 GLOSTER, Hugh M. *Negro Voices in American Fiction.* Chapel Hill: Univ. of North Carolina Press, 1948.

176 HERRON, Ima Honaker. *The Small Town in American Literature.* Durham, N.C.: Duke Univ. Press, 1939.

177 HOFFMAN, Daniel G. *Form and Fable in American Fiction.* New York: Oxford Univ. Press 1961.† [Hawthorne, Melville, and Twain.]

178 HUBBELL, Jay B. *The South in American Literature, 1607–1900.* Durham, N.C.: Duke Univ. Press, 1954. [Very detailed to 1865.]

179 JONES, Howard Mumford. *Jeffersonianism and the American Novel.* Introduction by Martin S. Dvorkin. New York: Teachers College Press, 1966.†

180 KAUL, A. N. *The American Vision: Actual and Ideal Society in Nineteenth-Century Fiction.* New Haven: Yale Univ. Press, 1963. [Cooper, Hawthorne, Melville, and Twain.]†

181 KEISER, Albert. *The Indian in American Literature.* New York: Oxford Univ. Press, 1933.

182 KUHLMANN, Susan. *Knave, Fool, and Genius: The Confidence Man as He Appears in Nineteenth-Century American Fiction.* Chapel Hill: Univ. of North Carolina Press, 1973.

183 LAWRENCE, D. H. *Studies in Classic American Literature.* New York: Thomas Seltzer, 1923.†

184 LEVIN, Harry. *The Power of Blackness.* New York: Alfred A Knopf, 1958. [Hawthorne, Poe, and Melville.]†

185 LEWIS, Richard W. B. *The American Adam: Innocence, Tragedy, and Tradition in the Nineteenth Century.* Chicago: Univ. of Chicago Press, 1955.†

186 LOGGINS, Vernon. *The Negro Author: His Development in America.* New York: Columbia Univ. Press, 1931.

187 LYNN, Kenneth S. *The Dream of Success: A Study of the Modern American Imagination.* Boston: Little, Brown, 1955 [Deals with Dreiser, London, Norris, Herrick, and Alger among others.]

188 LYONS, John O. *The College Novel in America.* Carbondale: So. Illinois Univ. Press, 1962.

189 MCILWAINE, Shields. *The Southern Poor-White From Lubberland to Tobacco Road.* Norman: Univ. of Oklahoma Press, 1939.

190 MAXWELL, D. E. S. *American Fiction: The Intellectual Background.* New York: Columbia Univ. Press, 1963.

191 MAY, John R. *Toward a New Earth: Apocalypse in the American Novel.* South Bend: Univ. of Notre Dame Press. 1972.

192 MEYER, Roy W. *The Middle Western Farm Novel in the Twentieth Century.* Lincoln: Univ. of Nebraska Press, 1965. [Early sections have much on nineteenth century midwestern novelists.]†

193 MILLS, Nicolaus. *American and English Fiction in the Nineteenth Century: An Anti-Genre Critique and Comparison.* Bloomington: Indiana Univ. Press, 1973.

SPECIAL STUDIES OF THE AMERICAN NOVEL

194 MINTER, David L. *The Interpreted Design as a Structural Principle in American Prose.* New Haven: Yale Univ. Press, 1969.

195 NELSON, John H. *The Negro Character in American Literature.* Lawrence: Univ. of Kansas Press, 1926.

196 PEARCE, Roy Harvey. *Savagism and Civilization.* Baltimore: Johns Hopkins Press, 1967.

197 PORTE, Joel. *The Romance in America: Studies in Cooper, Poe, Hawthorne, Melville, and James.* Middletown, Conn.: Wesleyan Press, 1969.†

198 RIDEOUT, Walter B. *The Radical Novel in the United States, 1900–1954.* Cambridge: Harvard Univ. Press, 1956.†

199 ROURKE, Constance. *American Humor: A Study of the National Character.* New York: Harcourt, Brace and Co., 1931. [Incidental to novel but much on Twain and James.]†

200 RUBIN, Louis D., Jr., ed. *The Comic Imagination in American Literature.* New Brunswick, N.J.: Rutgers Univ. Press, 1973.

201 RUBIN, Louis D., Jr, and MOORE, John Rees, eds. *The Idea of an American Novel.* New York: Crowell, 1961. [Essays on "Americanism" in the novel, with special sections on Cooper, Hawthorne, Melville, Howells, James, Twain, Crane, Dreiser, and others.]

202 SMITH, Henry Nash. *Virgin Land: The American West as Symbol and Myth.* Cambridge: Harvard Univ. Press, 1950.†

203 SPENCER, Benjamin T. *The Quest for Nationality.* Syracuse, N.Y.: Syracuse Univ. Press, 1957. [To 1892.] Supplemented by Spencer, "Nationality During the Interregnum (1892–1912)," *AL*, XXXII (1961), 434–445.

204 SPINDLER, Russell S. *The Military Novel.* Madison, Wis.: U.S. Armed Forces Institute, 1964.

205 STEWART, Randall. *American Literature and Christian Doctrine.* Baton Rouge: Louisiana State Univ. Press, 1958. [Deals with Hawthorne, Melville, James, and Dreiser among others.]

206 TAYLOR, Gordon O. *The Passages of Thought: Psychological Representation in the American Novel 1870–1900.* New York: Oxford Univ. Press, 1969.

207 TUTTLETON, James W. *The Novel of Manners in America.* Chapel Hill: Univ. of North Carolina Press, 1972.†

208 WALCUTT, Charles C. *Man's Changing Mask: Modes and Methods of Characterization in Fiction.* Minneapolis: Univ. of Minnesota Press, 1966.†

209 WESTBROOK, Percy D. *Acres of Flint: Writers of Rural New England, 1870–1900.* Washington: Scarecrow Press, 1951.

210 WHITE, George L. *Scandinavian Themes in American Fiction.* Philadelphia: [the author], 1937.

211 WILLIAMS, Stanley T. *The Spanish Background of American Literature.* 2 vols. New Haven: Yale Univ. Press, 1955.

212 WRIGHT, Nathalia. *American Novelists in Italy: The Discoverers: Allston to James.* Philadelphia: Univ. of Pennsylvania Press, 1965. [Cooper, Stowe, Hawthorne, Howells, and James.]†

213 YELLIN, Jean F. *The Intricate Knot: Black Figures in American Literature 1776–1863.* New York: New York Univ. Press, 1972.†

Collections of Studies of the American Novel

214 AUCHINCLOSS, Louis. *Pioneers and Caretakers: A Study of Nine American Women Novelists.* Minneapolis: Univ. of Minnesota Press, 1965. [Sarah Orne Jewett, Edith Wharton, Ellen Glasgow, Willa Cather, and others.]

215 BROWNELL, William Crary. *American Prose Masters: Cooper, Hawthorne, Emerson, Poe, Lowell, Henry James.* Ed. H. M. Jones. Cambridge: Harvard Univ. Press, 1963.†

216 BRUCCOLI, Matthew J., ed. *The Chief Glory of Every People: Essays on Classic American Writers.* Carbondale and Edwardsville: So. Illinois Univ. Press, 1973.

217 ERSKINE, John. *Leading American Novelists.* New York: Holt, 1910. [Brown, Cooper, Simms, Hawthorne, Stowe, and Harte.]

218 FEIDELSON, Charles, Jr., and BRODTKORB, Paul, Jr., eds. *Interpretations of American Literature.* New York: Oxford Univ. Press, 1959. [Reprints critical essays from Poe to present.]†

219 FOSTER, Richard, ed. *Six American Novelists of the Nineteenth Century: An Introduction.* With introduction. Minneapolis: Univ. of Minnesota Press, 1968. [Reprints of UMPAW on Cooper, Hawthorne, Melville, Twain, Howells, and James.]

220 HOYT, Charles A., ed. *Minor American Novelists.* Carbondale: So. Illinois Univ. Press, 1971.

221 LITZ, A. Walton, ed. *Modern American Fiction: Essays in Criticism.* New York: Oxford Univ. Press, 1963. [Essays on Crane, Dreiser, Stein, and most contemporary novelists.]

222 MIZENER, Arthur. *Twelve Great American Novels.* New York: New American Library, 1967. [Includes Cooper's *Deerslayer,* Hawthorne's *Scarlet Letter,* Melville's *Moby Dick,* Twain's *Huckleberry Finn,* James's *Ambassadors,* and Wharton's *Age of Innocence.*]

223 MORGAN, H. Wayne. *American Writers in Rebellion from Twain to Dreiser.* New York: Hill and Wang, 1965. [Mark Twain, Frank Norris, Hamlin Garland, Theodore Dreiser, and W. D. Howells.]†

224 MORGAN, H. Wayne. *Writers in Transition.* New York: Hill and Wang, 1963. [Stephen Crane, Edith Wharton, Ellen Glasgow, Willa Cather, and others.]

225 O'CONNOR, William Van. *The Grotesque: An American Genre and Other Essays.* Carbondale: So. Illinois Univ. Press, 1962. [Hawthorne, Melville, Twain, James, and the Realistic Novel.]

226 SHAPIRO, Charles, ed. *Twelve Original Essays on Great American Novels.* Detroit: Wayne State Univ. Press, 1958. [Cooper, Hawthorne, Melville, Twain, Crane, James, Wharton, Dreiser, and others.]†

227 STEGNER, Wallace, ed. *The American Novel from James Fenimore Cooper to William Faulkner.* New York: Basic Books, 1965. [Essays on novels by Cooper, Hawthorne, Melville, DeForest, James, Twain, Howells, Crane, Norris, Dreiser, Wharton, London, Cather, and six post-World War I writers.]

228 WEGELIN, Christof, ed. *The American Novel: Criticism and Background Readings.* New York: Free Press, 1972. [Cooper, Hawthorne, Melville, Twain, Howells, Crane, Dreiser, James, and Wharton.]†

Major American Novelists

Although the entries have not been indicated, students working on any of the following figures should always consult Alexander Cowie, *The Rise of the American Novel* (**97**), Arthur Hobson Quinn, *American Fiction: An Historical and Critical Survey* (**98**), Edward Wagenknecht, *The Cavalcade of the American Novel* (**101**), and *The Literary History of the United States* (**47**).

Bellamy, Edward (1850–1898)

Texts

There is no standard edition. The following reprint editions, however, have useful editorial apparatus.

229 *The Duke of Stockbridge: A Romance of Shay's Rebellion.* Edited with introduction by Joseph Schiffman. Cambridge: Harvard Univ. Press, 1962.

230 *Looking Backward 2000–1887.* Ed. Robert C. Elliot. Boston: Houghton Mifflin, 1966.†

231 *Looking Backward.* Ed. with an introduction by Joseph Schiffman. New York: Harper, 1959.

232 *Looking Backward 2000–1887.* Ed John L. Thomas. Cambridge: Harvard Univ. Press, 1967.

233 MORGAN, Arthur E., ed. *The Philosophy of Edward Bellamy.* New York: King's Crown Press, 1945.

Bibliography

See Bibliographies in **3, 18,** and **237.**

234 BOWMAN, Sylvia E. "Edward Bellamy (1850–1898)." *ALR,* I (1967), 7–12.

Biographical and Critical Books

235 AARON, Daniel, and LEVIN, Harry. *Edward Bellamy, Novelist and Reformer.* Foreword by Harold C. Martin. (Union Worthies 23) Schenectady, N.Y.: Union College, 1968.

236 BOWMAN, Sylvia E. *The Year 2000: A Critical Biography of Edward Bellamy.* New York: Bookman, 1958.

237 MORGAN, Arthur E. *Edward Bellamy.* New York: Columbia Univ. Press, 1944.

Critical Essays

The first item is a collection, followed by individual essays.

238 BOWMAN, Sylvia E., et al. *Edward Bellamy Abroad: An American Prophet's Influence.* New York: Twayne, 1962. [Essays.]

239 BECKER, George J. "Edward Bellamy: Utopia, American Plan." *AR,* XIV (1954), 181–194.

240 BLEICH, David. "Eros and Bellamy." *AQ,* XVI (1964), 445–459.

241 BOGGS, W. Arthur. "*Looking Backward* at the Utopian Novel, 1888–1900." *BNYPL,* LXIV (1960), 329–336.

242 BOWMAN, Sylvia E. "Utopian Views of Man and the Machine." *SLitI,* VI (1973), 105–120.

243 DUDDEN, Arthur P. "Edward Bellamy: *Looking Backward, 2000–1887.*" *Landmarks of American Writing.* Ed. Hennig Cohen. New York: Basic Books, 1969, 207–218.

244 FRANKLIN, John Hope. "Edward Bellamy and the Nationalist Movement." *NEQ,* XI (1938), 739–772.

245 LEVI, Albert W. "Edward Bellamy: Utopian." *Ethics,* LV (1945), 131–144.

246 MADISON, Charles A. "Edward Bellamy, Social Dreamer." *NEQ,* XV (1942), 444–466.

247 PARSSINEN, T. M. "Bellamy, Morris, and the Image of the Industrial City in Victorian Social Criticism." *MQ,* XIV (1973), 257–266.

248 SADLER, Elizabeth. "One Book's Influence: Edward Bellamy's *Looking Backward.*" *NEQ,* XVII (1944), 530–555.

249 SANCTON, Thomas A. "Looking Inward: Edward Bellamy's Spiritual Crisis." *AQ,* XXV (1973), 538–557.

250 SCHIFFMAN, Joseph. "Edward Bellamy's Altruistic Man." *AQ,* VI (1954), 195–209.

251 SCHIFFMAN, Joseph. "Edward Bellamy's Religious Thought." *PMLA,* LXVIII (1953), 716–732.

252 SCHIFFMAN, Joseph. "Mutual Indebtedness: Unpublished Letters of Edward Bellamy to William Dean Howells." *HLQ,* XII (1958), 363–374.

253 SHURTER, Robert L. "The Literary Work of Edward Bellamy." *AL,* V (1933), 229–234.

254 SHURTER, Robert L. "The Writing of *Looking Backward.*" *SAQ,* XXXVIII (1939), 255–261.

255 TAYLOR, Walter Fuller. "Edward Bellamy." See **153.**

256 TRIMMER, Joseph F. "American Dreams: A Comparative Study of the Utopian Novels of Bellamy and Howells." *BSUF,* XII (1971), 13–21.

Brown, Charles Brockden (1771–1810)

Texts

An edition of the Works of Brown is in preparation under the general editorship of Sydney P. Krause at the Kent State University Press.

257 *The Novels of Charles Brockden Brown.* 7 vols. Boston: 1827. Reprinted in 6 vols. Philadelphia: 1887. [Standard, but out of print.]

258 *Arthur Mervyn; or, Memoirs of the Year 1793.* Introduction by Warner Berthoff. New York: Holt, Rinehart and Winston, 1962.†

259 *Edgar Huntly, or Memoirs of a Sleepwaker.* Ed. David Stineback. New Haven: College and University Press, 1973.†

260 *Ormond.* Edited with an introduction by Ernest Marchand. New York: American Book Co., 1937.†

261 *The Rhapsodist and Other Uncollected Writing.* Ed Harry R. Warfel. New York: Scholars' Facsimiles and Reprints, 1943.

262 *Wieland; or, The Transformation, Together with Memoirs of Carwin the Biloquist: A Fragment.* Edited with an introduction by Fred Lewis Pattee. New York: Harcourt, Brace and Co., 1926.†

Bibliography

See bibliographies in **3, 18, 260,** and **261.**

263 HEMENWAY, Robert E., and KELLER, Dean H. "Charles Brockden Brown: America's First Important Novelist: A Checklist of Biography and Criticism." *PBSA,* XL (1966), 349–362.

Biographical and Critical Books

264 CLARK, David Lee. *Charles Brockden Brown, Pioneer Voice of America.* Durham, N.C.: Duke Univ. Press, 1952.

265 DUNLAP, William. *The Life of Charles Brockden Brown.* 2 vols. Philadelphia: 1815. [Still useful.]

266 RINGE, Donald A. *Charles Brockden Brown.* (*TUSAS,* 98.) New York: Twayne, 1966.†

267 WILEY, Lulu Rumsey. *The Sources and Influences of the Novels of Charles Brockden Brown.* New York: Vantage Press, 1950.

268 WARFEL, Harry R. *Charles Brockden Brown, American Gothic Novelist.* Gainesville: Univ. of Florida Press, 1949.

Critical Essays

269 BERNARD, Kenneth. "*Arthur Mervyn:* The Ordeal of Innocence." *TSLL,* VI (1965), 441–459.

270 BERNARD, Kenneth. "Charles Brockden Brown and the Sublime." *Person,* XLV (1964), 235–249.

271 BERNARD, Kenneth. "Charles Brockden Brown." See **220,** pp. 1–9.

272 BERNARD, Kenneth. *"Edgar Huntly:* Charles Brockden Brown's Unsolved Murder." *LC,* XXXIII (1967), 30–53.

273 BERTHOFF, W. B. "Adventures of the Young Man: An Approach to Charles Brockden Brown." *AQ,* IX (1957), 421–434.

274 BERTHOFF, W. B. " 'A Lesson on Concealment': Brockden Brown's Method in Fiction." *PQ,* XXXVII (1958), 45–57.

275 BRANCACCIO, Patrick. "Studied Ambiguities: *Arthur Mervyn* and the Problem of the Unreliable Narrator." *AL,* XLII (1970), 18–27.

276 ERSKINE, John. "Charles Brockden Brown." See **217.**

277 FLECK, Richard F. "Symbolic Landscapes in *Edgar Huntly.*" *RS,* XXXIX (1971), 229–232.

278 GARROW, Scott. "Character Transformation in *Wieland.*" *SoQ,* IV (1966), 308–318.

279 GREINER, Donald J. "Brown's Use of the Narrator in *Wieland:* An Indirect Plea for the Acceptance of Fiction." *CLAJ,* XIII (1969), 131–136.

280 HAVILAND, Thomas P. "Precosité Crosses the Atlantic." *PMLA,* LIX (1944), 131–141.

281 HEDGES, William L. "Benjamin Rush, Charles Brockden Brown, and the American Plague Year." *EAL,* VIII (1973), 295–309.

282 HEMENWAY, Robert. "Brockden Brown's Twice Told Insanity Tale." *AL,* XL (1968), 211–215.

283 HINTZ, Howard W. "Charles Brockden Brown." *The Quaker Influence in American Literature.* New York: Fleming H. Revell, 1940, 34–40.

284 HUGHES, Philip R. "Archetypal Patterns in *Edgar Huntly.*" *SNNTS,* V (1973), 176–190.

285 HUME, Robert D. "Charles Brockden Brown and the Use of Gothicism: A Reassessment." *ESQ,* LXVI (1972), 10–18.

286 JENKINS, R. B. "Invulnerable Virtue in *Wieland* and 'Comus'." *SAB,* XXXVIII (1973), 72–75.

287 JUSTUS, James H. "Arthur Mervyn, American." *AL,* XLII (1970), 304–324.

288 KATZ, Joseph. "Analytical Bibliography and Literary History: The Writing and Printing of *Wieland.*" *Proof,* I (1971), 8–34.

289 KIMBALL, Arthur G. "Savages and Savagism: Brockden Brown's Dramatic Irony." *SIR,* VI (1967), 214–225.

290 KRAUSE, Sydney J. *"Ormond:* Seduction in a New Key." *AL,* XLIV (1973), 570–584.

291 LEVINE, Paul. "The American Novel Begins." *ASch,* XXXV (1966), 134–148.

292 LYTTLE, David. "The Case Against Carwin." *NCF,* XXVI (1971), 257–269.

293 LOSHE, Lillie Deming. See **106,** pp. 29–58.

294 MANLY, William M. "The Importance of Point of View in Brockden Brown's *Wieland.*" *AL,* XXXV (1963), 311–321.

295 MARCHAND, Ernest C. "The Literary Opinions of Charles Brockden Brown." *SP,* XXXI (1934), 541–566.

296 MORRIS, Mabel. "Charles Brockden Brown and the American Indian." *AL,* XVIII (1946), 244–247.

297 MULQUEEN, James E. "The Plea for a Deistic Education in Charles Brockden Brown's *Wieland.*" *BSUF,* X (1969), 70–77.

298 NELSON, Carl. "A Just Reading of Charles Brockden Brown's *Ormond.*" *EAL,* VIII (1973), 163–178.

299 PRESCOTT, F. C. "*Wieland* and *Frankenstein.*" *AL,* II (1930), 172–173.

300 RIDGELY, J. V. "The Empty World of *Wieland.*" In *Individuality and Community: Variations on a Theme in American Fiction,* edited by Kenneth H. Baldwin and David K. Kirby. Durham, N.C.: Duke Univ. Press, 1975, pp. 3–16.

301 RINGE, Donald A. "Charles Brockden Brown." In *Major Writers of Early American Literature,* Edited by Everett Emerson. Madison: Univ. of Wisconsin Press, 1972, pp. 273–294.

302 RINGE, Donald A. "Early American Gothic: Brown, Dana and Allston." *ATQ,* XIX (1973), 3–8.

303 SCHULZ, Dieter. "*Edgar Huntly* as Quest Romance." *Al,* XLIII (1971), 323–335.

304 SCHULZ, Max F. "Brockden Brown: An Early Casualty of the American Experience." In *Americana-Austriaca: Beiträge zur Amerikakunde,* edited by Klaus Lanzinger. Band 2, Vienna: W. Braumüller, 1970, 81–90.

305 SICKLES, Eleanor. "Shelley and Charles Brockden Brown." *PMLA,* XLV (1930), 1116–1128.

306 SNELL, George J. "Charles Brockden Brown: Apocalypticalist." *UKCR,* XI (1944), 131–138. See also **99.**

307 SOLVE, Melvin T. "Shelley and the Novels of Brown." *Fred Newton Scott Anniversary Papers.* Chicago: Univ. of Chicago Press, 1929, pp. 141–156.

308 STROZIER, Robert. "*Wieland* and Other Romances: Horror in Parentheses." *ESQ,* L Sup (1968), 24–29.

309 TILTON, Eleanor M. " 'The Sorrows' of Charles Brockden Brown." *PMLA,* LXIX (1954), 1304–1308.

310 VAN DER BEETS, Richard, and WITHERINGTON, Paul. "My Kinsman, Brockden Brown: Robin Molineux and Arthur Mervyn." *ATQ,* I (1969), 13–15.

311 VAN DOREN, Carl. "Minor Tales of Brockden Brown, 1798–1800." *Nation,* C (1915), 46–47.

312 WARD, William S. "Charles Brockden Brown, His Contemporary British Reviewers, and Two Minor Bibliographical Problems." *PBSA,* LXV (1971), 399–402.

313 WARFEL, Harry R. "Charles Brockden Brown's German Sources." *MLQ,* I (1940), 357–365.

314 WITHERINGTON, Paul. "Benevolence and the 'Utmost Stretch': Charles Brockden Brown's Narrative Dilemma." *Criticism,* XIV (1972), 175–191.

315 WITHERINGTON, Paul, "Image and Idea in *Wieland* and *Edgar Huntly.*" *Serif,* III (1966), 19–26.

316 ZIFF, Larzer. "A Reading of *Wieland.*" *PMLA,* LXXVII (1962), 51–57.

Cable, George Washington (1844–1925)

Texts

There is no collected edition. The following reprints and collections, however, have useful editorial apparatus.

317 *Creoles and Cajuns: Stories of Old Louisiana.* Edited with an introduction by Arlin Turner. Garden City, N.Y.: Doubleday, 1959.

318 *The Grandissimes.* Introduction by Newton Arvin. New York: Hill & Wang, 1957.†

319 *The Negro Question, A Selection of Writings on Civil Rights in the South by George W. Cable.* Edited with an introduction by Arlin Turner. Garden City, N.Y.: Doubleday, 1958.†

Bibliography

See bibliographies in **3, 18,** and **321.**

320 BUTCHER, Philip. "George Washington Cable (1844–1925)." *ALR,* I (1967), 20–25.

Biographical and Critical Books

321 BIKLÉ, Lucy Leffingwell Cable. *George W. Cable: His Life and Letters.* New York: Scribner's, 1928.

322 BUTCHER, Philip. *George Washington Cable.* New York: Twayne, 1962.†

323 BUTCHER, Philip. *George W. Cable: The Northampton Years.* New York: Columbia Univ. Press, 1959.

324 CARDWELL, Guy A. *Twins of Genius: Letters of Mark Twain, George W. Cable, and Others.* East Lansing: Michigan State College Press, 1953.

325 EKSTRÖM, Kjell. *George Washington Cable.* Cambridge: Harvard Univ. Press, 1950. [Cable's early life and works.]

326 RUBIN, Louis D., Jr. *George W. Cable: The Life and Times of a Southern Heretic.* New York: Pegasus, 1969.

327 TURNER, Arlin. *George W. Cable: A Biography.* Durham, N.C.: Duke Univ. Press, 1956.†

328 TURNER, Arlin. *George W. Cable.* (*SoWS* 1.) Austin, Texas: Steck-Vaughn, 1969.

329 TURNER, Arlin. *Mark Twain and George W. Cable: The Record of a Literary Friendship.* East Lansing: Michigan State College Press, 1960. [Letters and interlinking commentary.]

Critical Essays

330 BOWEN, Edwin W. "George Washington Cable: An Appreciation." *SAQ*, XVIII (1919), 145–155.

331 BUTCHER, Philip. "George W. Cable and George W. Williams: An Abortive Collaboration." *JNH*, LIII (1968), 334–344.

332 CHASE, Richard. "Cable and His *Grandissimes.*" *KR*, XVIII (1956), 373–383.

333 DOUGHTY, Nanelia S. "Realistic Negro Characterization in Post-bellum Fiction." *NALF*, III (1969), 62, 68.

334 EIDSON, John Olin. "George W. Cable's Philosophy of Progress." *SWR*, XXI (1936), 211–216.

335 HEARN, Lafcadio. "The Scenes of Cable's Romances." *Century Mag.*, XXVII (1883), 40–47.

336 HOWELL, Elmo. "George Washington Cable's Creoles: Art and Reform in *The Grandissimes.*" *MissQ*, XXVI (1973), 43–53.

337 PERRET, J. John. "The Ethnic and Religious Prejudices of G. W. Cable." *LaS*, XI (1972), 263–273.

338 PUGH, Griffith T. "George Washington Cable." *MissQ*, XX (1967), 69–76.

339 PUGH, Griffith T. "George W. Cable's Theory and Use of Folk Speech." *SFQ*, XXIV (1960), 287–293.

340 RINGE, Donald A. "The 'Double Center': Character and Meaning in Cable's Early Novels." *SNNTS*, V (1973), 52–62.

341 RUBIN, Louis D., Jr. "The Division of the Heart: Cable's *The Grandissimes.*" *SLJ*, I (1969), 27–47.

342 RUBIN, Louis D., Jr. "The Road to Yoknapatawpha: George W. Cable and *John March, Southerner.*" *VQR*, XXXV (1959), 119–132; also in Rubin's *The Faraway Country: Writers of the Modern South.* Seattle: Univ. of Washington Press, 1963.

343 TINKER, Edward Larocque. "Cable and the Creoles." *AL*, V (1934), 313–326.

344 TOULMIN, Harry Aubrey, Jr. *Social Historians.* Boston: Richard G. Badger, 1911, 35–56.

345 TURNER, Arlin. "A Novelist Discovers a Novelist: The Correspondence of H. H. Boyesen and George W. Cable." *WHR*, V (1951), 343–372.

346 TURNER, Arlin. "George W. Cable, Novelist and Reformer." *SAQ*, XLVIII (1949), 539–545.

347 TURNER, Arlin. "George W. Cable on Prison Reform." *HLQ*, XXXVI (1972), 69–75.

348 WILSON, Edmund. "The Ordeal of George Washington Cable." *NY*, XXXIII (Nov. 9, 1957), 172–216. Reprinted in *Patriotic Gore: Studies in the Literature of the American Civil War.* New York: Oxford Univ. Press, 1962. [Review-essay of Turner's *George W. Cable*, which becomes an important study of Cable.]

Chesnutt, Charles Waddell (1858–1932)

Texts

There is no collected edition. The following volumes have useful introductory material.

349 *The Conjure Woman.* Introduction by Robert M. Farnsworth. Ann Arbor: Univ. of Michigan Press, 1969.†

350 *The House Behind the Cedars.* Introduction by Darwin Turner. New York: Collier, 1969.

351 *The Marrow of Tradition.* Introduction by Robert M. Farnsworth. Ann Arbor: Univ. of Michigan Press, 1969.†

Bibliography

See **18, 21,** and **159.**

352 FREENEY, Mildred, and HENRY, Mary T., comps. *A List of the Manuscripts, Published Works and Related Items in the Charles Waddell Chesnutt Collection of the Erastus Milo Cravath Memorial Library, Fisk Univ.* Nashville, 1954.

353 KELLER, Dean H. "Charles Waddell Chesnutt (1858–1932)." *ALR,* III (1968), 1–4.

Biographical and Critical Books

354 CHESNUTT, Helen M. *Charles Waddell Chesnutt: Pioneer of the Color Line.* Chapel Hill: Univ. of North Carolina Press, 1952.

355 HEERMANCE, J. Noel. *Charles W. Chesnutt: America's First Great Black Novelist.* Hamden, Conn.: Archon Books, 1974.

Critical Essays

356 AMES, Russell. "Social Realism in Charles W. Chesnutt." *Phylon,* XIV (1953), 199–206.

357 ANDREWS, William L. "Chesnutt's Patesville: The Presence and Influence of the Past in *The House Behind the Cedars.*" *CLAJ,* XV (1972), 284–294.

358 BALDWIN, Richard E. "The Art of *The Conjure Woman.*" *AL,* XLIII (1971), 385–398.

359 BRITT, David D. "Chesnutt's Conjure Tales: What You See Is What You Get." *CLAJ,* XV (1972), 269–283.

360 CHAMETZKY, Jules. "Regional Literature and Ethnic Realities." *AR,* XXXI (1971), 385–396.

361 FARNSWORTH, Robert M. "Charles Chesnutt and the Color Line." See **220,** pp. 28–40.

362 GARTNER, Carol B. "Charles W. Chesnutt: Novelist of a Cause." *MarkhamR,* III (1968), 5–12.

363 GILES, James R. "Chestnutt's Primus and Annie: A Contemporary View of *The Conjure Woman.*" *MarkhamR,* III (1972), 46–49.

364 GLOSTER, Hugh M. "Charles W. Chesnutt: Pioneer in the Fiction of Negro Life." *Phylon,* II (1941), 57–66.

365 MASON, Julian D., Jr. "Charles W. Chesnutt as Southern Author." *MissQ,* XX (1967), 77–89.

366 REILLY, John M. "The Dilemma in Chesnutt's *The Marrow of Tradition.*" *Phylon,* XXXII (1971), 31–38.

367 RENDER, Sylvia Lyons. "Tar Heelia in Chesnutt." *CLAJ,* IX (1965), 39–50.

368 SILLEN, Samuel. "Charles W. Chesnutt: A Pioneer Negro Novelist." *Masses & Mainstream,* VI (1953), 8–14.

369 SMITH, Robert A. "A Pioneer Black Writer and the Problems of Discrimination and Miscegenation." *Costerus,* XI (1973), 181–185.

370 SOCKEN, June. "Charles Waddell Chestnutt and the Solution to the Race Problem." *NALF,* III (1969), 52–56.

371 WINKELMAN, Donald M. "Three American Authors as Semi-Folk Artists." *JAF,* LXXVIII (1965), 130–135. [Mark Twain, Manly Wade Wellman, and Charles W. Chesnutt.]

372 WINTZ, Cary D. "Race and Realism in the Fiction of Charles W. Chesnutt." *Ohio Hist.,* LXXXI (1972), 122–130.

Clemens, Samuel L. ("Mark Twain"), (1835–1910)

Texts

373 *The California Edition of the Writings of Mark Twain* (Berkeley: Univ. of Calif. Press) is underway. The manuscript material is under the general editorship of Frank Anderson, and the published works under that of John C. Gerber. This edition, under the sponsorship of the CEAA, will be definitive. So far, none of the novels have appeared.

374 *The Writings of Mark Twain.* Ed. Albert B. Paine. 37 vols. New York: Harper, 1922–1925. [Standard, but will be superseded by new collected edition now in progress at the University of California.]

The following volumes contain material which is pertinent to Clemens as a fiction writer but which is not in *The Writings:*

375 *The Autobiography of Mark Twain, Including Chapters Now Published for the First Time.* Edited with an introduction by Charles Neider. New York: Harper, 1959.†

376 *Mark Twain in Eruption: Hitherto Unpublished Pages About Men and Events.* Edited with an introduction by Bernard De Voto. New York: Harper, 1940.

377 SMITH, Henry Nash, and GIBSON, William M., eds. *Mark Twain—Howells Letters: The Correspondence of Samuel L. Clemens and William D. Howells, 1872–1910.* 2 vols. Cambridge: Harvard Univ. Press, 1960.

There have been numerous reprints of Mark Twain's fiction. Among those whose editorial apparatus is useful are:

378 BRADLEY, Sculley; BEATTY, R. C.; and LONG, E. H., eds. *Adventures of Huckleberry Finn: An Annotated Text, Backgrounds, and Sources, Essays in Criticism.* New York: Norton, 1962.†

379 HILL, Hamlin, and BLAIR, Walter, eds. *The Art of Huckleberry Finn: Text, Sources, Criticisms.* San Francisco: Chandler Publishing Co., 1962. [Facsimile of first edition with sources and critical essays by various hands.]†

380 LETTIS, Richard; MORRIS, William E.; and MCDONNELL, Robert F., eds. *Huck Finn and His Critics.* New York: Macmillan, 1962.†

381 LYNN, Kenneth S., ed. *Huckleberry Finn: Text, Sources, and Criticism.* New York: Harcourt, Brace & World Co., 1961.†

382 *Pudd'nhead Wilson and Those Extraordinary Twins.* Facsimile of 1st edition. With introduction, note on text, and bibliography by Frederick Anderson. San Francisco: Chandler, 1968.

383 SMITH, Henry Nash, ed. *Adventures of Huckleberry Finn.* With introduction. Boston: Houghton Mifflin, 1958.†

Bibliography

See **3** and **18**.

384 BEEBE, Maurice, and FEASTER, John. "Criticism of Mark Twain: A Selected Checklist." *MFS,* XIV (1968), 93–139.

385 CLARK, Harry Hayden. "Mark Twain." See **22**, pp. 273–320.

386 JOHNSON, Merle. *A Bibliography of the Works of Mark Twain.* Rev. ed. New York: Harper, 1935. [The standard bibliography.]

387 KOLIN, Philip C. "Mark Twain's *Pudd'nhead Wilson:* A Selected Checklist." *BB,* XXVIII (1971), 58–59, 48.

Biographical and Critical Books

388 ALLEN, Jerry. *The Adventures of Mark Twain.* Boston: Little, Brown, 1954.†

389 ANDERSON, Frederick, ed. *Mark Twain: The Critical Heritage.* With introduction. London: Routledge & K. Paul; New York: Barnes & Noble, 1971.

390 ANDREWS, Kenneth R. *Nook Farm: Mark Twain's Hartford Circle.* Cambridge: Harvard Univ. Press, 1950.†

391 BAETZHOLD, Howard G. *Mark Twain and John Bull: The British Connection.* Bloomington: Indiana Univ. Press, 1970.

392 BALDANZA, Frank. *Mark Twain: An Introduction and Interpretation.* New York: Barnes & Noble, 1961.†

393 BELLAMY, Gladys Carmen. *Mark Twain as a Literary Artist.* Norman: Univ. of Oklahoma Press, 1950. [One of the best works of literary criticism.]

394 BLAIR, Walter. *Mark Twain and Huck Finn.* Berkeley, Calif.: Univ. of California Press, 1960. [An excellent critical-historical study of *Huck Finn.*]

395 BLAIR, Walter, ed. *Mark Twain's Hannibal, Huck and Tom.* With introduction. Berkeley: Univ. of California Press, 1969.

396 BLUES, Thomas. *Mark Twain and the Community.* Lexington: Univ. of Kentucky Press, 1970.

397 BRANCH, Edgar Marquess. *The Literary Apprenticeship of Mark Twain.* Urbana: Univ. of Illinois Press, 1950.

398 BRASHEAR, Minnie M. *Mark Twain, Son of Missouri.* Chapel Hill: Univ. of North Carolina Press, 1934.

399 BROOKS, Van Wyck. *The Ordeal of Mark Twain.* Rev. ed. New York: E. P. Dutton & Co., 1933. [A provocative study of Mark Twain.]†

400 BUDD, Louis J. *Mark Twain: Social Philosopher.* Bloomington: Indiana Univ. Press, 1962.

401 CANBY, Henry Seidel. *Turn West, Turn East.* Boston: Houghton Mifflin, 1951. [A biographical comparison with Henry James.]

402 CARDWELL, Guy A. See 324.

403 COVICI, Pascal, Jr. *Mark Twain's Humor: The Image of a World.* Dallas: So. Methodist Univ. Press, 1962.

404 COX, James M. *Mark Twain: The Fate of Humor.* Princeton: Princeton Univ. Press, 1966.

405. DE VOTO, Bernard. *Mark Twain at Work.* Cambridge: Harvard Univ. Press, 1942.

406 DE VOTO, Bernard. *Mark Twain's America.* Boston: Little, Brown, 1932. [Spirited reply to Brooks, **399.**]

407 ENSOR, Allison. *Mark Twain and the Bible.* Lexington: Univ. of Kentucky Press, 1969.

408 FATOUT, Paul. *Mark Twain in Virginia City.* Bloomington: Indiana Univ. Press, 1964.

409 FATOUT, Paul. *Mark Twain on the Lecture Circuit.* Bloomington: Indiana Univ. Press, 1960.†

410 FERGUSON, De Lancey. *Mark Twain: Man and Legend.* Indianapolis: Bobbs-Merrill, 1943. [Best single biography.]†

411 FONER, Philip S. *Mark Twain: Social Critic.* New York: International Publishers, 1958.†

412 FRANKLIN, H. Bruce. See **127.**

413 GEISMAR, Maxwell. *Mark Twain: An American Prophet.* Boston: Houghton Mifflin, 1970.†

414 GRANT, Douglas. *Mark Twain.* Edinburgh: Oliver and Boyd; New York: Grove Press, 1962.

415 HILL, Hamlin. *Mark Twain: God's Fool.* New York: Harper & Row, 1973.†

416 HOWELLS, W. D. *My Mark Twain.* New York: Harper, 1910.†

417 KAPLAN, Justin. *Mr. Clemens and Mark Twain, a Biography.* New York: Simon and Schuster, 1966.†

418 KRAUSE, Sydney J. *Mark Twain as Critic.* Baltimore: Johns Hopkins Press, 1967.

419 LEARY, Lewis G. *Southern Excursions: Essays on Mark Twain and Others.* Preface by Author. Baton Rouge: Louisiana State Univ. Press, 1971. [Contains *Mark Twain*, University of Minnesota Pamphlets on American Writers, no. 5.]

420 LONG, E. Hudson. *Mark Twain Handbook.* New York: Hendricks House, 1957. [Indispensable guide to works, criticism, and problems.]

421 LYNN, Kenneth S. *Mark Twain and Southwestern Humor.* Boston: Little, Brown, 1960.

422 MASTERS, Edgar Lee. *Mark Twain: A Portrait.* New York: Scribner's, 1938.

423 MAY, John R. See **191.**

424 PAINE, Albert B. *Mark Twain: A Biography.* 3 vols. New York: Harper, 1912. [Very detailed but not completely trustworthy.]

425 REGAN, Robert. *Unpromising Heroes: Mark Twain and His Characters.* Berkeley: Univ. of California Press, 1966.

426 ROGERS, Franklin R. *Mark Twain's Burlesque Patterns as Seen in the Novels and Narratives, 1855–1885.* Dallas: So. Methodist Univ. Press, 1960.

427 SALOMON, Roger B. *Twain and the Image of History.* New Haven: Yale Univ. Press, 1961.

428 SMITH, Henry Nash. *Mark Twain: The Development of a Writer.* Cambridge: Harvard Univ. Press, 1962. [With Bellamy **(393)**, one of two best critical studies.]†

429 SMITH, Henry Nash. *Mark Twain's Fable of Progress: Political and Economic Ideas in A CONNECTICUT YANKEE.* New Brunswick, N.J.: Rutgers Univ. Press, 1964.

430 SPENGEMANN, William C. *Mark Twain and the Backwoods Angel: The Matter of Innocence in the Works of Samuel L. Clemens.* Kent, Ohio.: Kent State Univ. Press, 1966.

431 STONE, Albert E., Jr. *The Innocent Eye: Childhood in Mark Twain's Imagination.* New Haven: Yale Univ. Press, 1961.

432 TUCKEY, John S., ed. *Mark Twain's 'The Mysterious Stranger' and the Critics.* Belmont, Calif.: Wadsworth, 1968.

433 TURNER, Arlin. See **329.**

434 WAGENKNECHT, Edward. *Mark Twain: The Man and His Work.* Norman: Univ. of Oklahoma Press, 1967.

435 WECTER, Dixon. *Sam Clemens of Hannibal.* Ed. Elizabeth Wecter. Boston: Houghton Mifflin, 1952. [Clemens' childhood and adolescence.]†

436 WIGGINS, Robert A. *Mark Twain: Jackleg Novelist.* Seattle: Univ. of Washington Press, 1964.

Critical Essays

The collections listed first **(437–446)** represent the bulk of the best Mark Twain criticism in essay form up to their dates of publication, as do **378, 379, 380, 381.**

437 CAMP, James E., and KENNEDY, X. J., eds. *Mark Twain's Frontier: A Textbook of Primary Source Materials for Student Research and Writing.* New York: Holt, Rinehart, and Winston, 1963.†

438 CARDWELL, Guy A., ed. *Discussions of Mark Twain.* Boston: D.C. Heath & Co., 1963.†

439 KESTERSON, David B., ed. *Critics on Mark Twain.* (*RLitC* 21) Coral Gables: Univ. of Miami Press, 1973.

440 LEARY, Lewis G. ed. *A Casebook on Mark Twain's Wound.* New York: T. Y. Crowell, 1962. [Reprints critical essays on the Brooks-De Voto controversy in excellent arrangement.]†

441 MARKS, Barry A., ed. *Mark Twain's HUCKLEBERRY FINN.* Boston: D.C. Heath & Co., 1959. [Essays on the novel.]†

442 Mark Twain Issue. *American Quarterly,* XVI, iv (March, 1964).

443 MARK Twain Special Number. *MFS,* XIV (1968).

444 SCOTT, Arthur L., ed. *Mark Twain, Selected Criticism.* Dallas: So. Methodist Univ. Press, 1955.†

445 SIMPSON, Claude M., ed. *Twentieth Century Interpretations of ADVENTURES OF HUCKLEBERRY FINN.* With introduction. Englewood Cliffs, N.J.: Prentice-Hall, 1968.†

446 SMITH, Henry Nash, ed. *Mark Twain: A Collection of Critical Essays.* Englewood Cliffs, N.J.: Prentice-Hall, 1963.†

447 ADAMS, Richard P. "The Unity and Coherence of *Huckleberry Finn.*" *TSE,* VI (1956), 87–103.

448 ALTENBERND, Lynn. "Huck Finn, Emancipator." *Criticism,* I (1959), 298–307.

449 ALTICK, Richard D. "Mark Twain's Despair: An Explanation in Terms of His Humanity." *SAQ,* XXXIV (1935), 359–367.

450 ANDERSEN, Kenneth. "Mark Twain, W. D. Howells, and Henry James: Three Agnostics in Search of Salvation." *MTJ,* XV (1970), 13–16.

451 BAETZHOLD, Howard G. " 'The Autobiography of Sir Robert Smith of Camelot': Mark Twain's Original Plan for *A Connecticut Yankee.*" *AL,* XXXII (1961), 456–461.

452 BAETZHOLD, Howard G. "The Course of Composition of *A Connecticut Yankee:* A Reinterpretation." *AL,* XXXIII (1961), 195–214.

453 BALDANZA, Frank. "The Structure of *Huckleberry Finn.*" *AL,* XXVII (1955), 347–355.

454 BANTA, Martha. "Rebirth or Revenge: The Endings of *Huckleberry Finn* and *The American. MFS,* XV (1969), 191–207.

455 BELSON, Joel J. "The Nature and Consequences of the Loneliness of Huckleberry Finn." *ArQ,* XXVI (1970), 243–248.

456 BENARDETE, Jane J. "*Huckleberry Finn* and the Nature of Fiction." *MR,* IX (1968), 209–226.

457 BOLAND, Sally. "The Seven Dialects in *Huckleberry Finn.*" *NDQ,* XXXVI (1968), 30–40.

458 BRADBURY, Malcolm. "Mark Twain in the Gilded Age." *CritQ,* XI (1969), 65–73.

459 BRANCH, Edgar M. "Mark Twain and J. D. Salinger: A Study in Literary Continuity." *AQ,* IX (1957), 144–158.

460 BRAND, John M. "The Incipient Wilderness: A Study of *Pudd'nhead Wilson.*" *WAL,* VII (1972), 125–134.

461 BRODWIN, Stanley. "Blackness and the Adamic Myth in Mark Twain's *Pudd'n-head Wilson.*" *TSLL,* XV (1973), 167–176.

462 BROWN, Spencer. "*Huckleberry Finn* for Our Time: A Re-Reading of the Concluding Chapters." *MQR,* VI (1967), 41–46.

463 BUDD, Louis J. "Twain, Howells, and the Boston Nihilists." *NEQ,* XXXII (1959), 351–371.

464 BURG, David F. "Another View of *Huckleberry Finn. NCF,* XXIX (1974), 299–319.

465 BURNS, Graham. "Time and Pastoral: *The Adventures of Huckleberry Finn.*" *CR,* XV (1972), 52–63.

466 BUTCHER, Philip. " 'The Godfathership' of *A Connecticut Yankee.*" *CLAJ,* XII (1969), 189–198.

467 CARDWELL, Guy A. "Mark Twain's Failures in Comedy." *GaR,* XIII (1959), 424–436.

468 CECIL, L. Moffitt. "Tom Sawyer: Missouri Robin Hood." *WAL,* IV (1969), 125–131.

469 CHELLIS, Barbara A. "Those Extraordinary Twins: Negroes and Whites." *AQ,* XXI (1969), 100–112.

470 CHRISTOPHER, J. R. "On the *Adventures of Huckleberry Finn* as a Comic Myth." *CimR,* XVIII (1972), 18–27.

471 COARD, Robert L. "Mark Twain's *The Gilded Age* and Sinclair Lewis's *Babbitt. MQ,* XIII (1972), 319–333.

472 COBURN, Mark D. " 'Training is Everything': Communal Opinion and the Individual in *Pudd'nhead Wilson.*" *MLQ,* XXXI (1970), 209–219.

473 COLWELL, James L. "Huckleberries and Humans: On the Naming of Huckleberry Finn." *PMLA,* LXXXVI (1971), 70–76.

474 COX, James M. "*A Connecticut Yankee in King Arthur's Court:* The Machinery of Self-Preservation." *YR,* L (1960), 89–102.

475 COX, James M. "Mark Twain: The Height of Humor." See **200,** pp. 139–148.

476 COX, James M. "Mark Twain: The Triumph of Humor." See **216,** pp. 213–230.

477 COX, James M. "Pudd'nhead Wilson: The End of Mark Twain's American Dream." *SAQ,* LVIII (1959), 351–363.

478 COX, James M. "Remarks on the Sad Initiation of Huckleberry Finn." *SR,* LXII (1954), 389–405.

479 CROWE, Charles. "Mark Twain's *Huckleberry Finn* and the American Journey." *Archiv,* CXCIX (1962), 145–158.

480 DYSON, A. E. "Huckleberry Finn and the Whole Truth." *CritQ,* III (1961), 29–40.

481 ELLIOTT, George P. "Wonder for *Huckleberry Finn.*" See **226.**

482 ENSOR, Allison. "The 'Tennessee Land' of *The Gilded Age:* Fiction and Reality." *TSL,* XV (1970), 15–23.

483 FALK, Robert P. See **140.**

484 FETTERLEY, Judith. "Disenchantment: Tom Sawyer in *Huckleberry Finn.*" *PMLA,* LXXXVII (1972), 69–74.

485 FETTERLEY, Judith. "Yankee Showman and Reformer: The Character of Mark Twain's Hank Morgan." *TSLL,* XIV (1973), 667–680.

486 FIEDLER, Leslie A. "Come Back to the Raft Ag'in Huck Honey!" *PR,* XV (1948), 664–671; reprinted in Fiedler's *An End to Innocence.* Boston: Beacon Press, 1955. pp. 142–151.†

487 FISHER, Marvin, and ELLIOTT, Michael. *"Pudd'nhead Wilson:* Half a Dog is Worse Than None." *SoR,* VIII (1972), 533–547.

488 FLECK, Richard F. "Mark Twain's Social Criticism in *The Innocents Abroad."* *BRMMLA,* XXV (1971), 39–48.

489 FRANTZ, Ray W., Jr. "The Role of Folklore in *Huckleberry Finn."* *AL,* XXVIII (1956), 314–327.

490 FRASER, John. "In Defense of Culture: *Huckleberry Finn."* *OR,* VI (1967), 5–22.

491 FREIMARCK, John. *"Pudd'nhead Wilson:* A Tale of Blood and Brotherhood." *UR,* XXXIV (1968), 303–306.

492 FRENCH, Bryant Morey. *"The Gilded Age* Manuscript." *YULG,* XXXV (1960), 35–41.

493 FRENCH, Bryant M. "James Hammond Trumbull's Alternative Chapter: Mottoes for *The Gilded Age."* *PQ,* L (1971), 271–280.

494 FULLER, Daniel J. "Mark Twain and Hamlin Garland: Contrarieties in Regionalism." *MTJ,* XVII (1973–74), 14–18.

495 FUSSELL, Edwin S. "The Structural Problem of *The Mysterious Stranger."* *SP,* LXIX (1952), 95–104.

496 GARDNER, Joseph H. "Mark Twain and Dickens." *PMLA,* LXXXIV (1969), 90–101.

497 GERBER, John C. "Mark Twain." See **22.**

498 GERBER, John C. "Mark Twain's Search for Identity." In *Essays in American and English Literature Presented to Bruce Robert McElderry, Jr.,* edited by Max F. Schulz, William Templeman, and Charles R. Metzger. Athens: Ohio Univ. Press, 1968, pp. 27–47.

499 GERBER, John C. "The Relation Between Point of View and Style in the Works of Mark Twain." *Style in Prose Fiction* (English Institute Essays, 1958). New York: Columbia Univ. Press, 1959, pp. 142–171.

500 GOOLD, Edgar H., Jr. "Mark Twain on the Writing of Fiction." *AL,* XXVI (1954), 141–153.

501 GOUDIE, Andrea. " 'What Fools These Mortals Be!': A Puckish Interpretation of Mark Twain's Narrative Stance." *KanQ,* V (1973), 19–31.

502 HANSEN, Chadwick. "The Character of Jim and the Ending of *Huckleberry Finn."* *MR,* V (1963), 45–66.

503 HANSEN, Chadwick. "The Once and Future Boss: Mark Twain's Yankee." *NCF,* XXVIII (1973), 62–73.

504 HANSEN, Chadwick. "There Warn't No Home Like a Raft Floating Down the Mississippi, or Like a Raft Floating Down the Neckar, or Like A Balloon Ballooning Across the Sahara: Mark Twain as Improviser." *Directions in Literary Criticism: Contemporary Approaches to Literature.* Festschrift for Henry W. Sams. Ed. Stanley Weintraub and Philip Young. University Park and London: Pennsylvania State Univ. Press, 1973, pp. 160–167.

505 HARRELL, Don W. "A Chaser of Phantoms: Mark Twain and Romanticism." *MQ*, XIII (1972), 201–212.

506 HOFFMAN, Daniel G. See **177**.

507 HOFFMAN, Michael J. "Huck's Ironic Circle." *GaR*, XXIII (1969), 307–322.

508 HOWELL, Elmo. "Huckleberry Finn in Mississippi." *LaS*, VII (1968), 167–172.

509 KAUL, A. N. See **180**.

510 KETTERER, David. "Epoch-Eclipse and Apocalypse: Special 'Effects' in *A Connecticut Yankee.*" *PMLA*, LXXVIII (1973), 1104–1114.

511 KING, Bruce. *"Huckleberry Finn." ArielE*, II (1971), 69–77.

512 KRUSE, Horst H. "Annie and Huck: A Note on *The Adventures of Huckleberry Finn.*" *AL*, XXXIX (1967), 207–214.

513 LANE, Lauriat, Jr. "Why *Huckleberry Finn* Is a Great World Novel." *CE*, XVII (1955), 1–5.

514 LEARY, Lewis. "Tom and Huck: Innocence on Trial." *VQR*, XXX (1954), 417–430.

515 LEAVIS, F. R. "Mark Twain's Neglected Classic: The Moral Astringency of 'Pudd'nhead Wilson'." *Commentary*, XXI (1956), 128–136.

516 LORCH, Fred W. "A Note on Tom Blankenship (Huckleberry Finn)." *AL*, XII (1940), 351–353.

517 LYNN, Kenneth S. "Huck and Jim." *YR*, XLVII (1958), 421–431.

518 MACDONALD, Dwight. "Mark Twain: An Unsentimental Journey." *NY*, XXXVI (1960), 160–196. Reprinted in Macdonald's *Against the American Grain: Essays on the Effects of Mass Culture.* New York: Random House, 1962.† [A very valuable history of his literary reputation.]

519 MCKEITHAN, D. M. *Court Trials in Mark Twain and Other Essays.* The Hague: Martinus Nijhoff, 1958.

520 MCMAHAN, Elizabeth E. "The Money Motif: Economic Implications in *Huckleberry Finn.*" *MTJ*, XV (1971), 5–10.

521 MANIERRE, William R. "On Keeping the Raftsmen's Passage in *Huckleberry Finn.*" *ELN*, VI (1968), 118–122.

522 MARX, Leo. "Mr. Eliot, Mr. Trilling and *Huckleberry Finn.*" *ASch*, XXII (1953), 423–440.

523 MILLER, J. Hillis. "Three Problems of Fictional Form: First-Person Narration in *David Copperfield* and *Huckleberry Finn.*" *Experience in the Novel.* Ed. Roy Harvey Pearce. New York: Columbia Univ. Press, 1968, pp. 21–48.

524 MIXON, Wayne. "Mark Twain, *The Gilded Age*, and the New South Movement." *SHR*, VII (1973), 403–409.

525 MOORE, Olin Harris. "Mark Twain and Don Quixote." *PMLA*, XXXVII (1922), 324–346.

526 MORGAN, H. Wayne. "Mark Twain: The Optimist as Pessimist." See **223.**

527 O'CONNOR, William Van. "Why *Huckleberry Finn* Is Not the Great American Novel." *CE,* XVII (1955), 6–10.

528 OSTROM, Alan. "Huck Finn and the Modern Ethos." *CentR,* XVI (1972), 162–179.

529 PARSONS, Coleman O. "Down the Mighty River with Mark Twain." *MissQ,* XXII (1969), 1–18.

530 PIZER, Donald. See **115.**

531 POWER, William. "Huck Finn's Father." *UKCR,* XXVIII (1961), 83–94.

532 POWERS, Lyall H. "The Sweet Success of Twain's Tom." *DR,* LIII (1973), 310–324.

533 ROSS, Michael L. "Mark Twain's *Pudd'nhead Wilson:* Dawson's Landing and the Ladder of Nobility." *Novel,* VI (1973), 244–256.

534 RUBENSTEIN, Gilbert M. "The Moral Structure of *Huckleberry Finn.*" *CE,* XVIII (1956), 72–76. Reprinted in **378.**

535 RUBIN, Louis D., Jr. "How Mark Twain Threw Off His Inhibitions and Discovered the Vitality of Formless Form." *SR,* LXXIX (1971), 426–433. Reprinted in **87.**

536 RUBIN, Louis D., Jr. "Mark Twain: *The Adventures of Tom Sawyer.*" See **243,** pp. 157–171.

537 RUBIN, Louis D., Jr. "Tom Sawyer and the Use of Novels." *AQ,* IX (1957), 209–216. Reprinted in *The Faraway Country.* See **342.**

538 SALOMON, Roger B. "Mark Twain and Victorian Nostalgia." In *Patterns of Commitment in American Literature,* edited by Marston LaFrance. Toronto: Univ. of Toronto Press, 1967, pp. 73–91.

539 SAPPER, Neil. " 'I Been There Before': Huck Finn as Tocquevillian Individual." *MissQ,* XXIV (1971), 35–45.

540 SCHMITZ, Neil. "The Paradox of Liberation in *Huckleberry Finn.*" *TSLL,* XIII (1971), 125–136.

541 SCHMITZ, Neil. "Twain, *Huckleberry Finn,* and the Reconstruction." *AmerS,* XII (1971), 59–67.

542 SIMONSON, Harold P. "*Huckleberry Finn* as Tragedy." *YR,* LIX (1970), 532–548.

543 SKERRY, Philip J. "*The Adventures of Huckleberry Finn* and *Intruder in the Dust:* Two Conflicting Myths of the American Experience." *BSUF,* XIII (1972), 4–13.

544 SMITH, Henry Nash. "Mark Twain's Images of Hannibal: From St. Petersburg to Eseldorf." *TexSE,* XXXVII (1958), 3–23.

545 SPANGLER, George M. "*Pudd'nhead Wilson:* A Parable of Property." *AL,* XLII (1970), 28–37.

546 STEIN, Allen F. "Return to Phelps Farm: *Huckleberry Finn* and the Old Southwestern Framing Device." *MissQ,* XXIV (1971), 111–116.

547 TAYLOR, Walter Fuller. See **153.**

548 TOWERS, Tom H. "Mark Twain's *Connecticut Yankee:* The Trouble in Came-lot." In *Challenges in American Culture,* edited by Ray B. Browne, Larry N. Landrum, and William K. Bottorff. Bowling Green, Ohio: Bowling Green Univ. Popular Press, 1970, pp. 190–198.

549 TRACHTENBERG, Alan. "The Form of Freedom in *Adventures of Huckleberry Finn.*" *SoR,* VI (1970), 954–971.

550 TRACY, Robert. "Myth and Reality in *The Adventures of Tom Sawyer.*" *SoR,* IV (1968), 530–541.

551 TURNER, Arlin. "Mark Twain and the South: An Affair of Love and Anger." *SoR,* IV (1968), 493–519.

552 VALES, Robert L. "Thief and Theft in *Huckleberry Finn.*" *AL,* XXXVII (1966), 420–429.

553 VANDERSEE, Charles. "The Mutual Awareness of Mark Twain and Henry Adams." *ELN,* V (1968), 285–292.

554 VOGELBACK, Arthur Lawrence. "*The Prince and the Pauper:* A Study in Critical Standards." *AL,* XIV (1942), 48–54.

555 WALTERS, Thomas N. "Twain's Finn and Alger's Gilman: Picaresque Counter-Directions." *MarkhamR,* III (1972), 53–58.

556 WARREN, Robert Penn. "Mark Twain." *SoR,* VIII (1972), 459–492.

557 WELLS, Anna M. "Huck Finn, Tom Sawyer, and Samuel Clemens." *PMLA,* LXXXVII (1972), 1130–1131.

558 WELLS, David M. "More on the Geography of *Huckleberry Finn.*" *SAB,* XXXVIII (1973), 82–86.

559 WEXMAN, Virginia. "The Role of Structure in *Tom Sawyer* and *Huckleberry Finn.*" *ALR,* VI (1973), 1–11.

560 WILLIAMS, James D. "Revision and Intention in Mark Twain's *A Connecticut Yankee.*" *AL,* XXXVI (1964), 288–297.

561 WINKELMAN, Donald M. See **371.**

562 WYSONG, Jack P. "Samuel Clemens' Attitude Toward the Negro as Demon-strated in *Pudd'nhead Wilson* and *A Connecticut Yankee at King Arthur's Court.*" *XUS,* VII (1968), 41–57.

563 ZWAHLEN, Christine. "Of Hell or of Hannibal?" *AL,* XLII (1971), 562–563.

Cooper, James Fenimore (1789–1851)

Texts

A definitive edition of Cooper's works, under the general editorship of James F. Beard and the sponsorship of the CEAA, is underway and will be published by the New York State University Press.

564 *Cooper's Novels.* Illustrated by F. O. C. Darley. 32 vols. New York: Townsend, 1859–1861. [Most nearly definitive; usually called the "Darley Edition."]

565 *J. Fenimore Cooper's Works.* "Household Edition." 32 vols. New York: Hurd & Houghton, 1876–1884. [Contains 15 prefaces by Cooper's daughter, Susan.]

566 *The Works of James Fenimore Cooper.* 33 vols. New York: Putnam's, 1895–1900. [Known as "Mohawk Edition"; contains *Ned Myers.*]

567 BEARD, James F., ed. *The Letters and Journal of James Fenimore Cooper.* 6 vols. Cambridge: Harvard Univ. Press, 1960–1968.

There are many reprint editions. The following have useful editorial apparatus:

568 *Home As Found.* Introduction by Lewis Leary. New York: Capricorn Books, 1961.†

569 *James Fenimore Cooper: Representative Selections, With Introduction, Bibliography, and Notes.* Ed. Robert E. Spiller. New York: American Book Co., 1936.

570 *The Leatherstocking Saga.* Ed. Allen Nevins. New York: Pantheon, 1954, and New York: Modern Library, 1965. [The parts of the Leatherstocking Tales which pertain to Natty Bumppo, arranged in chronological order, with an introduction.]

571 *Satanstoe.* Edited with introduction, chronology, and bibliography by Robert E. Spiller. New York: American Book Co., 1937.

Bibliographies

See **3, 8, 18,** and **569.**

572 BEARD, James F. "James Fenimore Cooper." *Fifteen American Authors Before 1900: Bibliographic Essays on Research and Criticism.* Ed. Robert A. Rees and Earl N. Harbert. Madison: Univ. of Wisconsin Press, 1971, pp. 63–96.

573 SPILLER, Robert E., and BLACKBURN, Philip C. *A Descriptive Bibliography of the Writings of James Fenimore Cooper.* New York: R. R. Bowker, 1934. [Standard.]

Biographical and Critical Books

574 BOYNTON, Henry Walcott. *James Fenimore Cooper.* New York: Century, 1931.

575 CUNNINGHAM, Mary, ed. *James Fenimore Cooper: A Re-Appraisal.* Cooperstown, N.Y.: New York State Historical Assn., 1954. [Twelve essays read by scholars at the Cooper Centennial Celebration, 1951.]

576 DEKKER, George. *James Fenimore Cooper: The American Scott.* New York: Barnes & Noble, 1967.

577 FREDERICK, John T. See **169.**

578 GROSSMAN, James. *James Fenimore Cooper.* New York: William Sloane, 1949.†

579 HOUSE, Kay Seymour. *Cooper's Americans.* Columbus: Ohio State Univ. Press, 1965.

580 KOLODNY, Annette. *The Lay of the Land: Metaphor as Experience and History in American Life and Letters.* Chapel Hill: Univ. of North Carolina Press, 1975, pp. 89–115.

581 LOUNSBURY, Thomas R. *James Fenimore Cooper.* Boston: Houghton Mifflin, 1882.

582 MCWILLIAMS, John P., Jr. *Political Justice in a Republic: James Fenimore Cooper's America.* Berkeley: Univ. of California Press, 1972.

583 OVERLAND, ORM. *The Making and Meaning of an American Classic: James Fenimore Cooper's 'The Prairie'.* Oslo: Universitetsforlaget, 1973.

584 PHILBRICK, Thomas. *James Fenimore Cooper and the Development of American Sea Fiction.* Cambridge: Harvard Univ. Press, 1961.

585 RINGE, Donald A. *James Fenimore Cooper.* New York: Twayne, 1962.†

586 RINGE, Donald A. *The Pictorial Mode: Space and Time in the Art of Bryant, Irving and Cooper.* Lexington: Univ. Press of Kentucky, 1971.

587 ROSS, John F. *The Social Criticism of Fenimore Cooper.* University of California Publications in English, III. Berkeley: Univ. of California Press, 1933.

588 SHULENBERGER, Arvid. *Cooper's Theory of Fiction: His Prefaces and Their Relation to His Novels.* University of Kansas Humanities Studies, no. 32. Lawrence: Univ. of Kansas Press, 1955.

589 SPILLER, Robert E. *Fenimore Cooper: Critic of His Times.* New York: Minton, Balch, 1931.

590 SPILLER, Robert E. *James Fenimore Cooper.* University of Minnesota Pamphlets on American Writers, no. 48. Minneapolis: Univ. of Minnesota Press, 1965. Reprinted in **219.**

591 WALKER, Warren S. *James Fenimore Cooper: An Introduction and Interpretation.* New York: Barnes & Noble, 1962.†

592 WAPLES, Dorothy. *The Whig Myth of James Fenimore Cooper.* New Haven: Yale Univ. Press, 1938.

Critical Essays

593 ABCARIAN, Richard. "Cooper's Critics and the Realistic Novel." *TSLL,* VIII (1966), 33–41.

594 ALDRIDGE, A. Owen. "Fenimore Cooper and the Picaresque Tradition." *NCF,* XXVII (1972), 283–292.

595 ANDERSON, Charles. "Cooper's Sea Novels Spurned in the Maintop." *MLN,* LXVI (1951), 388–391.

596 BALL, Roland C. "American Reinterpretations of European Romantic Themes: The Rebel-Hero in Cooper and Melville." Proceedings of the IVth Congress of the International Comparative Literature Association. The Hague: Mouton, 1966, pp. 1113–1121.

597 BAYM, Nina. "The Women of Cooper's Leatherstocking Tales." *AQ,* XXIII (1971), 696–709.

598 BECKER, George J. "James Fenimore Cooper and American Democracy." *CE,* XVII (1956), 325–334.

599 BEWLEY, Marius. "Fenimore Cooper and the Economic Age." *AL,* XXVI (1954), 166–195.

600 BEWLEY, Marius. See **155.**

601 BEWLEY, Marius. "Revaluations (XVI): James Fenimore Cooper." *Scrutiny,* XIX (1952–53), 98–125.

602 BEWLEY, Marius. "The Cage and the Prairie: Two Notes on Symbolism." *HR,* X (1957), 408–413.

603 BIER, Jesse. "The Bisection of Cooper: *Satanstoe* as Prime Example." *TSLL,* IX (1968), 511–521.

604 BIER, Jesse. "Lapsarians on *The Prairie:* Cooper's Novel." *TSLL,* IV (1962), 49–57.

605 BONNER, Willard Hallam. "Cooper and Captain Kidd." *MLN,* LXI (1946), 21–27.

606 BRADY, Charles A. "Myth-Maker and Christian Romancer." See **172.**

607 BRENNER, Gerry. "Cooper's 'Composite Order': *The Pioneers* as Structured Art." *SNNTS,* II (1970), 264–275.

608 BROWNELL, William C. See **215.**

609 CADY, Edwin Harrison. See **162.**

610 CLARK, Harry Hayden. "Fenimore Cooper and Science." *TWA,* XLVIII (1959), 179–204; XLIX (1960), 249–282. [In two parts.]

611 COLLINS, Frank M. "Cooper and the American Dream." *PMLA,* LXXXI (1966), 79–94.

612 DARNELL, Donald G. "Cooper and Faulkner: Land, Legacy, and the Tragic Vision." *SAB,* XXXIV (1969), 3–5.

613 DAVIS, David Brion. "The Deerslayer: A Democratic Knight of the Wilderness." See **226.**

614 DRYDEN, Edgar A. "History and Progress: Some Implications of Form in Cooper's Littlepage Novels." *NCF,* XXVI (1971), 49–64.

615 ERSKINE, John. "James Fenimore Cooper." See **217.**

616 FREDERICK, John T. "Cooper's Eloquent Indians." *PMLA,* LXXXI (1956), 1004–1017.

617 FRENCH, David P. "James Fenimore Cooper and Fort William Henry." *AL,* XXXII (1960), 28–38.

618 FRENCH, Florence H. "Cooper's Use of Proverbs in the Anti-Rent Novels." *NYFQ,* XXVI (1970), 42–49.

619 FRENCH, Florence H. "Cooper the Tinkerer." *NYFQ,* XXVI (1970), 229–239. [Cooper's use of proverbs.]

620 GATES, W. B. "Cooper's Indebtedness to Shakespeare." *PMLA,* LXVII (1952), 716–731.

621 GOETZMANN, William H. "James Fenimore Cooper." See **243,** pp. 66–78.

622 GRIFFIN, Max L. "Cooper's Attitude Toward the South." *SP,* LXVIII (1951), 67–76.

623 GROSSMAN, James. "Fenimore Cooper: The Development of the Novelist." See **216,** pp. 3–24.

624 GROSSMAN, James. "James Fenimore Cooper: An Uneasy American." *YR,* XL (1951), 696–709.

625 HALL, Joan J. "Romance as History: Cooper's Wyandotté." *KyR,* II (1968), 38–46.

626 HASTINGS, George E. "How Cooper Became a Novelist." *AL,* XII (1940), 20–51.

627 HOLMAN, C. Hugh. "The Influence of Scott and Cooper on Simms." *AL*, XXIII (1951), 203–218.

628 HOUSE, Kay Seymour. "James Fenimore Cooper: *The Pioneers.*" See **227**.

629 HOWARD, David. "James Fenimore Cooper's *Leatherstocking Tales:* 'without a cross'." In *Tradition and Tolerance in Nineteenth-Century Fiction: Critical Essays on Some English and American Novels,* edited by David Howard, John Lucas, and John Goode. London: Routledge & K. Paul, 1966; New York: Barnes & Noble, 1967, pp. 9–54.

630 JONES, Howard Mumford. "Prose and Pictures: James Fenimore Cooper." *TSE,* III (1952), 133–154.

631 KAUL, A. N. See **180**.

632 KAY, Donald. "Major Character Types in *Home as Found:* Cooper's Search for American Principles and Dignity." *CLAJ,* XIV (1971), 432–439.

633 KIRK, Russell. "Cooper and the European Puzzle." *CE,* VII (1946), 198–205.

634 LAWRENCE, D. H. See **183**.

635 LEWIS, Merrill. "Lost-and-Found In the Wilderness: The Desert Metaphor in Cooper's *The Prairie.*" *WAL,* V (1970), 195–204.

636 LOVELAND, Anne C. "James Fenimore Cooper and the American Mission." *AQ,* XXI (1969), 244–258.

637 MARTIN, Terence. "From the Ruins of History: *The Last of the Mohicans.*" *Novel,* II (1969), 221–229.

638 MCALEER, John J. "Biblical Analogy in the Leatherstocking Tales." *NCF,* XVII (1962), 217–235.

639 MCDOWELL, Tremaine. "James Fenimore Cooper as Self-Critic." *SP,* XXVII (1930), 508–516.

640 MCDOWELL, Tremaine. "The Identity of Harvey Birch." *AL,* II (1930), 111–120. [On *The Spy.*]

641 MAXWELL, D. E. S. See **190**.

642 MILLS, Gordon. "The Symbolic Wilderness: James Fenimore Cooper and Jack London." *NCF,* XIII (1959), 329–340.

643 MUSZYNSKA-WALLACE, E. Soteris. "The Sources of *The Prairie.*" *AL,* XXI (1949), 191–200.

644 NOBLE, David W. "Cooper, Leatherstocking and the Death of the American Adam." *AQ,* XVI (1964), 419–431.

645 O'DONNELL, Charles. "The Moral Basis of Civilization: Cooper's Home Novels." *NCF,* XVII (1962), 265–273.

646 PAINE, Gregory. "Cooper and the North American Review." *SP,* XXVIII (1931), 267–277.

647 PAINE, Gregory. "The Indians of *The Leatherstocking Tales.*" *SP,* XXIII (1926), 16–39.

648 PAUL, Jay S. "Home as Cherished: The Theme of Family in Fenimore Cooper." *SNNTS,* V (1973), 39–51.

649 PEARCE, Roy Harvey. "The Leatherstocking Tales Reexamined." *SAQ,* XLVI (1947), 524–536. Reprinted in *Historicism Once More.* Princeton: Princeton Univ. Press, 1969.

650 PHILBRICK, Thomas L. "Cooper's *The Pioneers:* Origins and Structure." *PMLA,* LXXIX (1964), 579–593.

651 PHILBRICK, Thomas L. "Language and Meaning in Cooper's *The Water-Witch.*" *ESQ,* LX (1970), 10–16.

652 PHILBRICK, Thomas L. "*The Last of the Mohicans* and the Sounds of Discord." *AL,* XLIII (1971), 25–41.

653 PHILBRICK, Thomas L. "The Sources of Cooper's Knowledge of Fort William Henry." *AL,* XXXVI (1964), 209–214. [On *The Last of the Mohicans.*]

654 PICKERING, James H. "New York in the Revolution: Cooper's *Wyandotté.*" *NYH,* XLIX (1968), 121–141.

655 PICKERING, James H. "*Satanstoe:* Cooper's Debt to William Dunlap." *AL,* XXXVIII (1967), 468–477.

656 RINGE, Donald A. "Chiaroscuro as an Artistic Device in Cooper's Fiction." *PMLA,* LXXVIII (1963), 349–357.

657 RINGE, Donald A. "Cooper's Last Novels, 1847–1850." *PMLA,* LXXV (1960), 583–590.

658 RINGE, Donald A. "Cooper's Littlepage Novels: Change and Stability in American Society." *AL,* XXXII (1960), 280–290.

659 RINGE, Donald A. "James Fenimore Cooper and Thomas Cole: An Analogous Technique." *AL,* XXX (1958), 26–36.

660 RINGE, Donald A. "Man and Nature in Cooper's *The Prairie.*" *NCF,* XV (1961), 313–323.

661 ROBINSON, E. Arthur. "Conservation in Cooper's *The Pioneers.*" *PMLA,* LXXXII (1967), 564–578.

662 SANDY, Alan F., Jr. "The Voices of Cooper's *The Deerslayer.*" *ESQ,* LX (1970), 5–9.

663 SMITH, Henry N. "Consciousness and Social Order: The Theme of Transcendence in the Leatherstocking Tales." *WAL,* V (1970), 177–194.

664 SNELL, George J. "J. Fenimore Cooper: Shaper of American Romance." See **99.**

665 STEIN, Paul. "Cooper's Last Fiction: The Theme of 'Becoming'." *SAQ,* LXX (1971), 77–87.

666 STEIN, William B. "*The Prairie:* The Scenario of the Wise Old Man." *BuR,* XIX (1971), 15–36.

667 SUTTON, Walter. "Cooper as Found—1949." *UKCR,* XVI (1959), 3–10.

668 VANCE, William L. "The Meaning of Cooper's *The Prairie.*" *PMLA,* LXXXIX (1974), 323–331.

669 VAN DER BEETS, Richard. "Cooper and the 'Semblance of Reality': A Source for *The Deerslayer.*" *AL,* XLII (1971), 544–546.

670 VANDIVER, Edward P., Jr. "Simms's Porgy and Cooper." *MLN,* LXX (1955), 272–274.

671 VLACH, John M. "Fenimore Cooper's Leatherstocking as Folk Hero." *NYFQ,* XXVII (1971), 323–338.

672 WALKER, Warren S. "Ames Vs. Cooper: The Case Re-Opened." *MLN,* LXX (1955), 27–32.

673 WALKER, Warren S. "Buckskin West: Leatherstocking at High Noon." *NYFQ*, XXIV (1968), 88–102.

674 WINTERS, Yvor. "Fenimore Cooper or The Ruins of Time." *In Defense of Reason*. Denver: Alan Swallow, 1947.

675 ZOELLNER, Robert H. "Conceptual Ambivalence in Cooper's Leatherstocking." *AL*, XXXI (1960), 397–420.

Crane, Stephen (1871–1900)

Texts

676 *The University of Virginia Edition of the Works of Stephen Crane*. Ed. Fredson Bowers. Charlottesville: Univ. of Virginia Press, 1969–
Vol. I. *Bowery Tales: Maggie; George's Mother*, 1969.
Vol. II. *The Red Badge of Courage*, 1975.
Vol. IV. *The O'Ruddy*, 1971.

677 *The Work of Stephen Crane*. Ed. Wilson Follett. 12 vols. New York: Knopf, 1925–1926. [Considered standard before the CEAA edition (676), but very incomplete. See following volumes which supplement this edition.]

678 *The Complete Novels of Stephen Crane*. With introduction and bibliography by Thomas A. Gullason. Garden City, N.Y.: Doubleday, 1967.

679 *Maggie, A Girl of the Streets*. Ed. Herbert van Thal. London: Cassell, 1966.

680 *Maggie: A Girl of the Streets (A Story of New York)*. Introduction by Philip D. Jordan. Lexington: Univ. Press of Kentucky, 1970.

681 *Maggie: A Girl of the Streets: A Story of New York*. Introduction by Joseph Katz. Gainesville, Fla.: Scholars' Facsimiles & Reprints, 1966.

682 *Maggie: A Girl of the Streets*. Facsimile of 1893. Edited with introduction by Donald Pizer. San Francisco: Chandler, 1968.

683 *The Red Badge of Courage*. (Merrill Editions.) Introduction by Joseph Katz. Columbus, Ohio: Charles E. Merrill, 1969.

684 *Stephen Crane: An Omnibus*. Ed. Robert W. Stallman. New York: Knopf, 1952. ["New" or "restored" text of *A Red Badge of Courage* with much unpublished material. Excellent introduction.]

685 *Stephen Crane's 'Maggie': Text and Context*. Ed. Maurice Bassan. Belmont, Calif.: Wadsworth, 1966.

686 *The Sullivan County Sketches*. Ed. Melvin Schoberlin. Syracuse, N.Y.: Syracuse Univ. Press, 1949.

687 STALLMAN, Robert W., and GILKES, Lillian, eds. *Stephen Crane: Letters*. New York: New York Univ. Press, 1960.

688 STALLMAN, Robert W., and HAGEMANN, E. R., eds. *The War Dispatches of Stephen Crane*. New York: New York Univ. Press, 1964.

There are numerous reprint editions of *The Red Badge of Courage* and other works by Crane.

Bibliographies

See **3, 8, 18, 684**, and **768**.

689 STALLMAN, Robert W. *Stephen Crane: A Critical Bibliography.* Ames: Iowa State Univ. Press, 1972.

690 WILLIAMS, Ames W., and STARRETT, Vincent. *Stephen Crane: A Bibliography.* Glendale, Calif.: John Valentine, 1948.

691 HUDSWORTH, Robert N., ed. "The *Thoth* Annual Bibliography of Stephen Crane Scholarship." *Thoth,* IV (1963) and annually thereafter with various editors.

692 GROSS, Theodore L., and WERTHEIM, Stanley, *Hawthorne, Melville, Stephen Crane: A Critical Bibliography.* New York: Free Press, 1971.

693 KATZ, Joseph. *Checklist of Stephen Crane.* (Merrill Checklists.) Columbus, Ohio: Charles E. Merrill, 1969.

694 PIZER, Donald. "Stephen Crane." See **572**, pp. 97–137.

Biographical and Critical Books

695 BEER, Thomas. *Stephen Crane: A Study in American Letters.* New York: Knopf, 1923; also in Beer's *Hanna, Crane, and the Mauve Decade.* New York: Knopf, 1941.

696 BERRYMAN, John. *Stephen Crane.* New York: Sloane, 1950.†

697 CADY, Edwin H. *Stephen Crane.* New York: Twayne, 1962.†

698 CAZEMAJOU, Jean. *Stephen Crane.* (*UMPAW* 76.) Minneapolis: Univ. of Minnesota Press, 1969.

699 GIBSON, Donald B. *The Fiction of Stephen Crane.* Carbondale: So. Illinois Univ. Press, 1968.

700 GILKES, Lillian. *Cora Crane: A Biography of Mrs. Stephen Crane.* Bloomington: Univ. of Illinois Press, 1960.

701 GULLASON, Thomas A., ed. *Stephen Crane's Career: Perspectives and Evaluations.* With preface. New York: New York Univ. Press, 1972.

702 HOLTON, Milne. *Cylinder of Vision: The Fiction and Journalistic Writing of Stephen Crane.* Baton Rouge: Louisiana State Univ. Press, 1972.

703 LAFRANCE, Marston. *A Reading of Stephen Crane.* Oxford: Clarendon, 1971.

704 LINSON, Corwin K. *My Stephen Crane.* Ed. Edwin H. Cady. Syracuse, N.Y.: Syracuse Univ. Press, 1958.

705 RAYMOND, Thomas L. *Stephen Crane.* Newark, N.J.: Carteret Book Club, 1923. [A pioneer study.]

706 SOLOMON, Eric. *Stephen Crane, From Parody to Realism.* Cambridge: Harvard Univ. Press, 1966.

707 STALLMAN, R. W. *Stephen Crane: A Biography.* New York: George Braziller, 1968.

708 WERTHEIM, Stanley, ed. *The Merrill Studies in 'Maggie' and 'George's Mother'.* With introduction. Columbus, Ohio: Charles E. Merrill, 1970.

Critical Essays

The bulk of the best critical essays are reprinted in the first five volumes. Additional essays are listed following these collections.

709 BASSAN, Maurice, ed. *Stephen Crane: A Collection of Critical Essays.* Englewood Cliffs, N.J.: Prentice-Hall, 1967.

710 BRADLEY, Sculley; BEATTY, R. C.; and LONG, E. H., eds. *The Red Badge of Courage: An Annotated Text, Backgrounds and Sources, Essays in Criticism.* New York: Norton, 1962. Revised Ed., New York: Norton, 1977.†

711 KATZ, Joseph, ed. *Stephen Crane in Transition: Centenary Essays.* Dekalb: No. Illinois Univ. Press, 1972.

712 LETTIS, Richard; MCDONNELL, Robert F.; and MORRIS, William E., eds. *Stephen Crane's The Red Badge of Courage: Text and Criticism.* New York: Harcourt, Brace and Co., 1960.†

713 WEATHERFORD, Richard M., ed. *Stephen Crane: The Critical Heritage.* With introduction. London: Routledge & K. Paul, 1973.

714 ANDERSON, Warren D. "Homer and Stephen Crane." *NCF,* XIX (1964), 77–86.

715 AYERS, Robert W. "W. D. Howells and Stephen Crane: Some Unpublished Letters." *AL,* XXVIII (1957), 469–477.

716 BASSAN, Maurice. "Misery and Society: Some New Perspectives on Stephen Crane's Fiction." *SN,* XXXV (1963), 104–120.

717 BERRYMAN, John. "Stephen Crane: *The Red Badge of Courage.*" See **227.**

718 BRADBURY, Malcolm. "Romance and Reality in *Maggie.*" *JAmS,* III (1969), 111–121.

719 BRENNAN, Joseph X. "Ironic and Symbolic Structure in Crane's *Maggie.*" *NCF,* XVI (1962), 303–315.

720 CADY, Edwin H. "Stephen Crane: *Maggie, a Girl of the Streets.*" See **243,** pp. 172–181.

721 COLVERT, James B. "The Origins of Stephen Crane's Literary Creed." *TexSE,* XXXIV (1954), 179–188.

722 COLVERT, James B. "Structure and Theme in Stephen Crane's Fiction." *MFS,* V (1959), 199–208.

723 DEAMER, Robert G. "Stephen Crane and the Western Myth." *WAL,* VII (1972), 111–123.

724 DILLINGHAM, William B. "Insensibility in *The Red Badge of Courage.*" *CE,* XXV (1963), 194–198.

725 DUSENBERY, Robert. "The Homeric Mood in *The Red Badge of Courage.*" *PCP,* III (1968), 31–37.

726 FORD, Philip H. "Illusion and Reality in Crane's *Maggie.*" *ArQ,* XXV (1969), 293–303.

727 FROHOCK, W. M. *The Red Badge* and the Limits of Parody." *SoR,* VI (1970), 137–148.

728 FRYCKSTEDT, Olov W. "Henry Fleming's Tupenny Fury: Cosmic Pessimism in Stephen Crane's *The Red Badge of Courage.*" *SN,* XXXIII (1961), 265–281.

729 FULWILER, Toby. "The Death of the Handsome Sailor: A Study of *Billy Budd* and *The Red Badge of Courage.*" *ArQ*, XXVI (1970), 101–112.

730 GEISMAR, Maxwell. "Stephen Crane: Halfway House." See **102.**

731 GILKES, Lillian B. "Stephen Crane and the Biographical Fallacy: The Cora Influence." *MFS*, XVI (1970), 441–461.

732 GORDON, Caroline. "Stephen Crane." *Accent*, IX (1949), 153–157.

733 GREENFIELD, Stanley B. "The Unmistakable Stephen Crane." *PMLA*, LXXIII (1958), 562–572. Reprinted in **710** and **712.**

734 GULLASON, Thomas Arthur. "The Jamesian Motif in Stephen Crane's Last Novels." *Person*, XLII (1961), 77–84.

735 GULLASON, Thomas Arthur. "New Light on the Crane-Howells Relationship." *NEQ*, XXX (1957), 389–392.

736 GULLASON, Thomas Arthur. "The Sources of Stephen Crane's *Maggie.*" *PQ*, XXXVIII (1959), 497–502.

737 HAFER, Carol B. "The Red Badge of Absurdity: Irony in *The Red Badge of Courage.*" *CLAJ*, XIV (1971), 440–443.

738 HARRISON, Stanley R. "Stephen Crane and Death: A Moment Between Two Romanticisms." *MarkhamR*, II (1971), 117–120.

739 HART, John E. "*The Red Badge of Courage* as Myth and Symbol." *UKCR*, XIX (1953), 249–256.

740 HUNGERFORD, Harold R. " 'That Was at Chancellorsville': The Factual Framework of *The Red Badge of Courage.*" *AL*, XXXIV (1963), 520–531.

741 IVES, C. B. "Symmetrical Design in Four of Stephen Crane's Stories." *BSUF*, X (1969), 17–26. [*Maggie, George's Mother, Red Badge,* and "The Monster."]

742 JACKSON, Agnes M. "Stephen Crane's Imagery of Conflict in *George's Mother.*" *ArQ*, XXV (1969), 313–318.

743 JOHNSON, George W. "Stephen Crane's Metaphor of Decorum." *PMLA*, LXXVIII (1963), 250–256.

744 KATZ, Joseph. "The *Maggie* Nobody Knows." *MFS*, XII (1966), 200–212.

745 KRAUTH, Leland. "Heroes and Heroics: Stephen Crane's Moral Imperative." *SDR*, XI (1973), 86–93.

746 KWIAT, Joseph J. "The Newspaper Experience: Crane, Norris, and Dreiser." *NCF*, VIII (1953), 99–117.

747 LAFRANCE, Marston. "Stephen Crane in Our Time." See **216**, pp. 27–51.

748 LAFRANCE, Marston. "Stephen Crane's *Private Fleming: His Various Battles.*" See **538**, pp. 113–133.

749 LAVERS, Norman. "Order in *The Red Badge of Courage.*" *UR*, XXXII (1966), 287–295.

750 LEAVER, Florence. "Isolation in the Work of Stephen Crane." *SAQ*, LXI (1962), 521–532.

751 LIEBLING, A. J. "The Dollars Damned Him." *NY*, XXXVII (Aug. 5, 1961), 48–60, 63–66, 69–72.

752 LORCH, Thomas M. "The Cylindrical Structure of *The Red Badge of Courage.*" *CLAJ*, X (1967), 229–238.

753 MCDERMOTT, John J. "Symbolism and Psychological Realism in *The Red Badge of Courage.*" *NCF,* XXIII (1968), 324–331.

754 MARCUS, Mordecai, and MARCUS, Erin. "Animal Imagery in *The Red Badge of Courage.*" *MLN,* LXXIV (1959), 108–111.

755 MORGAN, H. Wayne. "Stephen Crane: The Ironic Hero." See **224.**

756 OSBORN, Scott C. "The 'Rivalry-Chivalry' of Richard Harding Davis and Stephen Crane." *AL,* XXVIII (1956), 50–61.

757 PIZER, Donald. "Crane Reports Garland on Howells." *MLN,* LXX (1955), 37–38.

758 PIZER, Donald. "Romantic Individualism in Garland, Norris, and Crane." *AQ,* X (1958), 463–475.

759 PRATT, Lyndon Upson. "A Possible Source of *The Red Badge of Courage.*" *AL,* XI (1939), 1–10.

760 RATHBUN, John W. "Structure and Meaning in *The Red Badge of Courage.*" *BSUF,* X (1968), 8–16.

761 SCHMITZ, Neil. "Stephen Crane and the Colloquial Self." *MQ,* XIII (1972), 437–451.

762 SCHNEIDER, Robert W. "Stephen Crane: The Promethean Protest." See **109.**

763 SIMONEAUX, Katherine G. "Color Imagery in Crane's *George's Mother.*" *CLAJ,* XIV (1971), 410–419.

764 SNELL, George J. "Naturalism Nascent: Crane and Norris." See **99.**

765 STALLMAN, Robert W. *The Houses that James Built and Other Literary Studies.* East Lansing: Michigan State Univ. Press, 1961. [Essays on James, Crane, and recent authors.]

766 STALLMAN, Robert W. "Stephen Crane and Cooper's Uncas." *AL,* XXXIX (1967), 392–396.

767 STARRETT, Vincent. "An Estimate of Stephen Crane." *SR,* XXVIII (1920), 405–413. [Early modern estimate.]

768 *Stephen Crane Number. MFS,* V (1959), 199–291. [Critical essays on Crane and his works, with a bibliography of criticism.]

769 STEVENSON, John W. "The Literary Reputation of Stephen Crane." *SAQ,* LI (1951), 287–300.

770 TAMKE, Alexander R. "The Principal Source of Stephen Crane's *Red Badge of Courage.*" In *Essays in Honor of Esmond Linworth Marilla,* edited by Thomas A. Kirby and William J. Olive. Baton Rouge: Louisiana State Univ. Press, 1970, pp. 299–311.

771 TUTTLETON, James W. "The Imagery of *The Red Badge of Courage.*" *MFS,* VIII (1963), 410–415.

772 VANDERBILT, Kermit, and WEISS, Daniel. "From Rifleman to Flagbearer: Henry Fleming's Separate Peace in *The Red Badge of Courage.*" *MFS,* XI (1966), 371–380.

773 VAN DOREN, Carl. "Stephen Crane." *American Mercury,* I (1924), 11–14.

774 WALCUTT, Charles C. "Stephen Crane: Naturalist and Impressionist." See **710.**

775 WEBSTER, H. T. "Wilbur T. Hinman's *Corporal Si Klegg* and Stephen Crane's *The Red Badge of Courage.*" *AL,* XI (1939), 285–293.

776 WEISBERGER, Bernard. *"The Red Badge of Courage."* See **226.**

777 WERTHEIM, Stanley. *"The Red Badge of Courage* and Personal Narratives of the Civil War." *ALR,* VI (1973), 61–65.

778 WEST, Ray B., Jr. "Stephen Crane: Author in Transition." *AL,* XXXIV (1962), 215–228.

779 WESTBROOK, Max. "Stephen Crane: The Pattern of Affirmation." *NCF,* XIV (1959), 219–229.

780 WOGAN, Claudia C. "Crane's Use of Color in *The Red Badge of Courage."* *MFS,* VI (1960), 168–172.

De Forest, John William (1826–1906)

Texts

The following reprint editions have useful editorial apparatus:

781 *Honest John Vane.* Introduction by Joseph Jay Rubin. (Monument Ed.) State College, Pa.: Bald Eagle Press, 1960.

782 *Miss Ravenel's Conversion from Secession to Loyalty.* Edited with an introduction by Gordon S. Haight. New York: Rinehart, 1955. [Restores readings expunged from editions after the first.]†

783 *Miss Ravenel's Conversion from Secession to Loyalty.* (Merrill Ed.) With an introduction by Arlin Turner. Columbus, Ohio: Charles E. Merrill, 1969.

Bibliography

See **3** and **8.**

784 HAGEMANN, E. R. "A Checklist of the Writings of John William De Forest (1826–1906)." *SB,* VIII (1956), 185–194.

785 HAGEMANN, E. R. "A John William De Forest Supplement, 1970." *ALR,* III (1970), 148–152.

786 LIGHT, James F. "John William De Forest (1826–1906)." *ALR,* I (1967), 32–35.

Biographical and Critical Books

787 LIGHT, James F. *John William De Forest.* (TUSAS 82.) New York: Twayne, 1965.

Critical Essays

788 CECIL, L. Moffitt. *"Miss Ravenel's Conversion* and *Pilgrim's Progress."* *CE,* XXIII (1962), 352–357.

789 FALK, Robert P. "John W. De Forest: The Panoramic Novel of Realism." See **140.**

790 HAGEMANN, E. R. "John William De Forest's 'Great American Novel'." See **220,** pp. 10–27.

791 HAIGHT, Gordon S. "The John William De Forest Collection." *YULG,* XVI (1940), 41–46.

792 HANSEN, Chadwick. "Salem Witchcraft and De Forest's *Witching Times.*" *EIHC,* CIV (1968), 89–108.

793 HOWELLS, William Dean. "The Heroine of 'Kate Beaumont'." *Heroines of Fiction,* Vol. II. New York: Harper, 1901, pp. 152–163.

794 LEVY, Leo B. "Naturalism in the Making: De Forest's *Honest John Vane.*" *NEQ,* XXXVII (1964), 89–98.

795 MCINTYRE, Clara F. "John William De Forest, Pioneer Realist." *Univ. of Wyoming Publications,* IX (1942), no. 1.

796 O'DONNELL, Thomas F. "De Forest, Van Petten, and Stephen Crane." *AL,* XXVII (1956), 578–580.

797 SESSLER, Harvey M. "A Test for Realism in De Forest's *Kate Beaumont.*" *ALR,* II (1969), 274–276.

798 SIMPSON, Claude M., Jr. "John W. De Forest, *Miss Ravenel's Conversion.*" See **227.**

799 STONE, Albert E., Jr. "Reading, Writing, and History: Best Novel of the Civil War." *AH,* XIII (June, 1962), 84–88. [*Miss Ravenel's Conversion.*]

Dreiser, Theodore (1871–1945)

Texts

There is no definitive or collected edition, but there are many reprints.

800 *Sister Carrie.* Ed. Donald Pizer. With notes and introduction. New York: Norton, 1970.†

801 ELIAS, Robert H., ed. *Letters of Theodore Dreiser: A Selection.* 3 vols. Philadelphia: Univ. of Pennsylvania Press, 1959.

Bibliographies

See **3, 8,** and **18.**

802 ATKINSON, Hugh C. *Checklist of Theodore Dreiser.* (Merrill Checklists.) Columbus, Ohio: Charles E. Merrill, 1969.

803 ATKINSON, Hugh C. *Theodore Dreiser: A Checklist* (Serif Series of Bibliographies & Checklists 15) Kent, Ohio: Kent State Univ. Press, 1971.

804 DOWELL, Richard W., and RUSCH, Frederic E. "A Dreiser Checklist, 1970." *Dreiser Newsletter,* III (1972), 13–21, and annually thereafter, by Frederic E. Rusch.

805 ELIAS, Robert H. "Theodore Dreiser." See **4,** pp. 123–179.

806 KAZIN, Alfred, and SHAPIRO, Charles. "A Selected Bibliography of Dreiser Biography and Criticism." See **828.**

807 MCDONALD, Edward D. *A Bibliography of the Writings of Theodore Dreiser.* Philadelphia: The Centaur Book Shop, 1928.

808 MILLER, R. N. *A Preliminary Checklist of Books and Articles on Theodore Dreiser.* Kalamazoo: Western Michigan College Library, 1947.

809 ORTON, Vrest. *Dreiserana: A Book About His Books.* New York: The Chocurua Bibliographies, 1929.

810 PIZER, Donald. "The Publications of Theodore Dreiser: A Checklist." *Proof,* I (1971), 247–292.

811 SALZMAN, Jack. "Theodore Dreiser (1871–1945)." *ALR,* II (1969), 132–138.

812 SHAPIRO, Charles. *Guide to Theodore Dreiser* (Merrill Guides.) Columbus, Ohio: Charles E. Merrill, 1969.

Biographical and Critical Books

813 BLOCK, Haskell M. *Naturalistic Tryptych: The Fictive and the Real in Zola, Mann, and Dreiser.* New York: Random House, 1970.†

814 CAMPBELL, Louise. *Letters to Louise.* Philadelphia: Univ. of Pennsylvania Press, 1959. [Letters by Dreiser with commentary by Louise Campbell, his typist-editor.]

815 DREISER, Helen. *My Life with Dreiser.* Cleveland, Ohio: World, 1951.

816 DUDLEY, Dorothy. *Forgotten Frontiers: Dreiser and the Land of the Free.* New York: Harrison Smith & Robert Haas, 1932.

817 ELIAS, Robert H. *Theodore Dreiser: Apostle of Nature.* New York: Knopf, 1949. Emended edition. Ithaca, N.Y.: Cornell Univ. Press, 1970.†

818 GERBER, Philip L. *Theodore Dreiser.* New York: Twayne, 1964.†

819 KENNELL, Ruth E. *Dreiser and the Soviet Union (1927–1945): A First-Hand Chronicle.* New York: International Publishers, 1969.

820 LEHAN, Richard. *Theodore Dreiser: His World and His Novels.* Carbondale: So. Illinois Univ. Press, 1969.

821 LUNDÉN, Rolf. *The Inevitable Equation: The Antithetic Pattern of Theodore Dreiser's Thought and Art.* Uppsala: Almquist & Wiksell, 1973.

822 MATTHIESSEN, F. O. *Theodore Dreiser.* New York: Sloane, 1951.

823 MOERS, Ellen. *Two Dreisers.* New York: Viking, 1969.

824 RASCOE, Burton. *Theodore Dreiser.* New York: Robert McBride, 1926.

825 SHAPIRO, Charles. *Theodore Dreiser: Our Bitter Patriot.* Carbondale: So. Illinois Univ. Press, 1962.†

826 SWANBERG, W. A. *Dreiser.* New York: Scribner's, 1965. [Most detailed and reliable biography.]

827 WARREN, Robert Penn. *Homage to Theodore Dreiser: August 27, 1871–December 28, 1945: On the Centennial of His Birth.* New York: Random House, 1971.

Critical Essays

Many of the best essays on Dreiser are collected in the first three entries.

828 KAZIN, Alfred, and SHAPIRO, Charles, eds. *The Stature of Theodore Dreiser.* Bloomington: Indiana Univ. Press, 1955 [A collection of criticism from 1900 to 1955]†

829 LYDENBERG, John, ed. *Drieser: A Collection of Critical Essays.* With introduction. Englewood Cliffs, N.J.: Prentice-Hall, 1971.†

830 SALZMAN, Jack, ed. *Theodore Dreiser: The Critical Reception.* With introduction. New York: David Lewis, 1972.

831 ANDERSON, Sherwood. "An Apology for Crudity." See **828.**

832 ARNAVON, Cyrille. "Theodore Dreiser and Painting." *AL,* XVII (1945), 113–126.

833 BECKER, George J. "Theodore Dreiser: The Realist as Social Critic." *TCL,* I (1955), 117–127.

834 BELLOW, Saul. "Dreiser and the Triumph of Art." See **828.**

835 BERRYMAN, John. "Dreiser's Imagination." See **828.**

836 BOURNE, Randolph. "The Art of Theodore Dresier." See **828.**

837 BROOKS, Van Wyck. "Theodore Dreiser." *UKCR,* XVI (1950), 187–197.

838 BROOKS, Van Wyck. "Theodore Dreiser." See **35.**

839 BURGAN, Mary A. "*Sister Carrie* and the Pathos of Naturalism." *Criticism,* XV (1973), 336–349.

840 BURGUM, Edwin Berry. "Theodore Dreiser and the Ethics of American Life." *The Novel and the World's Dilemma.* New York: Oxford Univ. Press, 1947.

841 CAMPBELL, Charles L. "*An American Tragedy:* Or, Death in the Woods." *MFS,* XV (1969), 251–259.

842 CHAMBERLAIN, John. "Theodore Dreiser Remembered." See **828.**

843 COHEN, Lester. "Theodore Dreiser: A Personal Memoir." *discovery,* IV (1954), 99–126.

844 CRAWFORD, Bruce. "Theodore Dreiser: Letter-Writing Citizen." *SAQ,* LIII (1954), 231–237.

845 DANCE, Daryl C. "Sentimentalism in Dreiser's Heroines, Carrie and Jennie." *CLAJ,* XIV (1970), 127–142.

846 DAVIS, David Brion. "Dreiser and Naturalism Revisited." See **828.**

847 DRUMMOND, Edward J., S. J. "Theodore Dreiser: Shifting Naturalism." In *Fifty Years of the American Novel,* edited by Harold C. Gardiner, S. J. New York: Scribner's, 1951, pp. 33–47.

848 DUFFUS, Robert L. "Dreiser." *Am. Mercury,* VII (1926), 71–76.

849 FARRELL, James T. "Some Correspondence with Theodore Dreiser." See **828.**

850 FLANAGAN, John T. "Dreiser's Style in *An American Tragedy.*" *TSLL,* VII (1965), 285–294.

851 FLANAGAN, John T. "Theodore Dreiser in Retrospect." *SWR,* XXXI (1946), 408–411.

852 FORD, Ford Madox. "Portrait of Dreiser." See **828.**

853 FREEDMAN, William A. "A Look at Dreiser as Artist: The Motif of Circularity in *Sister Carrie.*" *MFS,* VIII (1963), 384–392.

854 FRIEDRICH, Gerhard. "Theodore Dreiser's Debt to Woolman's *Journal.*" *AQ,* VII (1955), 385–392.

855 GEISMAR, Maxwell. "Dreiser and the Dark Texture of Life." *ASch,* XXII (1953), 215–221.

856 GEISMAR, Maxwell. "Theodore Dreiser: The Double Soul." See **102.**

857 GELFANT, Blanche Housman. "Theodore Dreiser: The Portrait Novel." See **174.**

858 GERBER, Philip L. "The Alabaster Protégé: Dreiser and Berenice Fleming." *AL,* XLIII (1971), 217–230.

859 GERBER, Philip L. "Dreiser's Financier: A Genesis." *JML,* I (1971), 354–374.

860 GERBER, Philip L. "The Financier Himself: Dreiser and C. T. Yerkes." *PMLA,* LXXXVIII (1973), 112–121.

861 GOODFELLOW, Donald M. "Theodore Dreiser and the American Dream." *Six Novelists: Stendhal, Dostoevski, Tolstoi, Hardy, Dreiser, Proust.* Pittsburgh: Carnegie Institute of Technology, 1959, pp. 53–66.

862 GREBSTEIN, Sheldon N. *"An American Tragedy:* Theme and Structure." In *The Twenties, Poetry and Prose: 20 Critical Essays,* edited by Richard E. Langford and William E. Taylor. Deland, Fla.: Everett Edwards Press, 1966, pp. 62–66.

863 GRIFFIN, Robert J. "Carrie and Music: A Note on Dreiser's Technique." In *From Irving to Steinbeck: Studies of American Literature in Honor of Harry R. Warfel,* edited by Motley Deakin and Peter Lisca. Gainesville: Univ. of Florida Press, 1972, pp. 73–81.

864 HAKUTANI, Yoshinobu. "Dreiser and French Realism." *TSLL,* VI (1964), 200–212.

865 HAKUTANI, Yoshinobu. *"Sister Carrie* and the Problem of Literary Naturalism." *TCL,* XIII (1967), 3–17.

866 HANDY, William J. "A Re-Examination of Dreiser's *Sister Carrie."* *TSLL,* I (1959), 380–393.

867 HOVEY, Richard B., and RALPH, Ruth S. "Dreiser's *The 'Genius':* Motivation and Structure." *HSL,* II (1970), 169–183.

868 JURNAK, Sheila H. "Popular Art Forms in *Sister Carrie."* *TSLL,* XIII (1971), 313–320.

869 KANE, Patricia. "Reading Matter as a Clue to Dreiser's Characters." *SDR,* VIII (1970), 104–106.

870 KATOPE, Christopher G. *"Sister Carrie* and Spencer's *First Principles."* *AL,* LXI (1969), 64–75.

871 KATZ, Joseph. "Dummy: *The 'Genius',* by Theodore Dreiser." *Proof,* I (1971), 330–357.

872 KATZ, Joseph. "Theodore Dreiser and Stephen Crane: Studies in a Literary Relationship." See **711,** pp. 174–204.

873 KAZIN, Alfred. "Theodore Dreiser: His Education and Ours." See **828.**

874 KERN, Alexander. "Dreiser's Difficult Beauty." *WR,* XVI (1952), 129–136. See **828.**

875 KWIAT, Joseph J. "Dreiser and the Graphic Artist." *AQ,* III (1951), 127–141.

876 KWIAT, Joseph J. "The Newspaper Experience: Crane, Norris, and Dreiser." See **746.**

877 LANE, Lauriat, Jr. "The Double in *An American Tragedy*." *MFS*, XII (1966), 213–220.

878 LEHAN, Richard. "Dreiser's *An American Tragedy*: A Critical Study." *CE*, XXV (1963), 187–193.

879 LEONARD, Neil. "Theodore Dreiser and Music." See **548**, pp. 242–250.

880 LEWIS, Sinclair. "Our Formula for Fiction." See **828**.

881 LEWISOHN, Ludwig. "An American Memory." See **828**.

882 LORD, David. "Dreiser Today." *PrS*, XV (1941), 230–239.

883 LYDENBERG, John. "Theodore Dreiser: Ishmael in the Jungle." In *American Radicals: Some Problems and Personalities*, edited by Harvey Goldberg. New York: Monthly Review Press, 1957.

884 LYNN, Kenneth S. "Theodore Dreiser: The Man of Ice." See **187**.

885 MCALEER, John J. "*An American Tragedy* and *In Cold Blood*." *Thought*, LXVII (1972), 569–586.

886 MARKELS, Julian. "Dreiser and the Plotting of Inarticulate Experience." *MR*, II (1961), 431–448.

887 MENCKEN, H. L. "The Dreiser Bugaboo." See **828**.

888 MENCKEN, H. L. "Theodore Dreiser." *A Book of Prefaces*. New York: Knopf, 1920, 67–148.

889 MILLGATE, Michael. "Theodore Dreiser." See **142**.

890 MILLGATE, Michael. "Theodore Dreiser and the American Financier." *SA*, VII (1961), 133–145.

891 MOERS, Ellen. "The Finesse of Dreiser." *ASch*, XXXIII (1963), 109–114.

892 MOOKERJEE, R. N. "Dreiser's Use of Hindu Thought in *The Stoic*." *AL*, XLIII (1971), 273–278.

893 MOOKERJEE, R. N. "The Literary Naturalist as Humanist: The Last Phase of Theodore Dreiser." *MQ*, XII (1971), 369–381.

894 MORGAN, H. Wayne. "Theodore Dreiser: The Naturalist as Humanist." See **223**.

895 NOBLE, David W. "Dreiser and Veblen and the Literature of Cultural Change." In *Studies in American Culture: Dominant Ideas and Images*, edited by Joseph J. Kwiat and Mary C. Turple. Minneapolis: Univ. of Minnesota Press, 1960.

896 PARRINGTON, Vernon L. Jr. "Theodore Dreiser: Chief of American Naturalists." See **44**, Vol. III.

897 PHILLIPS, William L. "The Imagery of Dreiser's Novels." *PMLA*, LXXVIII (1963), 572–585.

898 PIZER, Donald. "The Problem of Philosophy in the Novel." *BuR*, XVIII (1970), 53–62.

899 PIZER, Donald. See **115**.

900 PURDY, Strother B. "*An American Tragedy* and *L'Etranger*." *CL*, XIX (1967), 252–268.

901 RICHMAN, Sidney. "Theodore Dreiser's *The Bulwark*: A Final Resolution." *AL*, XXXIV (1962), 229–245.

902 ROSS, Woodburn O. "Concerning Dreiser's Mind." *AL*, XVIII (1946). 233–243.

903 SALZMAN, Jack. "The Critical Recognition of *Sister Carrie*: 1900–1907." *JAmS,* III (1969), 123–133.

904 SALZMAN, Jack. "The Curious History of Dreiser's *The Bulwark.*" *Proof,* III (1973), 21–61.

905 SALZMAN, Jack. "The Publication of *Sister Carrie:* Fact and Fiction." *LC,* XXXIII (1967), 119–133.

906 SCHNEIDER, Isidor. "Theodore Dreiser." *SRL,* X (1934), 533–535.

907 SCHNEIDER, Robert W. "Theodore Dreiser: The Cry of Despair." See **109.**

908 SHAPIRO, Charles. "*Jennie Gerhardt*: The American Family and the American Dream." See **226.**

909 SHERMAN, Stuart P. "The Barbaric Naturalism of Theodore Dreiser." See **828.**

910 SIMPSON, Claude M., Jr. "*Sister Carrie* Reconsidered." *SWR,* XLIV (1959), 44–53.

911 SIMPSON, Claude M., Jr. "Theodore Dreiser, *Sister Carrie.*" See **227.**

912 SNELL, George J. "Theodore Dreiser: Philosopher." See **99.**

913 SPATZ, Jonas. "Dreiser's Bulwark: An Archaic Masterpiece." In *The Forties: Fiction, Poetry, Drama,* edited by Warren French. Deland, Fla.: Everett/Edwards, 1969, pp. 155–162.

914 THOMAS, J. D. "Epimetheus Bound: Theodore Dreiser and the Novel of Thought." *SHR,* III (1969), 346–357.

915 THOMAS, J. D. "The Supernatural Naturalism of Dreiser's Novels." *RIP,* XLVI (1959) i, 53–69.

916 TRILLING, Lionel, "Reality in America." See **828.**

917 VANCE, William L. "Dreiserian Tragedy." *SNNTS,* IV (1972), 39–51.

918 VIVAS, Eliseo. "Dreiser, an Inconsistent Mechanist." See **828.**

919 WADLINGTON, Warwick. "Pathos and Dreiser." *SoR,* VII (1971), 411–429.

920 WALCUTT, Charles C. "*Sister Carrie:* Naturalism or Novel of Manners?" *Genre,* I (1968), 76–85.

921 WALCUTT, Charles C. "The Three Stages of Theodore Dreiser's Naturalism." *PMLA,* LV (1940), 266–289.

922 WALCUTT, Charles C. "Theodore Dreiser: The Wonder and Terror of Life." See **117.**

923 WARREN, Robert Penn. "*An American Tragedy.*" *YR,* LII (1962), 1–15.

924 WARREN, Robert Penn. "Homage to Theodore Dreiser on the Centenary of His His Birth." *SoR,* VII (1971), 345–410.

925 WEIR, Sybil B. "The Image of Women in Dreiser's Fiction." *PCP,* VII (1972), 65–71.

926 WESTLAKE, Neda M. "Dummy: *Twelve Men,* by Theodore Dreiser." *Proof,* II (1972), 153–174.

927 WHIPPLE, T. K. "Aspects of a Pathfinder." See **828.**

928 WILLEN, Gerald. "Dreiser's Moral Seriousness." *UKCR,* XXIII (1957), 181–187.

929 WILLIAMS, Philip. "The Chapter Titles of *Sister Carrie.*" *AL,* XXXVI (1964), 359–365.

930 WITEMEYER, Hugh. "Gaslight and Magic Lamp in *Sister Carrie.*" *PMLA,* LXXXVI (1971), 236–240.

Frederic, Harold (1856–1898)

Texts

There is no collected edition. The following reprinted editions have useful editorial apparatus:

931 *The Damnation of Theron Ware.* Ed. Everett Carter. The John Harvard Library. Cambridge: Harvard Univ. Press, 1960.

932 O'DONNELL, Thomas F., ed. *Harold Frederic's Stories of New York State.* Introduction by Edmund Wilson. Syracuse, N.Y.: Syracuse Univ. Press, 1966.

Bibliography

See **8, 18,** and **940.**

933 KATZ, Joseph. "Harold Frederic's *March Hares*: A Bibliographical Note." *Serif,* VI (1969), 36–37.

934 O'DONNELL, Thomas F. *Checklist of Harold Frederic.* (Merrill Checklists.) Columbus, Ohio: Charles E. Merrill, 1969.

935 O'DONNELL, Thomas F. "Harold Frederic (1856–1898)." *ALR,* I (1967), 39–44.

936 WOODWARD, Robert H. "Harold Frederic: Supplemental Critical Bibliography of Secondary Comment." *ALR,* III (1970), 95–147.

Biographical and Critical Books

937 BRIGGS, Austin, Jr. *The Novels of Harold Frederic.* Ithaca, N.Y.: Cornell Univ. Press, 1969.

938 GARNER, Stanton. *Harold Frederic.* (UMPAW 83.) Minneapolis: Univ. of Minnesota Press, 1969.

939 O'DONNELL, Thomas F. *Frederic in the Mohawk Valley.* Utica, N.Y.: Occasional Papers from Utica College, 1968.

940 O'DONNELL, Thomas F., and FRANCHERE, Hoyt C. *Harold Frederic.* New York: Twayne, 1961.†

Critical Essays

941 BLACKALL, Jean F. "Frederic's *Gloria Mundi* as a Novel of Education." *MarkhamR,* III (1972), 41–46.

942 BLACKALL, Jean F. "Perspectives on Harold Frederic's *Market-Place.*" *PMLA,* LXXXVI (1971), 388–405.

943 BREDAHL, A. Carl, Jr. "The Artist in *The Damnation of Theron Ware.*" *SNNTS,* IV (1972), 432–441.

944 CROWLEY, John W. "The Nude and the Madonna in *The Damnation of Theron Ware.*" *AL,* XLV (1973), 379–389.

945 DAVIS, Horton. *A Mirror of the Ministry in Modern Novels.* New York: Oxford Univ. Press, 1959, pp. 71–78. [Includes material on *The Damnation of Theron Ware.*]

946 GARMON, Gerald M. "Naturalism and *The Damnation of Theron Ware.*" *WGCR,* II (1969), 44–51.

947 GARNER, Stanton. "Harold Frederic and Swinburne's *Locrine*: A Matter of Clubs, Copyrights, and Character." *AL,* XLV (1973), 285–292.

948 JOHNSON, George W. "Harold Frederic's Young Goodman Ware: The Ambiguities of a Realistic Romance." *MFS,* VIII (1963), 361–374.

949 KANTOR, J. R. K. "Autobiography and Journalism: Sources for Harold Frederic's Fiction." *Serif,* IV (1967), 19–27.

950 KANTOR, J. R. K. "*The Damnation of Theron Ware* and *John Ward, Preacher.*" *Serif,* III (1966), 16–21.

951 MILNE, W. Gordon. "Frederic's 'Free' Woman." *ALR,* VI (1973), 258–260.

952 RALEIGH, John Henry. "*The Damnation of Theron Ware.*" *AL,* XXX (1958), 210–227.

953 STEIN, Allen F. "Evasions of an American Adam: Structure and Theme in *The Damnation of Theron Ware.*" *ALR,* V (1972), 23–36.

954 SUDERMAN, Elmer F. "*The Damnation of Theron Ware* as a Criticism of American Religious Thought." *HLQ,* XXXIII (1969), 61–75.

955 VAN DER BEETS, Richard. "The Ending of *The Damnation of Theron Ware.*" *AL,* XXXVI (1964), 358–359.

956 WALCUTT, Charles C. "Adumbrations: Harold Frederic." See **117.**

957 WALCUTT, Charles C. "Harold Frederic and American Naturalism." *AL,* XI (1939), 11–22.

958 WILLIAMS, David. "The Nature of the Damnation of Theron Ware." *MSE,* II (1969), 41–48.

959 WOODWARD, Robert H. "A Ghost Edition of *Theron Ware.*" *Frederic Herald,* I (1967), 4.

960 WOODWARD, Robert H. "Mohawk Valley Folk Life During the Civil War." *NYFQ,* XVIII (1962), 107–118. [On Frederic's regional novels and stories.]

961 WOODWARD, Robert H. "The Political Background of Harold Frederic's Novel *Seth's Brother's Wife.*" *NYH,* XLIII (1962), 239–248.

962 WOODWARD, Robert H. "Illusion and Moral Ambivalence in *Seth's Brother's Wife.*" *ALR,* II (1969), 279–282.

963 WOODWARD, Robert H. "Some Sources for Harold Frederic's *The Damnation of Theron Ware.*" *AL,* XXXIII (1961), 46–51.

964 ZLOTNICK, Joan. "*The Damnation of Theron Ware,* with a Backward Glance at Hawthorne." *MarkhamR,* II (1971), 90–92.

Garland, Hamlin (1860–1940)

Texts

There is no collected edition. The following reprinted editions have useful editorial apparatus:

965 *Crumbling Idols: Twelve Essays on Art, Dealing Chiefly with Literature, Painting, and the Drama.* Edited with an introduction by Jane Johnson. John Harvard Library. Cambridge: Harvard Univ. Press, 1960.

966 *Main-Travelled Roads.* Edited with a new preface by B. R. McElderry, Jr., and with the 1893 introduction by William Dean Howells. New York: Harper, 1956.

967 *Main-Travelled Roads.* (Merrill Editions) With an introduction by Donald Pizer. Columbus, Ohio: Charles E. Merrill, 1970.

968 *Rose of Dutcher's Coolly.* Ed. Donald Pizer. With introduction. Lincoln: Univ. of Nebraska Press, 1969.†

969 PIZER, Donald, ed. *Hamlin Garland's Diaries.* San Marco, Calif.: Huntington Library, 1969.

Bibliography

See **8, 18, 966,** and **974.**

970 ARVIDSON, Lloyd A., ed. *Centennial Tributes and a Checklist of the Hamlin Garland Papers in the University of Southern California Library.* Los Angeles: Univ. of Southern California Library, 1962.

971 BRYER, Jackson R., and HARDING, Eugene, [assisted by Robert A. Rees]. *Hamlin Garland and the Critics: An Annotated Bibliography.* Troy, N.Y.: Whitson, 1973.

972 PIZER, Donald. "Hamlin Garland (1860–1940)." *ALR,* I (1967), 45–51.

973 PIZER, Donald. "Hamlin Garland: A Bibliography of Newspaper and Periodical Publications (1885–1895)." *BB,* XXII (1957), 41–44.

Biographical and Critical Books

974 HOLLOWAY, Jean. *Hamlin Garland: A Biography.* Austin: Univ. of Texas Press, 1960.

975 MANE, Robert. *Hamlin Garland: l'homme et l'oeuvre, 1860–1940.* Paris: Didier, 1968. [*Études anglaises*, 30.]

976 PIZER, Donald. *Hamlin Garland's Early Works and Career.* Berkeley, Univ. of California Press, 1960.

Critical Essays

977 ÅHNEBRINK, Lars. "Garland and Dreiser: An Abortive Friendship." *MJ,* VII (1955–1956), 285–292.

978 ÅHNEBRINK, Lars. See **114.**

979 ALSEN, Eberhard. "Hamlin Garland's First Novel: *A Spoil of Office.*: *WAL*, IV (1969), 91–105.

980 CARTER, Joseph L. "Hamlin Garland's Liberated Woman." *ALR*, VI (1973), 255–258.

981 DALY, J. P., S. J. "Hamlin Garland's *Rose of Dutcher's Coolly.*" *English Language & Literature* (Korea), No. 11 (1962), 51–65.

982 DUFFEY, Bernard. "Hamlin Garland." *The Chicago Renaissance in American Letters.* East Lansing: Michigan State College Press, 1954, pp. 75–89.

983 DUFFEY, Bernard. "Hamlin Garland's 'Decline' from Realism." *AL*, XV (1953), 69–74.

984 EDWARDS, Herbert W. "Herne, Garland, and Henry George." *AL*, XXVIII (1956), 69–74.

985 EVANS, T. Jeff. "The Return Motif as a Function of Realism in *Main-Travelled Roads.*" *KanQ*, V (1973), 33–40.

986 FLANAGAN, John T. "Hamlin Garland, Occasional Minnesotan." *MH*, XXII (1941), 157–168.

987 FLANAGAN, John T. "Hamlin Garland Writes to His Chicago Publishers." *AL*, XXIII (1952), 447–457.

988 FRENCH, Warren. "What Shall We Do About Hamlin Garland?" *ALR*, III (1970), 283–289.

989 FULLER, Daniel J. See **494.**

990 HARRISON, Stanley R. "Hamlin Garland and the Double Vision of Naturalism." *SSF*, VI (1969), 548–556.

991 HENSON, Clyde E. "Joseph Kirkland's Influence on Hamlin Garland." *AL*, (1952), 458–463.

992 IRSFELD, John H. "The Use of Military Language in Hamlin Garland's 'The Return of a Private'." *WAL*, VII (1972), 145–147.

993 MCELDERRY, B. R., Jr. "Hamlin Garland and Henry James." *AL*, XXIII (1952), 433–446.

994 MENCKEN, H. L. "A Stranger on Parnassus." *Prejudices: First Series.* New York: Knopf, 1919.

995 MEYER, Roy W. "Hamlin Garland and the American Indian." *WAL*, II (1967), 109–125.

996 MILLER, Charles T. "Hamlin Garland's Retreat from Realism." *WAL*, I (1966), 119–129.

997 MORGAN, H. Wayne. "Hamlin Garland: The Rebel as Escapist." See **223.**

998 NEVINS, Allen. "Garland and the Prairies." *Literary Rev.,* II (1922), 881–882.

999 PIZER, Donald. "Crane Reports Garland on Howells." *MLN*, LXX (1955), 37–39.

1000 PIZER, Donald. "Hamlin Garland in the *Standard.*" *AL*, XXVI (1954), 401–405.

1001 PIZER, Donald. "Hamlin Garland's *A Son of the Middle Border:* An Appreciation." *SAQ*, LXV (1966), 448–459.

1002 PIZER, Donald. "Hamlin Garland's *A Son of the Middle Border:* Autobiography as 'Art'." See **498**, pp. 76–107.

1003 PIZER, Donald. "Romantic Individualism in Garland, Norris, and Crane." *AQ,* X (1958), 463–475.

1004 RAW, Ruth M. "Hamlin Garland, the Romanticist." *SR,* XXXVI (1928), 202–210.

1005 SAUM, Lewis O. "Hamlin Garland and Reform." *SDR,* X (1972), 36–62.

1006 SCHORER, C. E. "Hamlin Garland of Wisconsin." *WMH,* XXXVIII (1954), 147–150; 182–185.

1007 SIMPSON, Claude M., Jr. "Hamlin Garland's Decline." *SWR,* XXVI (1941), 223–234.

1008 STRONKS, James B. "Garland's Private View of Crane in 1898 (with a Postscript)." *ALR,* VI (1973), 249–250.

1009 STRONKS, James B. "A Realist Experiments with Impressionism; Hamlin Garland's 'Chicago Sketches'." *AL,* XXXVI (1964), 38–52.

1010 TAYLOR, Walter Fuller. "Hamlin Garland." See **153**.

1011 WALCUTT, Charles C. "Adumbrations: Hamlin Garland." See **117**.

1012 WHITFORD, Kathryn. "Patterns of Observation: A Study of Hamlin Garland's Middle Border Landscape." *TWA,* L (1961), 331–338.

Glasgow, Ellen (1874–1945)

Texts

1013 *The Works of Ellen Glasgow.* 12 vols. "The Virginia Edition." New York: Scribner's, 1938. [Standard but incomplete, with prefaces by author.)

1014 GORE, Luther Y., ed. *Beyond Defeat: An Epilogue to an Era.* With introduction. Charlottesville: Univ. Press of Virginia, 1966.

1015 *A Certain Measure: An Interpretation of Prose Fiction.* New York: Harcourt, Brace, 1943. [Contains prefaces from "Virginia Edition," plus one for *In This Our Life.*]

1016 *The Woman Within.* New York: Harcourt, Brace, 1954. [Intellectual and emotional autobiography.]

1017 ROUSE, Blair, ed. *Letters of Ellen Glasgow.* New York: Harcourt, Brace, 1958.

Bibliography

See **3, 8, 18,** and **1026.**

1018 EGLY, William H. "Bibliography of Ellen Andersen Gholson Glasgow." *BB,* XVII (1940), 47–50.

1019 KELLY, William W. *Ellen Glasgow, A Bibliography.* Charlottesville: Univ. Press of Virginia, 1964. [Standard with complete data on her works and the criticism of them.]

1020 MACDONALD, Edgar E. "Ellen Glasgow: An Essay in Bibliography." *RALS,* II (1972), 131–156.

1021 QUESENBERY, W. D., Jr. "Ellen Glasgow: A Critical Bibliography." *BB,* XXII (1959), 201–206; 230–236.

Biographical and Critical Books

1022 AUCHINCLOSS, Louis. *Ellen Glasgow.* University of Minneapolis Pamphlets on American Writers, No. 33. Minneapolis: Univ. of Minnesota Press, 1964. Reprinted with revisions in *Pioneers and Caretakers.* See **214.**

1023 GODBOLD, E. Stanly, Jr. *Ellen Glasgow and the Woman Within.* Baton Rouge: Louisiana State Univ. Press, 1972.

1024 HOLMAN, C. Hugh. *Three Modes of Modern Southern Fiction: Glasgow, Faulkner, Wolfe.* Athens: Univ. of Georgia Press, 1966.

1025 MCDOWELL, Frederick P. W. *Ellen Glasgow and the Ironic Art of Fiction.* Madison: University of Wisconsin Press, 1960.

1026 RAPER, J. W. *Without Shelter: The Early Career of Ellen Glasgow.* Baton Rouge: Louisiana State Univ. Press, 1971.

1027 RICHARDS, Marion K. *Ellen Glasgow's Development as a Novelist.* (SAmL 24.) The Hague: Mouton, 1971.

1028 ROUSE, H. Blair. *Ellen Glasgow.* New York: Twayne, 1962.†

1029 RUBIN, Louis D., Jr. *No Place on Earth: Ellen Glasgow, James Branch Cabell, and Richmond-in-Virginia.* Austin: Univ. of Texas Press, 1960.

1030 SANTAS, Joan Foster. *Ellen Glasgow's American Dream.* Charlottesville: Univ. Press, of Virginia, 1965.

Critical Essays

1031 BALDWIN, Alice M. "Ellen Glasgow." *SAQ,* LIV (1955), 394–404.

1032 BECKER, Allen W. "Ellen Glasgow's Social History." *TexSE,* XXXVI 1957), 12–19.

1033 BECKER, Allen W. "Ellen Glasgow and the Southern Literary Tradition." *MFS,* V (1959), 295–303.

1034 BRICKELL, Herschel. "Miss Glasgow and Mr. Marquand." *VQR,* XVII (1941), 405–417.

1035 CABELL, James Branch. "Two Sides of the Shielded." *Some of Us.* New York: Robert M. McBride, 1930, pp. 47–58.

1036 CANBY, Henry Seidel. "Ellen Glasgow: Ironic Tragedian." *SRL,* XVIII (Sept. 10, 1938), 3–4; 14.

1037 CLARK, Emily. "Appreciation of Ellen Glasgow and Her Work." *VQR,* V (1929), 182–191.

1038 EWING, Majl. "The Civilized Uses of Irony: Ellen Glasgow." In *English Studies in Honor of James Southall Wilson,* edited by Fredson Bowers. Charlottesville, Va.: *Univ. of Virginia Studies,* IV (1951), 81–91.

1039 GEISMAR, Maxwell. "Ellen Glasgow: The Armor of the Legend." See **102.**

1040 GILES, Barbara. "Character and Fate: The Novels of Ellen Glasgow." *Midstream*, IX (1956), 20–31.

1041 GLASGOW, Ellen. "One Way to Write Novels." *SRL*, XI (1934), 335; 344; 350; XXVII (Dec. 22, 1945), 12–13; 29–31.

1042 HARDY, John Edward. "Ellen Glasgow." In *Southern Renascence: The Literature of the Modern South*, edited by Louis D. Rubin, Jr., and Robert D. Jacobs. Baltimore: Johns Hopkins, 1953.

1043 HEINEMANN, K. A. "Ellen Glasgow: The Death of the Chivalrous Tradition." *ForumH*, IV (1967), 37–41.

1044 HOLLAND, Robert. "Miss Glasgow's 'Prufrock'." *AQ*, IX (1957), 435–440.

1045 HOLMAN, C. Hugh. "Ellen Glasgow and the Southern Literary Tradition." In *Virginia in History and Tradition*, edited by R. C. Simonini, Jr. Farmville, Va.: Longwood College, 1958. Reprinted and revised in *Southern Writers: Appraisals in Our Time*, edited by R. C. Simonini, Jr.. Charlottesville: Univ. Press of Virginia, 1964.

1046 HOLMAN, C. Hugh. "April in Queenborough: Ellen Glasgow's Comedies of Manners." *SR*, LXXXII (1974), 263–283.

1047 JESSUP, Josephine Lurie. *The Faith of Our Feminists: A Study of the Novels of Edith Wharton, Ellen Glasgow, Willa Cather*. New York: Richard R. Smith, 1950.

1048 KAZIN, Alfred. "Elegy and Satire." see **105**.

1049 MACDONALD, Edgar E. "Biographical Notes on Ellen Glasgow." *RALS*, III (1973), 249–253.

1050 MACDONALD, Edgar E. "The Glasgow-Cabell Entente." *AL*, XLI (1969), 76–91.

1051 MCDOWELL, Frederick P. W. "Ellen Glasgow and the Art of the Novel." *PQ*, XXX (1951), 328–347.

1052 MCDOWELL, Frederick P. W. " 'The Old Pagan Scorn of Everlasting Mercy'— Ellen Glasgow's *The Deliverance.* " *TCL*, IV (1959), 135–142.

1053 MIMS, Edwin. "The Social Philosophy of Ellen Glasgow." *Social Forces*, IV (1926), 495–503.

1054 MONROE, N. Elizabeth. "Contemplation of Manners in Ellen Glasgow." *The Novel and Society*. Chapel Hill: Univ. of North Carolina Press, 1941, pp. 139–187.

1055 MORGAN, H. Wayne. "Ellen Glasgow: The Qualities of Endurance." See **224**.

1056 PARKER, William R. "Ellen Glasgow: A Gentle Rebel." *EJ*, XX (1931), 187–194.

1057 PATTERSON, Daniel W. "Ellen Glasgow's Plan for a Social History of Virginia." *MFS*, V (1959), 353–360.

1058 ROUSE, H. Blair. "Ellen Glasgow in Retrospect." *EUQ*, VI (1950), 30–40.

1059 ROUSE, H. Blair. "Ellen Glasgow: Manners and Art." *Cabellian*, IV (1972), 96–98.

1060 ROUSE, H. Blair. "Ellen Glasgow: The Novelist in America." *Cabellian*, IV (1971), 25–35.

1061 STONE, Grace. "Ellen Glasgow and Her Novels." *SR*, L (1942), 289–301.

1062 WAGENKNECHT, Edward. "*Great Expectations* and Ellen Glasgow." *BUSE*, III (1957), 57–60.

1063 WELSH, John R. "Egdon Heath Revisited: Ellen Glasgow's *Barren Ground.*" In
Reality and Myth, edited by William E. Walker and Robert L. Welker. Nashville:
Vanderbilt Univ. Press, 1964.

Hawthorne, Nathaniel (1804–1864)

Texts

1064 *The Complete Works of Nathaniel Hawthorne, With Introductory Notes.* Ed.
George P. Lathrop. "The Riverside Edition." 12 vols. Boston: Houghton Mifflin,
1883. [Standard, but being superseded by **1065.**]

1065 *The Centenary Edition of the Works of Nathaniel Hawthorne.* General editors:
William Charvat, Roy H. Pearce, C. M. Simpson. Introductions by R. H. Pearce.
Textual introductions by Fredson Bowers. Columbus: Ohio State Univ. Press,
1962–.
> Vol. I. *The Scarlet Letter.* Ed. Fredson Bowers, 1963.
> Vol. II. *The House of the Seven Gables.* Ed. Fredson Bowers, 1965.
> Vol. III. *The Blithedale Romance* and *Fanshawe.* Ed. William Charvat and
> others, 1964.
> Vol. IV. *The Marble Faun: or The Romance of Monte Beni.* 1968. [Ed. William
> Charvat and others.]
> Vol. VIII. *The American Notebooks.* Ed. Claude Simpson, 1972.

1066 *Complete Novels and Selected Tales of Nathaniel Hawthorne.* Edited with an
introduction by Norman Holmes Pearson. New York: Modern Library, 1937.
[Best immediately available edition.]

1067 *The American Notebooks of Nathaniel Hawthorne.* Edited (from manuscripts) by
Randall Stewart. New Haven: Yale Univ. Press, 1932.

1068 *The English Notebooks of Nathaniel Hawthorne.* Edited (from manuscripts) by
Randall Stewart. New York: Modern Language Association, 1941.

1069 WARREN, Austin, ed. *Nathaniel Hawthorne: Representative Selections, With
Introduction, Bibliography, and Notes.* New York: American Book Co., 1934.

Bibliography

See **3, 8, 18, 1069,** and **1120.**

1070 BROWNE, Nina Eliza. *A Bibliography of Nathaniel Hawthorne.* Boston: Houghton Mifflin, 1905.

1071 CAMERON, Kenneth W. *Hawthorne Index to Themes, Motifs, Topics, Arche-
types, Sources, and Key Words Dealt with in Recent Criticism.* Hartford, Conn.:
Transcendental Books, 1968.

1072 CATHCART, Wallace H. *Bibliography of the Works of Nathaniel Hawthorne.*
Cleveland, Ohio: Rowfant Club, 1905.

1073 CLARK, C. E. Frazer, Jr. *Checklist of Nathaniel Hawthorne.* Columbus, Ohio:
Charles E. Merrill, 1970.

1074 FRANCIS, Gloria A. "Recent Hawthorne Scholarship, 1970–1971." *NHJ,* II
(1972), 273–278.

1075 GROSS, Theodore L., and WERTHEIM, Stanley. See **692**.

1076 JONES, Buford. "A Checklist of Hawthorne Criticism 1951–1966." *ESQ*, LII (1968), 1–90.

1077 PHILLIPS, Robert S. "*The Scarlet Letter*: A Selected Checklist of Criticism (1850–1962)." *BB*, XXII (1962), 213–216.

1078 PHILLIPS, Robert; KLIGERMAN, Jack; LONG, Robert E.; and HASTINGS, Robert. "Nathaniel Hawthorne: Criticism of the Four Major Romances: A Selected Bibliography." *Thoth*, III (1962), 39–50.

Biographical and Critical Books

1079 ARVIN, Newton. *Hawthorne*. Boston: Little, Brown, 1929.

1080 BELL, Michael D. *Hawthorne and the Historical Romance of New England*. Princeton: Princeton Univ. Press, 1971.

1081 BELL, Millicent. *Hawthorne's View of the Artist*. Albany: State Univ. of New York Press, 1962.

1082 CAMERON, Kenneth W. *Hawthorne Among His Contemporaries*. Hartford, Conn.: Transcendental Books, 1968.

1083 CANTWELL, Robert. *Nathaniel Hawthorne: The American Years*. New York: Rinehart, 1948. [To 1850.]

1084 CHANDLER, Elizabeth L. *A Study of the Sources of the Tales and Romances Written by Nathaniel Hawthorne before 1853*. Northampton, Mass.: Smith College, 1926.

1085 CREWS, Frederick C. *The Sins of the Fathers: Hawthorne's Psychological Themes*. New York: Oxford Univ. Press, 1966. [Non-doctrinaire Freudian interpretations.]†

1086 CROWLEY, Joseph D. *Nathaniel Hawthorne*. New York: Humanities, 1971.

1087 DAVIDSON, Edward Hutchins. *Hawthorne's Last Phase*. New Haven: Yale Univ. Press, 1949.

1088 ELDER, Marjorie J. *Nathaniel Hawthorne: Transcendental Symbolist*. Athens: Ohio Univ. Press, 1969.

1089 FAIRBANKS, Henry G. *The Lasting Loneliness of Nathaniel Hawthorne: A Study of the Sources of Alienation in Modern Man*. Albany, N.Y.: Magi Books, 1965.

1090 FAUST, Bertha. *Hawthorne's Contemporaneous Reputation: A Study of Literary Opinion in America and England, 1828–1864*. Philadelphia: Univ. of Pennsylvania Press, 1939.

1091 FICK, Leonard J. *The Light Beyond: A Study of Hawthorne's Theology*. Westminster, Md.: Newman Press, 1955.

1092 FOGLE, Richard Harter. *Hawthorne's Fiction: The Light and the Dark*. Norman: Univ. of Oklahoma Press, 1952.

1093 FOGLE, Richard Harter. *Hawthorne's Imagery: The "Proper Light and Shadow" in the Major Romances*. Norman: Univ. of Oklahoma Press, 1969.

1094 FOLSOM, James K. *Man's Accidents and God's Purposes: Multiplicity in Hawthorne's Fiction*. New Haven: College and University Press, 1963.†

1095 FOSSUM, Robert H. *Hawthorne's Inviolable Circle: The Problem of Time.* Deland, Fla.: Everett/Edwards, 1972.

1096 GALE, Robert L. *Plots and Characters in the Fiction and Sketches of Nathaniel Hawthorne.* Foreword by Norman H. Pearson. Hamden, Conn.: Archon, 1968.†

1097 HALL, Lawrence Sargent. *Hawthorne, Critic of Society.* New Haven: Yale Univ. Press, 1944.

1098 HAWTHORNE, Julian. *Nathaniel Hawthorne and His Wife.* 2 vols. Boston: Houghton Mifflin, 1885. [By his son.]

1099 HOELTJE, Hubert H. *Inward Sky: The Mind and Art of Nathaniel Hawthorne.* Durham, N.C.: Duke Univ. Press, 1962. [Most complete.]

1100 JACOBSON, Richard J. *Hawthorne's Conception of the Creative Process.* Cambridge: Harvard Univ. Press, 1966.

1101 JAMES, Henry. *Hawthorne.* English Men of Letters Series. London: Macmillan, 1879.†

1102 KESSELRING, Marion Louise. *Hawthorne's Reading, 1828–1850.* New York: New York Public Library, 1949.

1103 LATHROP, George Parsons. *A Study of Hawthorne.* Boston: J. R. Osgood, 1876. [By his son-in-law.]

1104 LOGGINS, Vernon. *The Hawthornes: The Story of Seven Generations of an American Family.* New York: Columbia Univ. Press, 1951.

1105 LUNDBLAD, Jane. *Hawthorne and the Tradition of Gothic Romance.* Cambridge: Harvard Univ. Press, 1946.

1106 LUNDBLAD, Jane. *Nathaniel Hawthorne and European Literary Tradition.* Cambridge: Harvard Univ. Press, 1947.

1107 MCPHERSON, Hugo. *Hawthorne as Myth-Maker: A Study in Imagination.* Univ. of Toronto Dept. of English Studies & Texts, 16. Toronto: Univ. of Toronto Press, 1969.

1108 MALE, Roy R. *Hawthorne's Tragic Vision.* Austin: Univ. of Texas, 1957.†

1109 MARTIN, Terence J. *Nathaniel Hawthorne.* New York: Twayne, 1965.†

1110 MATHER, Edward. *Nathaniel Hawthorne: A Biography.* New York: Crowell, 1940.

1111 MAY, John R. See **191**.

1112 MORRIS, Lloyd. *The Rebellious Puritan: A Portrait of Mr. Hawthorne.* New York: Harcourt, Brace, 1927.

1113 NORMAND, Jean. *Nathaniel Hawthorne: An Approach to an Analysis of Artistic Creation.* Trans. Derek Coltman and foreword by Henri Peyre. Cleveland: Press of Case Western Reserve Univ., 1970.

1114 REID, Alfred S. *The Yellow Ruff & The Scarlet Letter: A Source of Hawthorne's Novel.* Gainesville: Univ. of Florida Press, 1955.

1115 SCHUBERT, Leland. *Hawthorne, the Artist: Fine-Art Devices in Fiction.* Chapel Hill: Univ. of North Carolina Press, 1944.

1116 STEIN, William Bysshe. *Hawthorne's Faust: A Study of the Devil Archetype.* Gainesville: Univ. of Florida Press, 1953.

1117 STEWART, Randall. *Nathaniel Hawthorne: A Biography.* New Haven: Yale Univ. Press, 1948. [Authoritative.]

CAMROSE LUTHERAN COLLEGE
Library

1118 STUBBS, John C. *The Pursuit of Form: A Study of Hawthorne and the Romance.* Urbana: Univ. of Illinois Press, 1970.

1119 THARPE, Jac. *Nathaniel Hawthorne: Identity and Knowledge.* Preface by Harry T. Moore. Carbondale: So. Illinois Univ. Press, 1967.

1120 TURNER, Arlin. *Nathaniel Hawthorne: An Introduction and Interpretation.* New York: Barnes and Noble, 1961. [Succinct and sensible.]†

1121 VAN DOREN, Mark. *Nathaniel Hawthorne: A Critical Biography.* New York: Sloane, 1949.†

1122 WAGENKNECHT, Edward C. *Nathaniel Hawthorne: Man and Writer.* New York: Oxford Univ. Press, 1961.

1123 WAGGONER, Hyatt H. *Hawthorne: A Critical Study.* Rev. ed. Cambridge: Harvard Univ. Press, 1963.

1124 WAGGONER, Hyatt H. *Nathaniel Hawthorne.* University of Minnesota Pamphlets on American Writers, No. 23. Minneapolis: Univ. of Minnesota Press, 1962.

1125 WOODBERRY, George Edward. *Nathaniel Hawthorne.* Boston: Houghton Mifflin, 1902.

Critical Essays

The first ten titles are collections of some of the best criticism. Following them, other critical essays of note are listed.

1126 BRADLEY, Sculley; BEATTY, R. C.; and LONG, E. H., eds. *The Scarlet Letter: An Annotated Text, Backgrounds and Sources, Essays in Criticism.* New York: Norton, 1962. Revised ed., New York: Norton, 1976.†

1127 GROSS, Seymour L., ed. *A "Scarlet Letter" Handbook.* San Francisco: Wadsworth Publishing Co., 1960. [Essays with excellent bibliography.]†

1128 COHEN, B. Bernard, ed. *The Recognition of Nathaniel Hawthorne: Selected Criticism Since 1828.* With preface. Ann Arbor: Univ. of Michigan Press, 1969.

1129 GERBER, John C., ed. *Twentieth-Century Interpretations of 'The Scarlet Letter': A Collection of Critical Essays.* With introduction. Englewood Cliffs, N.J.: Prentice-Hall, 1968.†

1130 KAUL, A. N., ed. *Hawthorne: A Collection of Critical Essays.* With introduction. Englewood Cliffs, N.J.: Prentice-Hall, 1966.†

1131 KESTERSON, David B., ed. *The Merrill Studies in 'The Marble Faun'.* With preface. Columbus, Ohio: Charles E. Merrill, 1971.

1132 LYNN, Kenneth S., ed. *The Scarlet Letter: Text, Sources, Criticism.* New York: Harcourt, Brace & World, Inc., 1961.†

1133 PEARCE, Roy Harvey, ed. *Hawthorne Centenary Essays.* Columbus: Ohio State Univ. Press, 1964. [Collection of original "definitive" essays on Hawthorne's works, texts, ideas, and reception. Reflects current "received opinions" on Hawthorne's work.]

1134 ROUNTREE, Thomas J., ed. *Critics on Hawthorne.* With introduction. Coral Gables: Univ. of Miami Press, 1972.

1135 TURNER, Arlin, ed. *Studies in 'The Scarlet Letter'.* Columbus, Ohio: Charles E. Merrill, 1970.

1136 ABEL, Darrel. "Giving Lustre to Gray Shadows: Hawthorne's Potent Art." *AL*, XLI (1969), 373–388.

1137 ABEL, Darrel. "Hawthorne on the Strong Division-Lines of Nature." *ATQ*, XIV (1972), 23–31.

1138 ABEL, Darrel. "Hawthorne's Dimmesdale: Fugitive from Wrath." *NCF*, XI (1956), 81–105.

1139 ABEL, Darrel. "Hawthorne's Hester." *CE*, XIII (1952), 303–309.

1140 ABEL, Darrel. "Hawthorne's Pearl: Symbol and Character." *ELH*, XVIII (1951), 50–66.

1141 ABEL, Darrel. "Hawthorne's Skepticism About Social Reform with Especial Reference to *The Blithedale Romance*." *UKCR*, XIX (1953), 181–193.

1142 ABEL, Darrel. "The Devil in Boston." *PQ*, XXXII (1953), 366–381.

1143 ALLEN, Mary. "Smiles and Laughter in Hawthorne." *PQ*, LII (1973), 119–128.

1144 ANDOLA, John A. "Pearl: Symbolic Link Between Two Worlds." *BSUF*, XIII (1972), 60–67.

1145 ARDEN, Eugene. "Hawthorne's 'Case of Arthur D'." *AI*, XVIII (1961), 45–55. [Psychoanalytic interpretation of *The Scarlet Letter*.]

1146 AUCHINCLOSS, Louis. "*The Blithedale Romance:* A Study of Form and Point of View." *NHJ*, II (1972), 53–58.

1147 AUSTIN, Allen. "Satire and Theme in *The Scarlet Letter*." *PQ*, XLI (1962), 508–511.

1148 AXELSSON, Arne I. "Isolation and Interdependence as Structure in Hawthorne's Four Major Romances." *SN*, XLV (1973), 392–402.

1149 BALES, Kent. "*The Blithedale Romance:* Coverdale's Mean and Subversive Egotism." *BuR*, XXI (1973), 60–82.

1150 BARNES, Daniel R. "Orestes Brownson and Hawthorne's Holgrave." *AL*, XLV (1973), 271–278.

1151 BARNES, Daniel R. "Two Reviews of *The Scarlet Letter* in *Holden's Dollar Magazine*." *AL*, XLIV (1973), 648–652.

1152 BATTAGLIA, Francis J. "*The House of the Seven Gables:* New Light on Old Problems." *PMLA*, LXXXII (1967), 579–590.

1153 BAUGHMAN, Ernest W. "Public Confession and *The Scarlet Letter*." *NEQ*, XL (1967), 532–550.

1154 BAUMGARTNER, Alex M., and HOFFMAN, Michael J. "Illusion and Role in *The Scarlet Letter*." *PLL*, VII (1971), 168–184.

1155 BAYM, Nina. "*The Blithedale Romance:* A Radical Reading." *JEGP*, LXVII (1968), 545–569.

1156 BAYM, Nina. "Hawthorne's Women: The Tyranny of Social Myths." *CentR*, XV (1971), 250–272.

1157 BAYM, Nina. "*The Marble Faun:* Hawthorne's Elegy for Art." *NEQ*, XLIV (1971), 355–376.

1158 BAYM, Nina. "Passion and Authority in *The Scarlet Letter*." *NEQ*, XLIII (1970), 209–230.

1159 BAYM, Nina. "The Romantic *Malgré Lui:* Hawthorne in the Custom House." *ESQ,* XL (1973), 14–25.

1160 BEEBE, Maurice. "The Fall of the House of Pyncheon." *NCF,* XI (1956), 1–17. [On *The House of Seven Gables.*]

1161 BEIDLER, Peter G. "Theme of the Fortunate Fall in *The Marble Faun.*" *ESQ,* XLVII (1967), 56–62.

1162 BENOIT, Raymond. "Theology and Literature: *The Scarlet Letter.*" *BuR,* XX (1972), 83–92.

1163 BERCOVITCH, Sacvan. "Of Wise and Foolish Virgins: Hilda Versus Miriam in Hawthorne's *Marble Faun.*" *NEQ,* XLI (1968), 281–286.

1164 BEWLEY, Marius. "James's Debt to Hawthorne (I): *The Blithedale Romance and The Bostonians.*" *Scrutiny,* XVI (1949), 301–317. Reprinted in **155.**

1165 BEWLEY, Marius. "James's Debt to Hawthorne (II): *The Marble Faun* and *The Wings of the Dove.*" *Scrutiny,* XVI (1949), 301–317. Reprinted in **155.**

1166 BEWLEY, Marius. "Hawthorne's Novels. See **156.**

1167 BIER, Jesse. "Hawthorne on the Romance: His Prefaces Related and Examined." *MP,* LIII (1955), 17–24.

1168 BIRDSALL, Virginia Ogden. "Hawthorne's Fair-Haired Maidens: The Fading Light." *PMLA,* LXXV (1960), 250–256.

1169 BLAIR, Walter. "Color, Light, and Shadow in Hawthorne's Fiction." *NEQ,* XV (1942), 74–94.

1170 BLOW, Suzanne. "Pre-Raphaelite Allegory in *The Marble Faun.*" *AL,* LXIV (1972), 122–127.

1171 BODE, Carl. "Hawthorne's *Fanshawe:* The Promising of Greatness." *NEQ,* XXIII (1950), 235–242.

1172 BRODTKORB, Paul, Jr. "Art Allegory in *The Marble Faun.*" *PMLA,* LXXVII (1962), 254–267.

1173 BROWNELL, William C. See **215.**

1174 BROWNING, Preston M. "Hester Prynne as a Secular Saint." *MQ,* XIII (1972), 351–362.

1175 CALDWELL, Wayne T. "The Emblem Tradition and the Symbolic Mode: Clothing Imagery in *The House of the Seven Gables.*" *ESQ,* XIX (1973), 34–42.

1176 CANADAY, Nicholas, Jr. "Community and Identity at Blithedale." *SAQ,* LXXI (1972), 30–39.

1177 CARLETON, William G. "Hawthorne Discovers the English." *YR,* LIII (1964), 395–414.

1178 CARPENTER, Frederic I. "Puritans Preferred Blondes: The Heroines of Melville and Hawthorne." *NEQ,* IX (1936), 253–272.

1179 CARPENTER, Frederic I. "Scarlet A. Minus." *CE,* V (1944), 173–180. Reprinted in Carpenter's *American Literature and the Dream.* New York: Philosophical Library, 1955. Also in **1127.**

1180 CHARNEY, Maurice. "Hawthorne and the Gothic Style." *NEQ,* XXXIV (1961), 36–49.

1181 CLAY, Edward M. "The 'Dominating' Symbol in Hawthorne's Last Phase." *AL,* XXXIX (1968), 506–516.

1182 COANDA, Richard. "Hawthorne's Scarlet Alphabet." *Renascence,* XIX (1967), 161–166.

1183 COFFEE, Jessie A. "Margaret Fuller as Zenobia in *The Blithedale Romance.*" *Proceedings of Conference of College Teachers of English of Texas,* edited by J. F. Kobler, vol. 38, pp. 23–27. Denton: Conference of College Teachers of English of Texas, 1973.

1184 COLACURCIO, Michael J. "Footsteps of Ann Hutchinson: The Context of *The Scarlet Letter.*" *ELH,* XXXIX (1972), 459–494.

1185 COWLEY, Malcolm. "Hawthorne in the Looking-Glass." *SR,* LVI (1948), 545–563.

1186 COWLEY, Malcolm. "Five Acts of *The Scarlet Letter.*" *CE,* XIX (1957), 11–16. Reprinted in **226.**

1187 CREWS, Frederick C. "A New Reading of *The Blithedale Romance.*" *AL,* XXIX (1957), 147–170.

1188 CRONIN, M. "Hawthorne on Romantic Love and the Status of Woman." *PMLA,* LXIX (1954), 89–98.

1189 DARNELL, Donald G. " 'Doctrine by Ensample': The Emblem and *The Marble Faun.*" *TSLL,* XV (1973), 301–310.

1190 DAVIDSON, Edward H. "Dimmesdale's Fall." *NEQ,* XXXVI (1963), 358–370.

1191 DAVIDSON, Edward H. "Hawthorne and the Pathetic Fallacy." *JEGP,* LIV (1955), 486–497.

1192 DAVIDSON, Frank. "Toward a Re-evaluation of *The Blithedale Romance.*" *NEQ,* XXV (1952), 374–383.

1193 DENNIS, Carl. "*The Blithedale Romance* and the Problem of Self-Integration." *TSLL,* XV (1973), 93–110.

1194 DILLINGHAM, William B. "Arthur Dimmesdale's Confession." *SLitI,* II (1969), 21–26.

1195 DILLINGHAM, William B. "Structure and Theme in *The House of The Seven Gables.*" *NCF,* XIV (1959), 59–70.

1196 DOUBLEDAY, Neal F. "Hawthorne's Hester and Feminism." *PMLA,* LIV (1949), 825–828.

1197 DRYDEN, Edgar A. "Hawthorne's Castle in the Air: Form and Theme in *The House of the Seven Gables.*" *ELH,* XXXVIII (1971), 294–317.

1198 DRYDEN, Edgar A. "The Limits of Romance: A Reading of *The Marble Faun.*" See **300,** pp. 17–48.

1199 DUERKSEN, Roland A. "The Double Image of Beatrice Cenci in *The Marble Faun.*" *MichA,* I (1969), 47–55.

1200 DURR, Robert Allen. "Hawthorne's Ironic Mode." *NEQ,* XXX (1957), 486–495.

1201 EAKIN, Paul J. "Hawthorne's Imagination and the Structure of 'The Custom-House'." *AL,* XLIII (1971), 346–358.

1202 EISINGER, Chester E. "Pearl and the Puritan Heritage." *CE,* XII (1951), 323–329.

1203 ELDER, Marjorie. "Hawthorne's *The Marble Faun:* A Gothic Structure." *Costerus,* I (1972), 81–88.

1204 ERLICH, Gloria C. "Deadly Innocence: Hawthorne's Dark Women." *NEQ*, XLI (1968), 163–179.

1205 ERSKINE, John. See **217.**

1206 FAIRBANKS, Henry G. "Citizen Hawthorne and the Perennial Problem of American Society." *RUO*, XXIX (1959), 26–38.

1207 FAIRBANKS, Henry G. "Hawthorne and the Catholic Church." *BUSE*, I (1955), 148–165.

1208 FAIRBANKS, Henry G. "Hawthorne and the Nature of Man." *RUO*, XXVIII (1958), 309–322.

1209 FAIRBANKS, Henry G. "Man's Separation from Nature: Hawthorne's Philosophy of Suffering and Death." *ChS*, XLII (1959), 51–63.

1210 FERRELL, M. J. "Imbalance in Hawthorne's Characters." *SDR*, X (1972), 45–59.

1211 FLANAGAN, John T. "Point of View in 'The Marble Faun'." *NS* (1962), 218–224.

1212 FLINT, Allen. " 'essentially a day-dream, and yet a fact': Hawthorne's *Blithedale.*" *NHJ*, II (1972), 75–83.

1213 FLINT, Allen. "The Saving Grace of Marriage in Hawthorne's Fiction." *ESQ*, LXXI (1973), 112–116.

1214 FOGLE, Richard H. "Coleridge, Hilda, and *The Marble Faun.*" *ESQ*, XIX (1973), 105–111.

1215 FOGLE, Richard H. "Hawthorne and Coleridge on Credibility." *Criticism*, XIII (1971), 234–241.

1216 FOGLE, Richard H. "Hawthorne's Variegated Lighting." *BuR*, XXI (1973), 83–88.

1217 FOGLE, Richard H. "Nathaniel Hawthorne: *The House of the Seven Gables.*" See **243,** pp. 111–120.

1218 FOGLE, Richard H. "Priscilla's Veil: A Study of Hawthorne's Veil-Imagery in *The Blithedale Romance.*" *NHJ*, II (1972), 59–65.

1219 FUSSELL, Edwin S. "Nathaniel Hawthorne." See **170.**

1220 GARLITZ, Barbara. "Pearl: 1850–1955." *PMLA*, LXXII (1957), 689–699.

1221 GERBER, John C. "Form and Content in *The Scarlet Letter.*" *NEQ*, XVII (1944), 25–55. [Still the best study of its subject.]

1222 GOLDFARB, Clare R. "*The Marble Faun* and Emersonian Self-Reliance." *ATQ*, I (1969), 19–23.

1223 GOLLIN, Rita. " 'Dream-Work' in *The Blithedale Romance.*" *ESQ*, XIX (1973), 74–83.

1224 GORDON, John D. "Nathaniel Hawthorne, the Years of Fulfillment, 1804–1853." *BNYPL*, LIX (1955), 154–165; Part II, 198–217; Part III, 259–269; Part IV, 316–321.

1225 GRIFFITH, Kelley, Jr. "Form in *The Blithedale Romance.*" *AL*, XL (1968), 15–26.

1226 GROSS, Robert Eugene. "Hawthorne's First Novel: The Future of a Style." *PMLA*, LXXVII (1963), 60–68.

1227 GROSS, Seymour L. "Hawthorne Versus Melville." *BuR,* XIV (1966), 89–109.

1228 GROSS, Seymour L. " 'Solitude and Love and Anguish': The Tragic Design of *The Scarlet Letter.*" *CLAJ,* III (1960), 154–165.

1229 GUPTA, R. K. "Hawthorne's Theory of Art." *AL,* XL (1968), 309–324.

1230 GUPTA, R. K. "Hawthorne's Treatment of the Artist." *NEQ,* LXV (1972), 65–80.

1231 HALL, Spencer. "Beatrice Cenci: Symbol and Vision in *The Marble Faun.*" *NCF,* XXV (1970), 85–95.

1232 HART, John E. "*The Scarlet Letter:* One Hundred Years After." *NEQ,* XXIII, (1950), 381–395.

1233 Hawthorne Centenary Issue. *Nineteenth Century Fiction,* XIX ii (1964). [Articles by Blake R. Nevins, Robert E. Long, Gretchen G. Jordan, Peter L. Thorsley, Jr., Otis B. Wheeler, Arthur T. Broes, Oliver Evans, Bruce I. Granger, and Leo B. Levy.]

1234 HEDGES, William L. "Hawthorne's *Blithedale:* The Function of the Narrator." *NCF,* XIV (1960), 303–316.

1235 HIRSH, John C. "The Politics of Blithedale: The Dilemma of the Self." *SIR,* XI (1972), 138–146.

1236 HOELTJE, Hubert H. "The Writing of *The Scarlet Letter.*" *NEQ,* XXVII (1954), 326–346.

1237 HOFFMAN, Daniel G. See 177.

1238 HOLMES, Edward M. "Hawthorne and Romanticism." *NEQ,* XXXIII (1960), 476–488.

1239 HOWARD, David. "*The Blithedale Romance* and a Sense of Revolution." In *Tradition and Tolerance in Nineteenth-Century Fiction: Critical Essays on Some English and American Novels,* edited by David Howard, John Lucas, and John Goode. London: Routledge and K. Paul, 1966; New York: Barnes & Noble, 1967, pp. 55–97.

1240 HOWARD, David. "The Fortunate Fall and Hawthorne's *The Marble Faun.*" In *Romantic Mythologies,* edited by Ian Fletcher. London: Routledge and K. Paul; New York: Barnes & Noble, 1967, pp. 97–136.

1241 HOWARD, Leon. "Hawthorne's Fiction." *NCF,* VII (1953), 237–250.

1242 JANSSEN, James G. "Dimmesdale's 'Lurid Playfulness'." *ATQ,* I (1969), 30–34.

1243 JENKINS, R. B. "A New Look at an Old Tombstone." *NEQ,* XLV (1972), 417–421. [Hester Prynne's.]

1244 JOHNSON, Claudia D. "Hawthorne and Nineteenth-Century Perfectionism." *AL,* XLIV (1973), 585–595.

1245 JONES, Buford. "After Long Apprenticeship: Hawthorne's Mature Romances." *ESQ,* LXX (1973), 1–7.

1246 JONES, Buford. "The *Faery Land* of Hawthorne's Romances." *ESQ,* XLVIII (1967), 106–124.

1247 KATZ, Seymour. " 'Character,' 'Nature,' and Allegory in *The Scarlet Letter.*" *NCF,* XXIII (1968), 3–17.

1248 KAUL, A. N. "Character and Motive in *The Scarlet Letter.*" *CritQ,* X (1968), 373–384.

1249 KAUL, A. N. See **180**.

1250 KAY, Donald. "Five Acts of *The Blithedale Romance.*" *ATQ*, XIII (1972), 25–28.

1251 KEHL, D. G. "Hawthorne's 'Vicious' Circles: The Sphere-Circle Imagery in the Four Major Novels." *BRMMLA*, XXIII (1969), 9–20.

1252 KESTERSON, David B. "Journey to Perugia: Dantean Parallels in *The Marble Faun.*" *ESQ*, LXX (1973), 94–104.

1253 KLINKOWITZ, Jerome. "Ending the *Seven Gables:* Old Light on a New Problem." *SNNTS*, IV (1972), 396–401.

1254 KOSKENLINNA, Hazel M. "Setting, Image, and Symbol in Scott and Hawthorne." *ESQ*, LXX (1973), 50–59.

1255 KUSHEN, Betty. "Love's Martyrs: The Scarlet Letter as Secular Cross." *L & P*, XXII (1972), 109–120.

1256 LAWRENCE, D. H. See **183**.

1257 LEAVIS, Q. D. "Hawthorne as Poet." *SR*, LIX (1951), 429–440.

1258 LEFCOWITZ, Allan, and LEFCOWITZ, Barbara. "Some Rents in the Veil: New Light on Priscilla and Zenobia in *The Blithedale Romance.*" *NCF*, XXI (1966), 263–275.

1259 LEIBOWITZ, Herbert A. "Hawthorne and Spenser: Two Sources." *AL*, XXX (1959), 459–466.

1260 LEVIN, David. "Nathaniel Hawthorne, *The Scarlet Letter.*" See **227**.

1261 LEVIN, Harry. "Camera Obscura." See **184**, pp. 36–100.

1262 LEVY, Leo B. "*The Blithedale Romance:* Hawthorne's 'Voyage Through Chaos'." *SIR*, VIII (1968), 1–15.

1263 LEVY, Leo B. "The Landscape Modes of *The Scarlet Letter.*" *NCF*, XXIII (1969), 377–392.

1264 LEVY, Leo B. "*The Marble Faun:* Hawthorne's Landscape of the Fall." *AL*, XLII (1970), 139–156.

1265 LEVY, Leo B. "Picturesque Style in *The House of the Seven Gables.*" *NEQ*, XXXIX (1966), 147–160.

1266 LIEBMAN, Sheldon W. "The Design of *The Marble Faun.*" *NEQ*, XL (1967), 61–78.

1267 LOHMANN, Christoph K. "The Agency of the English Romance." *NHJ*, II (1972), 219–229.

1268 LOHMANN, Christoph. "The Burden of the Past in Hawthorne's American Romances." *SAQ*, LXVI (1967), 92–104.

1269 LUECKE, Sister Jane Marie, O.S.B. "Villains and Non-Villains in Hawthorne's Fiction." *PMLA*, LXXVIII (1963), 551–558.

1270 MCCALL, Dan E. "The Design of Hawthorne's 'Custom House'." *NCF*, XXI (1967), 349–358.

1271 MCCARTHY, Paul. "The Extraordinary Man as Idealist in Novels by Hawthorne and Melville." *ESQ*, LIV (1969), 43–51.

1272 MCCARTHY, Paul. "A Perspective in Hawthorne's Novels." *BSUF*, XIII (1972), 46–58.

1273 MCELROY, John. "The Hawthorne Style of American Fiction." *ESQ,* XIX (1973), 117–123.

1274 MACLEAN, Hugh N. "Hawthorne's *Scarlet Letter:* 'The Dark Problem of This Life'." *AL,* XXVII (1955), 12–24.

1275 MCNAMARA, Anne Marie. "The Character of Flame: The Function of Pearl in *The Scarlet Letter.*" *AL,* XXVII (1956), 537–553.

1276 MACSHANE, Frank. "The House of the Dead: Hawthorne's Custom House and *The Scarlet Letter.*" *NEQ,* XXXV (1962), 93–101.

1277 MAES-JELINEK, Hena. "Roger Chillingworth: An Example of the Creative Process in *The Scarlet Letter.*" *ES,* XLIX (1968), 341–348.

1278 MALE, Roy R. " 'From the Innermost Germ': The Organic Principle in Hawthorne's Fiction." *ELH,* XX (1953), 218–236.

1279 MALE, Roy R. "Hawthorne and the Concept of Sympathy." *PMLA,* LXVIII (1953), 138–149.

1280 MALE, Roy R. "Hawthorne's Fancy, or the Medium of *The Blithedale Romance.*" *NHJ,* II (1972), 67–73.

1281 MANIERRE, William R. "The Role of Sympathy in *The Scarlet Letter.*" *TSLL,* XIII (1971), 497–507.

1282 MARKS, Alfred H. "Ironic Inversion in *The Blithedale Romance.*" *ESQ,* LV (1969), 95–102.

1283 MARTIN, Terence. "Dimmesdale's Ultimate Sermon." *ArQ,* XXVII (1971), 230–240.

1284 MATHEWS, James W. "Hawthorne and the Chain of Being." *MLQ,* XVIII (1957), 282–294.

1285 MATHEWS, James W. "The House of Atreus and *The House of the Seven Gables.*" *ESQ,* LXIII (1971), 31–36.

1286 MATTHIESSEN, F. O. "Hawthorne." See **43,** pp. 179–369.

1287 MAXWELL, D. E. S. See **190.**

1288 MILLER, James E., Jr. "Hawthorne and Melville: The Unpardonable Sin." *PMLA,* LXX (1955), 91–114.

1289 MONTGOMERY, Judith H. "The American Galatea." *CE,* XXXII (1971), 890–899. [A feminist interpretation of *The Blithedale Romance, The Portrait of a Lady,* and *The House of Mirth.*]

1290 MOORE, Robert. "Hawthorne's Folk-Motifs and *The House of the Seven Gables.*" *NYFQ,* XXVIII (1972), 221–233.

1291 MORSBERGER, Katharine M. "Hawthorne's 'Borderland': The Locale of the Romance." *Costerus,* XII (1973), 93–112.

1292 MOSS, Sidney P. "The Symbolism of the Italian Background in *The Marble Faun.*" *NCF,* XXIII (1968), 332–336.

1293 MURPHY, John J. "The Function of Sin in Hawthorne's Novels." *ESQ,* L (1968), 65–71.

1294 MURRAY, Peter B. "Mythopoesis in *The Blithedale Romance.*" *PMLA,* LXXV (1960), 591–596.

1295 Nathaniel Hawthorne Special Number. *SNNTS,* II, iv (1970).

1296 NOBLE, David W. "The Analysis of Alienation by 20th Century Social Scientists and 19th Century Novelists: The Example of Hawthorne's *The Scarlet Letter.*" In *Myths and Realities: Conflicting Values in America,* edited by Berkley Kalin and Clayton Robinson. Memphis: John Willard Brister Library, Memphis State Univ., 1972, pp. 5–19.

1297 O'CONNOR, William Van. "Hawthorne and Faulkner: Some Common Ground." *VQR,* XXXIII (1957), 105–123. Reprinted in **225.**

1298 O'CONNOR, William Van. "The Hawthorne Museum: A Dialogue." See **225.**

1299 O'DONNELL, Charles R. "Hawthorne and Dimmesdale: The Quest for the Realm of Quiet." *NCF,* XIV (1960), 317–332.

1300 OSBORN, Robert, and OSBORN, Marijane. "Another Look at an Old Tombstone." *NEQ,* XLVI (1973), 278–279. [At end of *The Scarlet Letter.*]

1301 PANCOST, David W. "Hawthorne's Epistemology and Ontology." *ESQ,* LXX (1973), 8–13.

1302 PEARCE, Howard D. "Hawthorne's Old Moodie: *The Blithedale Romance* and *Measure for Measure.*" *SAB,* XXXVIII (1973), 11–15.

1303 PEARCE, Roy Harvey. "Day-Dream and Fact: The Import of *The Blithedale Romance.*" See **300,** pp. 49–63.

1304 PEARCE, Roy Harvey. "Hawthorne and the Twilight of Romance." *YR,* XXXVII (1948), 487–506.

1305 RAGAN, James F. "The Irony in Hawthorne's Blithedale." *NEQ,* XXXV (1962), 239–246.

1306 RAHV, Philip. "The Dark Lady of Salem." *PR,* VIII (1941), 362–381. Reprinted in Rahv's *Image and Idea.* Norfolk, Conn.: New Directions, 1949.

1307 REES, John O., Jr. "Shakespeare in *The Blithedale Romance.*" *ESQ,* LXXI (1973), 84–93.

1308 RINGE, Donald A. "Hawthorne's Psychology of the Head and Heart." *PMLA,* LXV (1950), 120–132.

1309 ROPER, Gordon. "The Originality of Hawthorne's *The Scarlet Letter.*" *DR,* XXX (1950), 62–79. Reprinted in **1127.**

1310 ROSS, Donald, Jr. "Dreams and Sexual Repression in *The Blithedale Romance.*" *PMLA,* LXXXVI (1971), 1014–1017.

1311 ROVIT, Earl H. "Ambiguity in Hawthorne's *Scarlet Letter.*" *Archiv,* CXCVIII (1961), 76–88.

1312 RYSKAMP, Charles. "The New England Sources of *The Scarlet Letter.*" *AL,* XXXI (1959), 257–272.

1313 SAMPSON, Edward C. "Sound-Imagery in *The House of the Seven Gables.*" *EngR,* XXII (1971), 26–29.

1314 SANDEEN, Ernest. "*The Scarlet Letter* as a Love Story." *PMLA,* LXXVII (1962), 425–435.

1315 SCANDON, Lawrence E. "The Heart of *The Scarlet Letter.*" *TSLL,* IV (1962), 198–213.

1316 SCHNEIDER, Daniel J. "The Allegory and Symbolism of Hawthorne's *The Marble Faun.*" *SNNTS,* I (1969), 38–50.

1317 SCHOER, Carol. "The House of the Seven Deadly Sins." *ESQ,* XIX (1973), 26–33.

1318 SCHWARTZ, Joseph. "Nathaniel Hawthorne and the Natural Desire for God." *NHJ,* II (1972), 159–171.

1319 SCOVILLE, Samuel. "Hawthorne's Houses and Hidden Treasures." *ESQ,* XIX (1973), 61–73.

1320 SCRIMGEOUR, Gary J. *"The Marble Faun:* Hawthorne's Faery Land." *AL,* XXXVI (1964), 271–287.

1321 SHEAR, Walter. "Characterization in *The Scarlet Letter." MQ,* XII (1971), 437–454.

1322 SHROEDER, John W. " 'That Inward Sphere': Notes on Hawthorne's Heart Imagery and Symbolism." *PMLA,* LXV (1950), 106–119.

1323 SIEGEL, Sally· D. "Hawthorne's Seven Veiled Ladies." *GyS,* I (1973), 48–53.

1324 SIMPSON, Claude M., Jr. "Correction or Corruption? Nathaniel Hawthorne and Two Friendly Improvers." *HLQ,* XXXVI (1973), 367–386.

1325 SLETHAUG, Gordon E. *"Felix Culpa* in Hawthorne's 'Custom House'." *EngR,* XXIII (1972), 32–41.

1326 SNELL, George. "Nathaniel Hawthorne: Bystander." See **102.**

1327 Special Hawthorne Issue. *Essex Institute Historical Collections,* C, iv (1964). [Articles by Norman H. Pearson, Ghulan Ali Chandry, Maurice Bassan, Ely Stork, and Edward C. Sampson.]

1328 SPRAGUE, Claire. "Dream and Disguise in *The Blithedale Romance." PMLA,* LXXXIV (1969), 596–597.

1329 STANTON, Robert. "The Trial of Nature: An Analysis of *The Blithedale Romance." PMLA,* LXXVI (1961), 528–538.

1330 STEPHENS, Rosemary. " 'A' is for 'Art' in *The Scarlet Letter." ATQ,* I (1969), 23–27.

1331 STEWART, Randall. "Guilt and Innocence." See **205.**

1332 STOUCK, David. "The Surveyor of the Custom-House: A Narrator for *The Scarlet Letter." CentR,* XV (1971), 309–329.

1333 STROUT, Cushing. "Hawthorne's International Novel." *NCF,* XXIV (1969), 169–181. [*The Marble Faun.*]

1334 STUBBS, John C. "Hawthorne's *The Scarlet Letter:* The Theory of the Romance and the Use of the New England Situation." *PMLA,* LXXXIII (1968), 1439–1447.

1335 SUMNER, D. Nathan. "The Function of Historical Sources in Hawthorne, Melville, and R. P. Warren." *RS,* XL (1972), 103–114.

1336 SWANN, Charles. "Hawthorne: History versus Romance." *JAmS,* VII (1973), 153–170.

1337 SWANSON, Donald R. "On Building *The House of the Seven Gables." BSUF,* X (1969), 43–50.

1338 TANSELLE, G. Thomas. "A Note on the Structure of *The Scarlet Letter." NCF,* XVII (1963), 283–285.

1339 TODD, Robert E. "The Magna Mater Archetype in *The Scarlet Letter." NEQ,* XLV (1972), 421–429.

1340 TURNER, Arlin. "Consistency in the Mind and Work of Hawthorne." See 216, pp. 99–116.

1341 TURNER, Arlin. "Hawthorne's Final Illness and Death: Additional Reports." *ESQ*, LXXI (1973), 124–127.

1342 TURNER, Arlin. "Hawthorne's Literary Borrowings." *PMLA*, LI (1936), 543–562.

1343 VAN CROMPHOUT, Gustaaf. "*Blithedale* and the Androgyne Myth: Another Look at Zenobia." *ESQ*, XVIII (1972), 141–145.

1344 VAN CROMPHOUT, Gustaaf. "Emerson, Hawthorne, and *The Blithedale Romance.*" *GaR*, XXV (1971), 471–480.

1345 VAN DEUSEN, Marshall. "Narrative Tone in 'The Custom House' and *The Scarlet Letter.*" *NCF*, XXI (1966), 61–71.

1346 VOGEL, Dan. "Hawthorne's Concept of Tragedy in *The Scarlet Letter.*" *NHJ*, II (1972), 183–193.

1347 WAPLES, Dorothy. "Suggestions for Interpreting *The Marble Faun.*" *AL*, XIII (1941), 224–239.

1348 WARREN, Austin. "Hawthorne, Margaret Fuller, and 'Nemesis'." *PMLA*, LIV (1939), 615–618.

1349 WARREN, Austin. "Hawthorne's Reading." *NEQ*, VIII (1935), 480–497.

1350 WARREN, Robert Penn. "Hawthorne Revisited." *SR*, LXXXI (1973), 75–112.

1351 WATERMAN, Arthur E. "Dramatic Structure in *The House of the Seven Gables.*" *SLitI*, II (1969), 13–19.

1352 WATSON, Charles N., Jr. "The Estrangement of Hawthorne and Melville." *NEQ*, XLVI (1973), 380–402.

1353 WEGELIN, Christof. "Europe in Hawthorne's Fiction." *ELH*, XIV (1947), 219–245.

1354 WENTERSDORF, Karl P. "The Element of Witchcraft in *The Scarlet Letter.*" *Folklore*, LXXXIII (1972), 132–153.

1355 WHELAN, Robert E., Jr. "*The Blithedale Romance:* The Holy War in Hawthorne's Mansoul." *TSLL*, XIII (1971), 91–109.

1356 WHELAN, Robert E., Jr. "Hester Prynne's Little Pearl: Sacred and Profane Love." *AL*, XXXIX (1968), 488–505.

1357 WHELAN, Robert E., Jr. "*The Marble Faun:* Rome as Hawthorne's Mansoul." *RS*, XL (1972), 163–175.

1358 WINTERS, Yvor. "Maule's Curse, or Hawthorne and the Problem of Allegory." *In Defense of Reason*. Denver, Colo.: Alan Swallow, 1947, pp. 157–175.

1359 WRIGHT, John. "Borges and Hawthorne." *TriQ*, XXV (1972), 334–355.

1360 WRIGHT, Nathalia. "The Influence of Italy on *The Marble Faun.*" In *Studies in Honor of John C. Hodges and Alwin Thaler*, edited by Richard B. Davis and John L. Lievsay. Knoxville: Univ. of Tennessee Press, 1961, pp. 141–149.

Howells, William Dean (1837–1920)

Texts

The following works have useful editorial apparatus.

1361 *The Selected Works of William Dean Howells* is being published by Indiana University Press, under the auspices of the CEAA and the editorship of Edwin H. Cady, Dan Cook, and David J. Nordloh.

1362 *Criticism and Fiction and Other Essays.* Edited with an introduction by Clara M. Kirk and Rudolf Kirk. New York: New York Univ. Press, 1959.

1363 SMITH, Henry Nash, and GIBSON, William. See **377.**

1364 *William Dean Howells: Representative Selections, with Introduction, Bibliography, and Notes.* Ed. Clara Kirk and Rudolf Kirk. New York: American Book Co., 1950. [The paperback reprint has augmented the bibliography.]†

Bibliography

See **3, 8, 18, 1364.**

1365 BEEBE, Maurice. "Criticism of William Dean Howells: A Selected Checklist." *MFS,* XVI (1970), 395–419.

1366 BRENNI, Vito J. *William Dean Howells: A Bibliography.* Metuchen, N.J.: Scarecrow, 1973.

1367 CADY, Edwin H. "Howells Bibliography: A 'Find' and a Clarification." *SB,* XII (1959), 230–234.

1368 FORTENBERRY, George. "William Dean Howells." See **572,** pp. 229–244.

1369 GIBSON, William M., and ARMS, George. *A Bibliography of William Dean Howells.* New York: New York Public Library and Arno Press, 1971. [Standard.]

1370 HALFMANN, Ulrich, and SMITH, Don R. "William Dean Howells: A Revised and Annotated Bibliography of Secondary Comment in Periodicals and Newspapers, 1868–1919." *ALR,* V (1972), 91–121.

1371 REEVES, John K., ed. "The Literary Manuscripts of W. D. Howells: A Descriptive Finding List." *BNYPL,* XLII (1958), 267–278; 350–363.

1372 WOODRESS, James, and ANDERSON, Stanley P. "A Bibliography of Writing About William Dean Howells." *ALR,* Special Number (1969), 1–139.

1373 WOODRESS, James. "Four Decades of Howells Scholarship." *TSLL,* II (1960), 115–123.

Biographical and Critical Books

1374 BENNETT, George N. *William Dean Howells: The Development of a Novelist.* Norman: Univ. of Oklahoma Press, 1959.

1375 BENNETT, George N. *The Realism of William Dean Howells, 1889–1920.* Nashville: Vanderbilt Univ. Press, 1973.

1376 BROOKS, Van Wyck. *Howells: His Life and World.* New York: E. P. Dutton, 1959.

1377 CADY, Edwin Harrison. *The Road to Realism: The Early Years, 1837–1885, of William Dean Howells.* Syracuse, N.Y.: Syracuse Univ. Press, 1956. [Vol. I of the definitive, two-volume biography.]

1378 CADY, Edwin Harrison. *The Realist at War: The Mature Years, 1885–1920, of William Dean Howells.* Syracuse, N.Y.: Syracuse Univ. Press, 1958. [Vol. II of the definitive biography.]

1379 CARRINGTON, George C., Jr. *The Immense Complex Drama: The World and Art of the Howells Novel.* Columbus: Ohio State Univ. Press, 1966.

1380 CARTER, Everett. *Howells and the Age of Realism.* See **138**.

1381 COOKE, Delmar Gross. *William Dean Howells: A Critical Study.* New York: E. P. Dutton, 1922.

1382 DEAN, James L. *Howells' Travels Toward Art.* Albuquerque: Univ. of New Mexico Press, 1970. [On Howells' travel writings.]

1383 DIETRICHSON, Jan W. *The Image of Money in the American Novel of the Gilded Age.* Oslo: Universitetsforlaget; New York: Humanities, 1969.

1384 FIRKINS, O. W. *William Dean Howells: A Study.* Cambridge: Harvard Univ. Press, 1924.

1385 FRYCKSTEDT, Olov W. *In Quest of America: A Study of Howells' Early Development as a Novelist.* Cambridge: Harvard Univ. Press, 1958.

1386 GIBSON, William M. *William D. Howells.* (UMPAW 63.) Minneapolis: Univ. of Minnesota Press, 1967.

1387 HARVEY, Alexander. *William Dean Howells: A Study of the Achievement of a Literary Artist.* New York: B. W. Huebach, 1917. [A very early study.]

1388 HOUGH, Robert L. *The Quiet Rebel: William Dean Howells as Social Commentator.* Lincoln: Univ. of Nebraska, 1959.

1389 HOWELLS, Mildred, ed. *Life in Letters of William Dean Howells.* 2 vols. Garden City, N.Y.: Doubleday, Doran, 1928.

1390 KIRK, Clara Marburg. *W. D. Howells and Art in His Time.* Brunswick, N.J.: Rutgers Univ. Press, 1965.

1391 KIRK, Clara Marburg. *W. D. Howells: Traveler from Altruria.* New Brunswick, N.J.: Rutgers Univ. Press, 1962. [Howells' view of America, 1889–1894.]

1392 KIRK, Clara Marburg, and KIRK, Rudolph. *William Dean Howells.* New York: Twayne, 1962.†

1393 KOLB, Harold H., Jr. *The Illusion of Life: American Realism as a Literary Form.* Charlottesville: Univ. Press of Virginia, 1969.

1394 LYNN, Kenneth S. *William Dean Howells: An American Life.* New York: Harcourt, Brace Jovanovich, 1971.

1395 MCMURRAY, William. *The Literary Realism of William Dean Howells.* Carbondale: So. Illinois Univ. Press, 1967.

1396 TANEYHILL, Richard H., and BENNETT, R. King. *'The Leatherwood God,' 1869–70: A Source of William Dean Howells' Novel of the Same Name, in Two Versions.* Introduction by George Kummer. Gainesville, Fla.: S F & R, 1966.

1397 TAYLOR, Gordon O. *The Passages of Thought: Psychological Representation in the American Novel 1870–1900.* New York: Oxford Univ. Press, 1969.

1398 VANDERBILT, Kermit. *The Achievement of William Dean Howells: A Reinterpretation.* Princeton: Princeton Univ. Press, 1968.

1399 WAGENKNECHT, Edward. *William Dean Howells: The Friendly Eye.* New York: Oxford Univ. Press, 1969.

1400 WOODRESS, James L., Jr. *Howells & Italy.* Durham, N.C.: Duke Univ. Press, 1952.

Critical Essays

The first two books are collections of reviews and critical essays. Additional essays are listed after them.

1401 CADY, Edwin H., and FRAZIER, David L., eds. *The War of the Critics over William Dean Howells.* Evanston, Ill.: Row, Peterson, 1962. [Reprints essays, largely contemporary with Howells' works.]†

1402 EBLE, Kenneth E., ed. *Howells: A Century of Criticism.* Dallas: So. Methodist Univ. Press, 1962. [Reprints critical essays in chronological order, forming a history of his reputation.]

1403 ABEL, Darrel, ed. " 'Howells or James?'—An essay by Henry Blake Fuller." *MFS,* III (1957), 159–164.

1404 ANDERSEN, Kenneth. See **450.**

1405 ARMS, George. " 'Ever Devotedly Yours': The Whitlock-Howells Correspondence." *JRUL,* X (1946), 1–19.

1406 ARMS, George. "Howells' English Travel Books: Problems in Technique." *PMLA,* LXXX (1967), 104–116.

1407 ARMS, George. "Howells' New York Novel: Comedy and Belief." *NEQ,* XXI (1948), 313–325. [On *A Hazard of New Fortunes.*]

1408 ARMS, George. "The Literary Background of Howells's Social Criticism." *AL,* XIV (1942), 260–276.

1409 AYERS, Robert W. "W. D. Howells and Stephen Crane: Some Unpublished Letters." *AL,* XXVIII (1957), 469–477.

1410 BALDWIN, Marilyn. "The Transcendental Phase of William Dean Howells." *ESQ,* LVII (1969), 57–61.

1411 BANTA, Martha. See **454.**

1412 BAXTER, Annette K. "Caste and Class: Howells' Boston and Wharton's New York." *MQ,* IV (1963), 353–361.

1413 BECKER, George J. "William Dean Howells: The Awakening of Conscience." *CE,* XIX (1958), 283–291.

1414 BEHRENS, Ralph. "Howells' Portrait of a Boston Brahmin." *MarkhamR,* III (1972), 71–74. [On *Silas Lapham.*]

1415 BERCES, Francis A. "Mimesis, Morality and *The Rise of Silas Lapham.*" *AQ,* XXII (1970), 190–202.

1416 BOARDMAN, Arthur. "Howellsian Sex." *SNNTS,* II (1970), 52–60.

1417 BOARDMAN, Arthur. "Social Point of View in the Novels of William Dean Howells." *AL*, XXXIX (1967), 42–59.

1418 BROOKS, Van Wyck. See **161**.

1419 BUDD, Louis J. *"Annie Kilburn."* *ALR*, IV (1968), 84–87.

1420 BUDD, Louis J. "Howells, *The Atlantic Monthly*, and Republicanism." *AL*, XXIV (1952), 139–156.

1421 BUDD, Louis J. "The Hungry Bear of American Realism." *ALR*, V (1972), 485–487.

1422 BUDD, Louis J. See **463**.

1423 CADY, Edwin Harrison. "The Gentleman as Socialist: William Dean Howells." See **162**.

1424 CADY, Edwin Harrison. "Howells in 1948." *UKCR*, XV (1948), 83–91.

1425 CADY, Edwin Harrison. "The Neuroticism of William Dean Howells." *PMLA*, LXI (1946), 229–238.

1426 CADY, Edwin Harrison. "A Note on Howells and 'The Smiling Aspects of Life'." *AL*, XVII (1945), 175–178.

1427 CANBY, Henry Seidel. See **401**.

1428 CARGILL, Oscar. "Henry James's 'Moral Policeman': William Dean Howells." *AL*, XXIX (1958), 371–398.

1429 CARTER, Everett. "William Dean Howells's Theory of Critical Realism." *ELH*, XVI (1949), 151–166.

1430 CECIL, L. Moffitt. "William Dean Howells and the South." *MissQ*, XX (1967), 13–24.

1431 COHN, Jan. "The House of Fiction: Domestic Architecture in Howells and Edith Wharton." *TSLL*, XV (1973), 537–549.

1432 COYLE, Leo P. "Mark Twain and William Dean Howells." *GaR*, X (1956), 302–311.

1433 CRONKHITE, G. Ferris. "Howells Turns to the Inner Life." *NEQ*, XXX (1957), 474–485.

1434 CROWLEY, John W. "The Length of Howells' *Shadow of a Dream*." *NCF*, XXVII (1972), 182–196.

1435 CROWLEY, John W. "The Oedipal Theme in Howells's *Fennel and Rue*." *SNNTS*, V (1973), 104–109.

1436 CUMPIANO, Marion W. "The Dark Side of *Their Wedding Journey*." *AL*, XL (1969), 472–486.

1437 DOVE, John Roland. "Howells' Irrational Heroines." *TexSE*, XXXV (1956), 64–80.

1438 EBLE, Kenneth E. "Howells' Kisses." *AQ*, IX (1957), 441–447.

1439 EBLE, Kenneth E. "The Western Ideals of William Dean Howells." *WHR*, XI (1957), 331–338.

1440 EDWARDS, Herbert W. "Howells and the Controversy over Realism in American Fiction." *AL*, III (1931), 237–248.

1441 EDWARDS, Herbert W. "The Dramatization of *The Rise of Silas Lapham*." *NEQ*, XXX (1957), 235–243.

1442 EICHELBERGER, Clayton L. "William Dean Howells: Perception and Ambivalence." See **216**, pp. 119–140.

1443 EKSTROM, William F. "The Equalitarian Principle in the Fiction of William Dean Howells." *AL*, XXIV (1952), 40–50.

1444 ESCHHOLZ, Paul A. "Howells' *A Modern Instance:* A Realist's Moralistic Vision of America." *SDR*, X (1972), 91–102.

1445 ESCHHOLZ, Paul A. "The Moral World of Silas Lapham: Howells' Romantic Vision of America in the 1880's." *RS*, XL (1972), 115–121.

1446 ESCHHOLZ, Paul A. "William Dean Howells' Recurrent Character Types: The Realism of *A Hazard of New Fortunes.*" *EngR*, XXIII (1973), 40–47.

1447 FALK, Robert P. See **140**.

1448 FERTIG, Walter L. "Maurice Thompson and *A Modern Instance.*" *AL*, XXXVIII (1966), 103–111.

1449 FIRKINS, O. W. "Last of the Mountineers." *SRL*, V (1929), 774–775.

1450 FISCHER, William C., Jr. "William Dean Howells: Reverie and the Nonsymbolic Aesthetic." *NCF*, XXV (1970), 1–30.

1451 FORD, Thomas W. "Howells and the American Negro." *TSLL*, V (1964), 530–537.

1452 FOSTER, Richard. "The Contemporaneity of Howells." *NEQ*, XXXII (1959), 54–78.

1453 FOX, Arnold B. "Howells' Doctrine of Complicity." *MLQ*, XIII (1952), 56–60.

1454 FRAZIER, David L. "Their Wedding Journey: Howells' Fictional Craft." *NEQ*, XLII (1969), 323–349.

1455 FRAZIER, David L. "Time and the Theme of *Indian Summer.*" *ArQ*, XVI (1960), 260–267.

1456 GIANNONE, Richard. "Howells' *A Foregone Conclusion:* Theme and Structure." *CLAJ*, VI (1963), 216–220.

1457 GIBSON, William M. "Materials and Form in Howells's First Novels." *AL*, XIX (1947), 158–166.

1458 GIFFORD, Henry. "W. D. Howells: His Moral Conservatism." *KR*, XX (1958), 124–133.

1459 GIRGUS, Sam B. "Bartley Hubbard: The Rebel in Howells' *A Modern Instance.*" *RS*, XXXIX (1971), 315–321.

1460 GIRGUS, Sam B. "Howells and Marcuse: A Forecast of the One-Dimensional Age." *AQ*, XXV (1973), 108–118.

1461 GOLDFARB, Clare R. "From Complicity to Altruria: The Use of Tolstoy in Howells." *UR*, XXXII (1966), 311–317.

1462 GOLDFARB, Clare R. "William Dean Howells' *The Minister's Charge:* A Study of Psychological Perception." *MarkhamR*, II (1969), 1–4.

1463 GRATTAN, C. Hartley. "Howells: Ten Years After." *American Mercury*, XX (1930), 42–50.

1464 GULLASON, Thomas Arthur. "New Light on the Crane-Howells Relationship." *NEQ*, XXX (1957), 389–392.

1465 HALFMANN, Ulrich, ed. "Interviews with William Dean Howells." *ALR,* VI (1973), 1–119.

1466 HARLOW, Virginia. "William Dean Howells and Thomas Sergeant Perry." *BPLQ,* I (1949), 135–150.

1467 HART, John E. "The Commonplace as Heroic in *The Rise of Silas Lapham.*" *MFS,* VIII (1963), 375–383.

1468 HEDGES, Elaine R. "César Birotteau and *The Rise of Silas Lapham:* A Study in Parallels." *NCF,* XVII (1962), 163–174.

1469 HOWELLS, William D. "Novel-Writing and Novel-Reading: An Impersonal Explanation." Ed. William M. Gibson. *BNYPL,* LXII (1958), 15–34. [Offprint is available.]

1470 KAZIN, Alfred. "Howells: A Late Portrait." *AR,* I (1941), 216–233.

1471 KIRK, Clara M., and KIRK, Rudolf. "Howells and the Church of the Carpenter." *NEQ,* XXXII (1959), 185–206.

1472 KIRK, Clara M., and KIRK, Rudolf. "Letters to an 'Enchanted Guest': W. D. Howells to Edmund Gosse." *JRUL,* XXII (1959), 1–25.

1473 KIRK, Clara M., and KIRK, Rudolf. "William Dean Howells, George William Curtis, and the Anarchist Affair." *AL,* XL (1969), 487–498.

1474 KIRK, Clara M. "Reality and Actuality in the March Family Narratives of W. D. Howells." *PMLA,* LXXIV (1959), 137–152.

1475 KRAUS, W. Keith. "The Convenience of Fatalism: Thematic Unity in William Dean Howells' *A Hazard of New Fortunes.*" *English Record,* XVIII (1967), 33–36.

1476 LUTWACK, Leonard. "William Dean Howells and the 'Editor's Study'." *AL,* XXIV (1952), 195–207.

1477 LYDENBERG, John, and CADY, Edwin H. "The Howells Revival: Rounds Two and Three." *NEQ,* XXXII (1959), 394–407.

1478 LYNN, Kenneth S. "Howells in the Nineties." *Perspectives in American History,* Vol. IV. Cambridge: Charles Warren Center for Studies in American History, Harvard Univ., 1970, pp. 27–82.

1479 MCMURRAY, William John. "Point of View in Howells' *The Landlord at Lion's Head.*" *AL,* XXXIV (1962), 207–214.

1480 MANIERRE, William R., II. "*The Rise of Silas Lapham:* Retrospective Discussion as Dramatic Technique." *CE,* XXIII (1962), 357–361.

1481 MATHEWS, James W. "Toward Naturalism: Three Late Novels of W. D. Howells." *Genre,* VI (1973), 362–375.

1482 MONTEIRO, George. "A Speech by W. D. Howells." *SB,* XX (1967), 262–263.

1483 MORGAN, H. Wayne. "William Dean Howells: The Realist as Reformer." See **223.**

1484 MORRIS, Lloyd. "Conscience in the Parlor: William Dean Howells." *ASch,* XVIII (1949), 407–416.

1485 NASH, Charles C. "Howell's Darker Vision: A Reading of *The Landlord at Lion's Head.*" *ELUD,* II (1973), 36–48.

1486 PARKER, Gail T. "William Dean Howells: Realism and Feminism." In *Uses of Literature* (Harvard English Studies 4), edited by Monroe Engel. Cambridge: Harvard Univ. Press, 1973, pp. 133–161.

1487 PARKS, Edd Winfield. "Howells and the Gentle Reader." *SAQ,* L (1951), 239–247.

1488 PAYNE, Alma J. "The Family in the Utopia of William Dean Howells." *GaR,* XV (1961), 217–229.

1489 PICHT, Douglas R. "William Dean Howells: Realistic-Realist." *RS,* XXXV (1967), 92–94.

1490 PIZER, Donald. "The Ethical Unity of *The Rise of Silas Lapham.*" *AL,* XXXII (1960), 322–327.

1491 PIZER, Donald. "The Evolutionary Foundation of W. D. Howells's *Criticism and Fiction.*" *PQ,* XL (1961), 91–103.

1492 PIZER, Donald. "Evolutionary Literary Criticism and Defense of Howellsian Realism." *JEGP,* LXI (1962), 296–304.

1493 PIZER, Donald. See **115.**

1494 REEVES, John K. "The Limited Realism of Howells' *Their Wedding Journey.*" *PMLA,* LXXVII (1962), 617–628.

1495 REEVES, John K. "The Way of a Realist: A Study of Howells' Use of the Saratoga Scene." *PMLA,* XLV (1950), 1035–1052.

1496 RIVIÈRE, Jean. "Howells and Whitman After 1881." *WWR,* XII (1966), 97–100.

1497 SCHNEIDER, Robert W. "William Dean Howells: The Mugwump Rebellion." See **109.**

1498 SINCLAIR, Robert B. "Howells in the Ohio Valley: An Example for a Generation of Novelists." *SRL,* XXVIII (Jan. 6, 1945), 22–23.

1499 SNELL, George J. "Howells' 'Grasshopper'." *CE,* VII (1946), 444–452. Reprinted in **99.**

1500 SOKOLOFF, B. A. "William Dean Howells and the Ohio Village: A Study in Environment and Art." *AQ,* XI (1959), 58–75.

1501 SOLOMON, Eric. "Howells, Houses, and Realism." *ALR,* IV (1968), 89–93.

1502 SPANGLER, George M. "Moral Anxiety in *A Modern Instance.*" *NEQ,* XLVI (1973), 236–249.

1503 SPANGLER, George M. "*The Shadow of a Dream:* Howells' Homosexual Tragedy." *AQ,* XXIII (1971), 110–119.

1504 SPRINGER, Haskell S. "*The Leatherwood God:* From Narrative to Novel." *Ohio Hist.,* LXXIV (1965), 191–202.

1505 STRONKS, James B. "*A Modern Instance.*" *ALR,* IV (1968), 87–89.

1506 SULLIVAN, Sister Mary Petrus, R. S. M. "The Function of Setting in Howells' *The Landlord at Lion's Head.*" *AL,* XXXV (1963), 38–52.

1507 SWEENEY, Gerard M. "The Medea Howells Saw." *AL,* XLII (1970), 83–89. [*A Modern Instance* and Grillparzer's *Medea.*]

1508 TANSELLE, G. Thomas. "The Architecture of *The Rise of Silas Lapham.*" *AL,* XXXVII (1966), 430–457.

1509 TANSELLE, G. Thomas. "The Boston Seasons of Silas Lapham." *SNNTS,* I (1969), 60–66.

1510 TAYLOR, Walter Fuller. "On the Origin of Howells' Interest in Economic Reform." *AL,* II (1930), 3–14.

1511 TAYLOR, Walter Fuller. "William Dean Howells: Artist and American." *SR,* XLVI (1938), 288–303.

1512 TAYLOR, Walter Fuller. "William Dean Howells and the Economic Novel." *AL,* IV (1932), 103–113.

1513 TAYLOR, Walter Fuller. "William Dean Howells." See **153.**

1514 THORBURN, Neil. "William Dean Howells as a Literay Model: The Experience of Brand Whitlock." *NOQ,* XXXIX (1967), 22–36.

1515 TOMLINSON, May. "Fiction and Mr. Howells." *SAQ,* XX (1921), 360–367.

1516 TOWERS, Tom H. "Savagery and Civilization: The Moral Dimensions of Howells's *A Boy's Town.*" *AL,* XL (1969), 499–509.

1517 TRILLING, Lionel. "W. D. Howells and the Roots of Modern Taste." *PR,* XVIII (1951), 516–536.

1518 TURAJ, Frank. "The Social Gospel in Howells' Novels." *SAQ,* LXVI (1967), 449–464.

1519 VANDERBILT, Kermit. "The Conscious Realism of Howells' *April Hopes.*" *ALR,* III (1970), 53–66.

1520 VANDERBILT, Kermit. "Howells Among the Brahmins: Why 'The Bottom Dropped Out' During *The Rise of Silas Lapham.*" *NEQ,* XXXV (1962), 291–317.

1521 VANDERBILT, Kermit. "Howells Studies: Past, or Passing, or to Come." *ALR,* VII (1974), 143–153.

1522 VANDERBILT, Kermit. "Marcia Gaylord's Electra Complex: A Footnote to Sex in Howells." *AL,* XXXIV (1962), 365–374.

1523 WALTS, Robert W. "William Dean Howells and His 'Library Edition'." *PBSA,* LII (1958), 283–294.

1524 WASSERSTROM, William. "William Dean Howells: The Indelible Stain." *NEQ,* XXXII (1959), 486–495.

1525 WESTBROOK, Max. "The Critical Implications of Howells' Realism." *TexSE,* XXXVII (1957), 71–79.

1526 William Dean Howells Special Number. *MFS,* XVI (1970).

1527 WILSON, Jack H. "Howells' Use of George Eliot's *Romola* in *April Hopes.*" *PMLA,* LXXXIV (1969), 1620–1627.

1528 WOODRESS, James L., Jr. "An Interview with Howells." *ALR,* III (1970), 71–75.

1529 WOODWARD, Robert H. "*Punch* on Howells and James." *ALR,* III (1970), 76–77.

1530 WRIGHT, Nathalia. "The Significance of the Legal Profession in *A Modern Instance.*" *From Irving to Steinbeck: Studies of American Literature in Honor of Harry R. Warfel.* Gainesville: Univ. of Florida Press, 1972, 57–70.

James, Henry (1843–1916)

Texts

1531   *The Novels and Tales of Henry James.* 26 vols. [including 2 posthumous vols.] New York: Scribner's, 1907–1917. [Known as "The New York Edition," this collection for which James revised texts and wrote prefaces is standard although incomplete. It has recently been reissued by Scribner's.]

1532   *The Novels and Tales of Henry James.* 35 vols. London: Macmillan, 1921–1923. [Reprints "New York Edition" with many added titles.]

1533   *The American Novels and Tales of Henry James.* Ed. F. O. Matthiessen. New York: Knopf, 1947.

1534   *The Art of the Novel.* Ed. Richard P. Blackmur. New York: Scribner's, 1934. [Prefaces to the "New York Edition," with excellent introduction.]†

1535   *The Complete Tales of Henry James.* Ed. Leon Edel. 12 vols. Philadelphia: Lippincott, 1962–1965. [Reprints short stories and short novels in text of their first book appearance.]

1536   *Henry James and H. G. Wells: A Record of Their Friendship, Their Debate on the Art of Fiction, and Their Quarrel.* Edited with an introduction by Leon Edel and Gordon N. Ray. London: Rupert Hart-Davis, 1959.

1537   *Henry James and Robert Louis Stevenson: A Record of Friendship and Criticism.* Edited with an introduction by Janet Adam Smith. London: Rupert Hart-Davis, 1948. [Letters and essays.]

1538   *Henry James: Representative Selections, with Introduction, Bibliography, and Notes.* Ed. Lyon Richardson. New York: American Book Co., 1941.†

1539   *The Letters of Henry James.* Ed. Percy Lubbock. 2 vols. New York: Scribner's, 1920.

1540   *The Notebooks of Henry James.* Ed. F. O. Matthiessen and Kenneth Murdock. New York: Oxford Univ. Press, 1947.

1541   *Letters of Henry James: Vol. I, 1843–1875.* Ed. Leon Edel. Cambridge: Harvard Univ. Press, 1974.

1542   *The Selected Letters of Henry James.* Ed. Leon Edel. Garden City, N.Y.: Doubleday, 1960.

Bibliography

See **1, 3, 8, 18, 1538.**

1543   BEEBE, Maurice, and STAFFORD, William T. "Criticism of Henry James: A Selected Checklist." *MFS,* XII (1966), 117–177.

1544   DUNBAR, Viola R. "Addenda to 'Biographical and Critical Studies of Henry James, 1941–1948'." *AL,* XX (1949), 424–435; XXII (1950), 56–61. See **1548.**

1545   EDEL, Leon, and LAURENCE, Dan H. *A Bibliography of Henry James.* 2d ed., rev. London: Rupert Hart-Davis, 1961. [Standard.]

1546   FOLEY, Richard Nicholas. *Criticism in American Periodicals of the Works of Henry James.* Washington: Catholic Univ. of America Press, 1944.

1547 HAGEMANN, E. R. "*Life* Buffets (and Comforts) Henry James, 1883–1916: An Introduction and an Annotated Checklist." *PBSA*, LXII (1968), 207–225.

1548 HAMILTON, Eunice C. "Biographical and Critical Studies of Henry James, 1941–1948." *AL*, XX (1949), 424–435.

1549 POWERS, Lyall H. *Guide to Henry James*. (Merrill Guides.) Columbus, Ohio: Charles E. Merrill, 1969.

1550 SPILLER, Robert E. "Henry James." See **22**.

1551 TINTNER, Adeline R. "Henry James Criticism: A Current Perspective." *ALR*, VII (1973), 155–168.

Biographical and Critical Books

1552 ANDERSON, Quentin. *The American Henry James*. New Brunswick, N.J.: Rutgers Univ. Press, 1957.

1553 ANDREAS, Osborn. *Henry James and the Expanding Horizon: A Study of the Meaning and Basic Themes of James's Fiction*. Seattle: Univ. of Washington Press, 1948.

1554 APPIGNANESI, Lisa. *Femininity and the Creative Imagination: A Study of Henry James, Robert Musil and Marcel Proust*. New York: Harper & Row, 1973.

1555 AUCHINCLOSS, Louis. See **134**.

1556 BANTA, Martha. *Henry James and the Occult: The Great Extension*. Bloomington and London: Indiana Univ. Press, 1972.

1557 BEACH, Joseph Warren. *The Method of Henry James*. Philadelphia: Alfred Saifer, 1954. [Originally published in 1918.]

1558 BELL, Millicent. *Edith Wharton and Henry James: The Story of Their Friendship*. New York: Braziller, 1965.

1559 BLACKALL, Jean Frantz. *Jamesian Ambiguity and 'The Sacred Fount'*. Ithaca, N.Y.: Cornell Univ. Press, 1965.

1560 BOWDEN, Edwin T. *The Themes of Henry James: A System of Observation Through the Visual Arts*. New Haven: Yale Univ. Press, 1956.†

1561 BROOKS, Van Wyck. *The Pilgrimage of Henry James*. New York: E. P. Dutton, 1925.

1562 BUITENHUIS, Peter. *The Grasping Imagination: The American Writings of Henry James*. Toronto: Toronto Univ. Press; London: Oxford Univ. Press, 1971.

1563 CARGILL, Oscar. *The Novels of Henry James*. New York: Macmillan, 1961. [A valuable guide to the novels, scholarship, and criticism.]

1564 CHATMAN, Seymour. *The Later Style of Henry James*. Oxford: Blackwell's, 1972.

1565 CREWS, Frederick C. *The Tragedy of Manners: Moral Drama in the Later Novels of Henry James*. New Haven: Yale Univ. Press, 1957.

1566 DELBAERE-GARANT, Jeanne. *Henry James: The Vision of France*. Paris: Belles Lettres, 1970.

1567 DUPEE, F. W. *Henry James*. New York: Sloane, 1951. Rev. ed. New York: William Morrow, 1974.

1568 EDEL, Leon. *Henry James.* University of Minnesota Pamphlets on American Writers, no. 4. Minneapolis: Univ. of Minnesota Press, 1960.

1569 EDEL, Leon. *Henry James: The Untried Years, 1843–1870.* (1953) *The Conquest of London, 1870–1881.* (1962) *The Middle Years, 1882–1895.* (1962) *The Treacherous Years, 1895–1901.* (1969) *The Master, 1901–1916.* (1972). Philadelphia: Lippincott. [The standard biography.]

1570 EDGAR, Pelham. *Henry James: Man and Author.* Boston: Houghton Mifflin, 1927.

1571 EGAN, Michael. *Henry James: The Ibsen Years.* London: Vision Press, 1972.

1572 GALE, Robert L. *The Caught Image: Figurative Language in the Fiction of Henry James.* Chapel Hill: Univ. of North Carolina Press, 1964.

1573 GALLOWAY, David. *Henry James: 'The Portrait of a Lady.'* London: Edward Arnold, 1967.

1574 GARD, Roger, ed. *Henry James: The Critical Heritage.* With Introduction. London: Routledge & K. Paul; New York: Barnes & Noble, 1968.

1575 GEISMAR, Maxwell. *Henry James and the Jacobites.* Boston: Houghton Mifflin, 1963. [A thoroughgoing attack on the novels, his reputation and political-social views.]†

1576 HEIMER, Jackson W. *The Lesson of New England: Henry James and His Native Religion.* Ball State Monograph 9. Muncie, Ind.: Ball State Univ., 1967.

1577 HOCKS, Richard A. *Henry James and Pragmatistic Thought.* Chapel Hill: Univ. of North Carolina Press, 1975.

1578 HOFFMAN, Charles G. *The Short Novels of Henry James.* New York: Bookman, 1957.

1579 HOLDER-BARELL, Alexander. *The Development of Imagery and Its Functional Significance in Henry James's Novels.* Bern: Francke, 1959.

1580 HOLLAND, Laurence B. *The Expense of Vision: Essays on the Craft of Henry James.* Princeton: Princeton Univ. Press, 1964.

1581 HYDE, H. Montgomery. *Henry James At Home.* New York: Farrar, Straus & Giroux, 1969.

1582 ISLE, Walter. *Experiments in Form: Henry James's Novels, 1896–1901.* Cambridge: Harvard Univ. Press, 1968.

1583 JEFFERSON, D. W. *Henry James.* Edinburgh: Oliver and Boyd, 1960; New York: Grove Press, 1961.†

1584 JEFFERSON, D. W. *Henry James and the Modern Reader.* Edinburgh: Oliver and Boyd, 1964.

1585 KELLEY, Cornelia Pulsifer. *The Early Development of Henry James.* Urbana: Univ. of Illinois Press, 1930. Rev. ed. 1965.

1586 KRAFT, James. *The Early Tales of Henry James.* Carbondale: So. Illinois Univ. Press, 1969.

1587 KROOK, Dorothea. *The Ordeal of Consciousness in Henry James.* Cambridge, Eng.: Univ. Press, 1962.†

1588 LEBOWITZ, Naomi. *The Imagination of Loving.* Detroit: Wayne State Univ. Press, 1965.

1589 LEYBURN, Ellen D. *Strange Alloy: The Relation of Comedy to Tragedy in the Fiction of Henry James.* Foreword by William Stafford. Chapel Hill: Univ. of North Carolina Press, 1968.

1590 MCELDERRY, B. R., Jr. *Henry James.* New York: Twayne, 1965.†

1591 MAINI, Darshan Singh. *Henry James: The Indirect Vision. Studies in Themes and Techniques.* Bombay and New Delhi: Tata McGraw-Hill, 1973.

1592 MARKOW-TOTEVY, Georges. *Henry James.* New York: Funk & Wagnalls, 1969.†

1593 MARKS, Robert. *James's Later Novels: An Interpretation.* New York: William-Frederick Press, 1960.

1594 MATTHIESSEN, F. O. *Henry James: The Major Phase.* New York: Oxford Univ. Press, 1944.†

1595 MATTHIESSEN, F. O. *The James Family: Including Selections from the Writings of Henry James, Senior, William, Henry, and Alice James.* New York: Knopf, 1947.

1596 MAVES, Carl. *Sensuous Pessimism: Italy in the Works of Henry James.* Bloomington: Indiana Univ. Press, 1973.

1597 MULL, Donald L. *Henry James's 'Sublime Economy': Money as Symbolic Center in the Fiction.* Middletown, Conn.: Wesleyan Univ. Press, 1973.

1598 NOWELL-SMITH, Simon. *The Lesson of the Master.* London: Constable, 1947.

1599 O'NEILL, John P. *Workable Design: Action and Situation in the Fiction of Henry James.* Port Washington, N.Y.: Kennikat, 1973.

1600 POIRIER, Richard. *The Comic Sense of Henry James: A Study of the Early Novels.* New York: Oxford Univ. Press, 1960.†

1601 POWERS, Lyall H. *Henry James and the Naturalist Movement.* East Lansing: Michigan State Univ. Press, 1971.

1602 POWERS, Lyall H. *Henry James: An Introduction and Interpretation.* New York: Holt, Rinehart and Winston, 1970.†

1603 PUTT, S. Gorley. *A Reader's Guide to Henry James.* Introduction by Arthur Mizener. London: Thames and Hudson; Ithaca, N.Y.: Cornell Univ. Press, 1966. [American title: *Henry James: A Reader's Guide.*]†

1604 SAMUELS, Charles T. *The Ambiguity of Henry James.* Urbana: Univ. of Illinois Press, 1971.

1605 SANFORD, Charles L. *The Quest for Paradise: Europe and the American Moral Imagination.* Urbana: Univ. of Illinois Press, 1961. [Myth of Eden in American history and literature, with special emphasis on Henry James.]

1606 SEARS, Sallie. *The Negative Imagination: Form and Perspective in the Novels of Henry James.* Ithaca, N.Y.: Cornell Univ. Press, 1968.

1607 SEGAL, Ora. *The Lucid Reflector: The Observer in Henry James' Fiction.* New Haven: Yale Univ. Press, 1970.

1608 SHARP, Sister M. Corona, O.S.U. *The Confidante in Henry James: Evolution and Moral Value of a Fictive Character.* Notre Dame: Univ. of Notre Dame Press, 1963.

1609 SHINE, Muriel G. *The Fictional Children of Henry James.* Chapel Hill: Univ. of North Carolina Press, 1969.

1610 SIEGEL, Eli. *James and the Children: A Consideration of Henry James's 'The Turn of the Screw.'* Ed. Martha Baird. New York: Definition Press, 1968.

1611 STEVENSON, Elizabeth. *The Crooked Corridor: A Study of Henry James.* New York: Macmillan, 1949.†

1612 STONE, Donald D. *Novelists in a Changing World: Meredith, James, and the Transformation of English Fiction in the 1880's.* Cambridge: Harvard Univ. Press, 1972. [The Princess Casamassima and *The Bostonians.*]

1613 STONE, Edward. *The Battle and the Books: Some Aspects of Henry James.* Athens: Ohio Univ. Press, 1964. [Excellent summary of the "critical wars" over James.]

1614 TILLEY, W. H. *The Backgrounds of THE PRINCESS CASAMASSIMA.* Gainesville: Univ. of Florida Press, 1961.

1615 VAID, Krishma B. *Technique in the Tales of Henry James.* Cambridge: Harvard Univ. Press, 1964.

1616 WARD, Joseph A. *The Imagination of Disaster: Evil in the Fiction of Henry James.* Lincoln: Univ. of Nebraska Press, 1961.

1617 WARD, Joseph A. *The Search for Form: Studies in the Structure of James's Fiction.* Chapel Hill: Univ. of North Carolina Press, 1967.

1618 WEINSTEIN, Philip M. *Henry James and the Requirements of the Imagination.* Cambridge: Harvard Univ. Press, 1971.

1619 WIESENFARTH, Joseph. *Henry James and the Dramatic Analogy: A Study of the Major Novels of the Middle Period.* New York: Fordham Univ. Press, 1963.

1620 WINNER, Viola H. *Henry James and the Visual Arts.* Charlottesville: Univ. Press of Virginia, 1970.

1621 WRIGHT, Walter F. *The Madness of Art: A Study of Henry James.* Lincoln: Univ. of Nebraska Press, 1962.

Critical Essays

The first fourteen titles are collections. Individual essays follow.

1622 BUITENHUIS, Peter, ed. *Twentieth Century Interpretations of 'The Portrait of a Lady': A Collection of Critical Essays.* With introduction. Englewood Cliffs, N.J.: Prentice-Hall, 1968.†

1623 DUPEE, F. W., ed. *The Question of Henry James.* London: Allan Wingate, 1947. [A collection of critical commentary so presented that it becomes a basic document.]

1624 EDEL, Leon, ed. *Henry James: A Collection of Critical Essays.* Englewood Cliffs, N.J.: Prentice-Hall, 1963.†

1625 GOODE, John, ed. *The Air of Reality: New Essays on Henry James.* With introduction. London: Metheun, 1972. [Essays on *The American, The Wings of the Dove, What Maisie Knew, The Golden Bowl, The Ambassadors, The Sacred Fount, The Awkward Age, The Tragic Muse,* and *The Bostonians.*]

1626 LEBOWITZ, Naomi, ed. *Discussions of Henry James.* Boston: D.C. Heath Co., 1962. [Reprints critical essays.]†

1627 POWERS, Lyall H., ed. *Henry James's Major Novels: Essays in Criticism.* With introduction. East Lansing: Michigan State Univ. Press, 1973.

1628 POWERS, Lyall H., ed. *Merrill Studies in 'The Portrait of a Lady'.* (Merrill Studies.) Columbus, Ohio: Charles E. Merrill, 1970.

1629 STAFFORD, William T. *James's Daisy Miller: The Story, the Play, the Critics.* New York: Scribner's, 1963.†

1630 STAFFORD, William T., ed. *Perspectives on James's 'Portrait of a Lady': A Collection of Critical Essays.* With introduction & bibliography. New York: N.Y.U. Press, 1967.

1631 STONE, Albert E., Jr., ed. *Twentieth Century Interpretations of 'The Ambassadors.'* With introduction. Englewood Cliffs, N.J.: Prentice-Hall, 1969.†

1632 TANNER, Tony, ed. *Henry James: Modern Judgments.* With introduction. London: Macmillan, 1968.†

1633 VANN, J. Don, ed. *Critics on Henry James.* Coral Gables: Univ. of Miami Press, 1972.

1634 WILLEN, Gerald, ed. *A Casebook on Henry James's THE TURN OF THE SCREW.* New York: Thomas Y. Crowell, 1960. [The text and 15 critical essays.]†

1635 WILLEN, Gerald, ed. *Henry James' 'Washington Square': A Critical Edition.* New York: Crowell, 1970. [Includes critical essays.]

1636 ABEL, Robert H. "Gide and Henry James: Suffering, Death, and Responsibility." *MQ,* IX (1968), 403–416.

1637 ADAMS, Percy G. "Young H. James and the Lesson of His Master Balzac." *RLC,* XXXV (1961), 458–467.

1638 ALLOTT, Miriam. "Form versus Substance in Henry James." *REL,* III (1962), 53–66.

1639 ANDERSON, Charles R. "James's Portrait of the Southerner." *AL,* XXVII (1955), 309–331. [On *The Bostonians.*]

1640 ANDERSON, Charles R. "Person, Place, and Thing in James's *The Portrait of a Lady.*" In *Essays on American Literature in Honor of Jay B. Hubbell,* edited by Clarence Gohdes. Durham, N.C.: Duke Univ. Press, 1967, pp. 164–182.

1641 ANDREACH, Robert J. "Henry James's *The Sacred Fount.* The Existentialist Predicament." *NCF,* XVII (1962), 197–216.

1642 ANTUSH, John V. "Money as Myth and Reality in the World of Henry James." *ArQ,* XXV (1969), 125–133.

1643 ANTUSH, John V. "The 'Much Finer Complexity' of History in *The American.*" *JAmS,* VI (1972), 85–95.

1644 AUSTIN, Deborah. "Innocents at Home: A Study of *The Europeans* of Henry James." *JEGP,* XIV (1962), 103–129.

1645 BAILEY, N. I. "Pragmatism in *The Ambassadors.*" *DR,* LIII (1973), 143–148.

1646 BAKER, Robert S. "Gabriel Nash's 'House of Strange Idols': Aestheticism in *The Tragic Muse.*" *TSLL,* XV (1973), 149–166.

1647 BARZUN, Jacques. "James the Melodramatist." *KR,* V (1943), 508–521. Reprinted in *The Energies of Art* by Barzun. New York: Vintage Books, 1962, pp. 230–249.†

1648 BASS, Eben. "Dramatic Scene and *The Awkward Age.*" *PMLA,* LXXIX (1964), 148–157.

1649 BAYM, Nina. "Fleda Vetch and the Plot of *The Spoils of Poynton.*" *PMLA,* LXXXIV (1969), 102–111.

1650 BAZZANELLA, Dominic J. "The Conclusion to *The Portrait of a Lady* Reexamined." *AL,* XLI (1969), 55–63.

1651 BEACH, Joseph Warren. "The Witness of the Notebooks." In *Forms of Modern Fiction,* ed. by William Van O'Connor. Minneapolis: Univ. of Minnesota Press, 1948, pp. 46–60.

1652 BEACH, Joseph Warren. See **69.**

1653 BEATTIE, Munro. "The Many Marriages of Henry James." In *Patterns of Commitment in American Literature,* edited by Marston La France. Toronto: Univ. of Toronto Press, 1967, pp. 93–112.

1654 BEEBE, Maurice. "The Turned Back of Henry James." *SAQ,* LIII (1954), 521–539.

1655 BELL, Millicent. "The Dream of Being Possessed and Possessing: Henry James's *The Wings of the Dove.*" *MR,* X (1969), 97–114.

1656 BELL, Millicent. "Edith Wharton and Henry James: The Literary Relation." *PMLA,* LXXIV (1959), 619–637.

1657 BELLRINGER, Alan W. "*The Tragic Muse:* The Objective Centre." *JAmS,* IV (1970), 73–89.

1658 BERLAND, Alwyn. "Henry James and the Grand Renunciation." *KM,* (1958), 82–90.

1659 BERSANI, Leo. "The Jamesian Lie." *PR,* XXXVI (1969), 53–79.

1660 BERSANI, Leo. "The Narrator as Center in *The Wings of the Dove.*" *MFS,* VI (1960), 131–144.

1661 BEWLEY, Marius. "Appearance and Reality in Henry James." *Scrutiny,* XVII (1950), 90–114.

1662 BEWLEY, Marius. "Henry James and 'Life'." *HR,* XI (1958), 167–185.

1663 BEWLEY, Marius. "James's Debt to Hawthorne (I): *The Blithedale Romance* and *The Bostonians.*" *Scrutiny,* XVI (1949), 178–195. Reprinted in **155.**

1664 BEWLEY, Marius. "James's Debt to Hawthorne (II): *The Marble Faun* and *The Wings of the Dove.*" *Scrutiny,* XVI (1949), 301–317. Reprinted in **155.**

1665 BEWLEY, Marius. "James's Debt To Hawthorne (III): The American Problem." *Scrutiny,* XVII (1950), 14–31.

1666 BEWLEY, Marius. "Maisie, Miles and Flora, the Jamesian Innocents: A Rejoinder." *Scrutiny,* XVII (1950), 255–263.

1667 BEWLEY, Marius. See **155** and **156.**

1668 BLACKALL, Jean Frantz, "James's *In the Cage:* An Approach Through the Figurative Language." *UTQ,* XXXI (1962), 164–179.

1669 BLACKALL, Jean Frantz. "*The Sacred Fount* as a Comedy of the Limited Observer." *PMLA,* LXXVIII (1963), 384–393.

1670 BLACKMUR, Richard P. "In the Country of the Blue." *KR,* V (1943), 595–617.

1671 BLACKMUR, Richard P. "The Loose and Baggy Monsters of Henry James." *Accent,* XI (1951), 129–146. [The "monsters" are traditional novelists like Dickens, Tolstoi, and Dostoevsky.]

1672 BLACKMUR, Richard P. *"The Sacred Fount." KR,* IV (1942), 328–352.

1673 BLASING, Mutlu. "Double Focus in *The American." NCF,* XXVIII (1973), 74–84.

1674 BLEHL, Vincent F., S. J. "Freedom and Commitment in James's *Portrait of a Lady." Person,* XLII (1961), 368–381.

1675 BOBBITT, Joan. "Aggressive Innocence in *The Portrait of a Lady." MSE,* IV (1973), 31–37.

1676 BOCHNER, Jay. "Life in a Picture Gallery: Things in *The Portrait of a Lady* and *The Marble Faun." TSLL,* XI (1969), 761–777.

1677 BONTLY, Thomas J. "The Moral Perspective of *The Ambassadors." Wisconsin Studies in Lit.,* VI (1969), 106–117.

1678 BREBNER, Adele. "How to Know Maisie." *CE,* XVII (1956), 283–285.

1679 BRODERICK, John C. "Nature, Art, and Imagination in *The Spoils of Poynton." NCF,* XIII (1959), 295–312.

1680 BROOKS, Peter. "The Melodramatic Imagination: The Example of Balzac and James." In *Romanticism: Vistas, Instances, Continuities;* edited by David Thorburn and Geoffrey Hartman. Ithaca and London: Cornell Univ. Press, 1973, pp. 198–222.

1681 BROOKS, Van Wyck. See **161.**

1682 BROWN, E. K. "James and Conrad." *YR,* XXXV (1945), 265–285. [On *The Golden Bowl.*]

1683 BROWN, E. K. "Two Formulas for Fiction: Henry James and H. G. Wells." *CE,* VIII (1946), 7–17.

1684 BROWNELL, William C. "Henry James." See **215.**

1685 BUITENHUIS, Peter. "Comic Pastoral: Henry James's *The Europeans." UTQ,* XXXI (1962), 152–163.

1686 BUITENHUIS, Peter. "From Daisy Miller to Julia Bride: 'A Whole Passage of Intellectual History'." *AQ,* XI (1959), 136–146.

1687 BUITENHUIS, Peter. "Henry James and American Culture." See **548,** pp. 199–208.

1688 BYRD, Scott. "The Fractured Crystal in *Middlemarch* and *The Golden Bowl." MFS,* XVIII (1972–73), 551–554.

1689 BYRD, Scott. "The Spoils of Venice: Henry James's 'Two Old Houses and Three Young Women' and *The Golden Bowl." AL,* XLIII (1971), 371–384.

1690 CANBY, Henry Seidel. See **401.**

1691 CARGILL, Oscar. "The First International Novel." *PMLA,* LXXIII (1958), 418–425. [On *The American.*]

1692 CARGILL, Oscar. "Gabriel Nash—Somewhat Less than Angel?" *NCF,* XIV (1959), 231–239. [On *The Tragic Muse.*]

1693 CARGILL, Oscar. "Mr. James's Aesthetic Mr. Nash." *NCF,* XII (1957), 171–187. [On *The Tragic Muse.*]

1694 CARGILL, Oscar. *"The Portrait of a Lady:* A Critical Reappraisal." *MFS,* III (1957), 11–32.

1695 CARTER, Everett. See **138.**

1696 CECIL, L. Moffitt. "'Virtuous Attachment' in James' *The Ambassadors.*" *AQ,* XIX (1967), 719–724.

1697 CHARTIER, Richard. "The River and the Whirlpool: Water Imagery in *The Ambassadors.*" *BSUF,* XII (1971), 70–75.

1698 CHASE, Richard. "James' *Ambassadors.*" See **226.**

1699 CHERNAIK, Judith. "Henry James as Moralist: The Case of the Late Novels." *CentR,* XVI (1972), 105–121.

1700 CLAIR, John A. "*The American*: A Reinterpretation." *PMLA,* LXXIV (1959), 613–618.

1701 CONGER, Syndy M. "The Admirable Villains in Henry James's *The Wings of the Dove.*" *ArQ,* XXVII (1971), 151–160.

1702 CONN, Peter J. "*Roderick Hudson:* The Role of the Observer." *NCF,* XXVI (1971), 65–82.

1703 COOK, David A. "James and Flaubert: The Evolution of Perception." *CL,* XXV (1973), 289–307.

1704 COOK, John A. "The Fool Show in *Roderick Hudson.*" *CRevAS,* IV (1973), 74–86.

1705 CORE, George. "Henry James and the Comedy of the New England Conscience." See **200,** pp. 179–193.

1706 COX, James M. "Henry James: The Politics of Internationalism." *SoR,* VIII (1972), 493–506.

1707 CROMPHOUT, G. Van. "Artist and Society in Henry James." *ES,* XLIX (1968), 132–140.

1708 CROW, Charles R. "The Style of Henry James: *The Wings of the Dove.*" *Sytle in Prose Fiction.* (English Institute Essays, 1958.) New York: Columbia Univ. Press, 1959, pp. 172–189.

1709 DAICHES, David. "Sensibility and Technique." *KR,* V (1943), 569–579.

1710 DAVIDSON, Arnold E. "James's Dramatic Method in *The Awkward Age.*" *NCF,* XXIX (1974), 320–335.

1711 DOOLEY, D. J. "The Hourglass Pattern in *The Ambassadors.*" *NEQ,* XLI (1968), 273–281.

1712 DUNBAR, Viola R. "A Source for *Roderick Hudson.*" *MLN,* LXIII (1948), 303–310.

1713 DUNN, Albert A. "The Articulation of Time in *The Ambassadors.*" *Criticism,* XIV (1972), 137–150.

1714 EDEL, Leon. "The Architecture of Henry James's 'New York Edition'." *NEQ,* XXIV (1951), 169–178.

1715 EDEL, Leon. "Henry James: *The Ambassadors.*" See **243,** pp. 182–193.

1716 EDEL, Leon. "Henry James: The Americano-European Legend." *UTQ,* XXXVI (1967), 321–324.

1717 EDEL, Leon. "The Text of *The Ambassadors.*" *HLB,* XIV (1960), 453–460.

1718 EDEL, Leon. See **139.**

1719 EDEL, Leon and POWERS, Lyall H. "Henry James and the Bazar Letters." *BNYPL,* LXII (1958), 75–103. [Offprint is available.]

1720 EDELSTEIN, Arnold. " 'The Tangle of Life': Levels of Meaning in *The Spoils of Poynton.*" *HSL,* II (1970), 133–150.

1721 EDWARDS, Herbert W. "Henry James and Ibsen." *AL,* XXIV (1952), 208–223.

1722 ENCK, John J. "Wholeness of Effect in *The Golden Bowl.*" *TWA,* XLVII (1958), 227–240.

1723 ENGSTRØM, Susanne. "Epistemological and Moral Validity in Henry James's *The Ambassadors.*" *Lang&L,* I (1971), 50–65.

1724 FALK, Robert P. "Henry James and the 'Age of Innocence'." *NCF,* VII (1952), 171–188.

1725 FALK, Robert P. "Henry James's Romantic 'Vision of the Real' in the 1870's." In *Essays Critical and Historical, Dedicated to Lily B. Campbell.* Berkeley, Univ. of California Press, 1950, pp. 235–255.

1726 FALK, Robert P. See **140.**

1727 FEIDELSON, Charles, Jr. "James and the 'Man of Imagination'." In *Literary Theory and Structure: Essays in Honor of William K. Wimsatt,* edited by Frank Brady, John Palmer, and Martin Price. New Haven and London: Yale Univ. Press, 1973, pp. 331–352.

1728 FERGUSON, Alfred R. "The Triple Quest of Henry James: Fame, Art, and Fortune." *AL,* XXVII (1956), 475–498.

1729 FERGUSSON, Francis. "*The Golden Bowl* Revisited." *SR,* LXIII (1955), 13–28.

1730 FINN, C. R. "Commitment and Identity in *The Ambassadors.*" *MLR,* LXVI (1971), 522–531.

1731 FIREBAUGH, Joseph J. "A Schopenhauerian Novel: James's *The Princess Casamassima.*" *NCF,* XIII (1958), 177–197.

1732 FIREBAUGH, Joseph J. "The Idealism of Merton Dasher." *TexSE,* XXXVII (1958), 141–154.

1733 FIREBAUGH, Joseph J. "The Pragmatism of Henry James." *VQR,* XXVII (1951), 419–435.

1734 FULLER, Roy. "The Two Sides of the Street." *SoR,* IX (1973), 579–594.

1735 GARGANO, James W. "*The Spoils of Poynton:* Action and Responsibility." *SR,* LXIX (1961), 650–660.

1736 GARGANO, James W. "The Theme of 'Salvation' in *The Awkward Age.*" *TSLL,* IX (1967), 273–287.

1737 GARGANO, James W. "*What Maisie Knew:* The Evolution of a 'Moral Sense'." *NCF,* XVI (1961), 33–46.

1738 GARIS, Robert E. "The Two Lambert Strethers: A New Reading of *The Ambassadors.*" *MFS,* VII (1961), 305–316.

1739 GETTMANN, Royal A. "Henry James's Revision of *The American.*" *AL,* XVI (1945), 279–295.

1740 GIBSON, Pricilla. "The Uses of James's Imagery: Drama Through Metaphor." *PMLA,* LXIX (1954), 1076–1084.

1741 GIBSON, William M. "Metaphor in the Plot of *The Ambassadors.*" *NEQ,* XXIV (1951), 291–305.

1742 GILLEN, Francis. "The Dramatist in His Drama: Theory vs. Effect in *The Awkward Age.*" *TSLL,* XII (1971), 663–674.

1743 GIRGUS, Sam B. "The Other Maisie: Inner Death and Fatalism in *What Maisie Knew.*" *ArQ,* XXIX (1973), 115–122.

1744 GIRLING, Harry K. "The Function of Slang in the Dramatic Poetry of *The Golden Bowl.*" *NCF,* XI (1956), 130–147.

1745 GOLDSMITH, Arnold L. "Henry James's Reconciliation of Free Will and Fatalism." *NCF,* XIII (1958), 109–126.

1746 GOODE, John. "The Art of Fiction: Walter Besant and Henry James." In *Tradition and Tolerance in Nineteenth-Century Fiction: Critical Essays on Some English and American Novels.* With introduction. London: Routledge & K. Paul, 1966; New York: Barnes & Noble, 1967, pp. 243–281.

1747 GOODMAN, Charlotte. "Henry James's *Roderick Hudson* and Nathaniel Parker Willis's *Paul Fane.*" *AL,* XLIII (1972), 642–645.

1748 GORDON, Caroline. "Mr. Verver, Our National Hero." *SR,* LXIII (1955), 29–47. [On *The Golden Bowl.*]

1749 GREENE, Mildred S. "*Les liaisons dangereuses* and *The Golden Bowl:* Maggie's 'Loving Readon'." *MFS,* XIX (1973–74), 531–540.

1750 GREENE, Philip L. "Point of View in *The Spoils of Poynton.*" *NCF,* XXI (1967), 359–368.

1751 GRENANDER, M. E.; RAHN, Beverly J.; and VALVO, Francine. "The Time-Scheme in *The Portrait of a Lady.*" *AL,* XXXII (1960), 127–135.

1752 HABEGGER, Alfred. "The Disunity of *The Bostonians.*" *NCF,* XXIV (1969), 193–209.

1753 HABEGGER, Alfred. "Reciprocity and the Market Place in *The Wings of the Dove* and *What Maisie Knew.*" *NCF,* XXV (1971), 455–473.

1754 HAGEMANN, E. R. " 'Unexpected light in shady places': Henry James and *Life,* 1883–1916." *WHR,* XXIV (1970), 241–250.

1755 HALL, William F. "Gabriel Nash: 'Famous Centre' of *The Tragic Muse.*" *NCF,* XXI (1966), 167–184.

1756 HALL, William F. "James's Conception of Society in *The Awkward Age.*" *NCF,* XXIII (1968), 28–48.

1757 HALVERSON, John. "Late Manner, Major Phase." *SR,* LXXIX (1971), 214–231.

1758 HAMBLEN, Abigail A. "Henry James and the Power of Eros: *What Maisie Knew.*" *MQ,* IX (1968), 391–399.

1759 HARTSOCK, Mildred E. "The Dizzying Crest: Strether as Moral Man." *MLQ,* XXVI (1965), 414–425.

1760 HARTSOCK, Mildred E. "The Princess Casamassima: The Politics of Power." *SNNTS,* I (1969), 297–309.

1761 HARVITT, Hélène. "How Henry James Revised *Roderick Hudson:* A Study in Style," *PMLA,* XXXIX (1924), 203–227.

1762 HASLAM, Gerald. "Olive Chancellor's Painful Victory in *The Bostonians.*" *RS,* XXXVI (1968), 232–237.

1763 HAVENS, Raymond D. "The Revision of *Roderick Hudson.*" *PMLA,* XL (1925), 433–434.

1764 HEMPHILL, George. "Hemingway and James." *KR,* XI (1949), 50–60.

1765 Henry James Number. *Modern Fiction Studies,* XII (1966).

1766 HINZ, Evelyn J. "Henry James's Names: Tradition, Theory, and Method." *CLQ,* IX (1972), 557–578.

1767 HOFFA, William. "The Final Preface: Henry James's Autobiography." *SR,* LXXVII (1969), 277–293.

1768 HOFFMAN, Frederick J. "Freedom and Conscious Form: Henry James and the American Self." *VQR,* XXXVII (1961), 269–285.

1769 HOPKINS, Viola. "Visual Art Devices and Parallels in the Fiction of Henry James." *PMLA,* LXXVI (1961), 561–574.

1770 HOROWITZ, Floyd R. "The Christian Time Sequence in Henry James's *The American.*" *CLAJ,* IX (1966), 234–245.

1771 HORRELL, Joyce T. "A 'Shade of Special Sense': Henry James and the Art of Naming." *AL,* XLII (1970), 203–220.

1772 HOSKINS, Katherine. "Henry James and the Future of the Novel." *SR,* LIV (1946), 87–101.

1773 HOXIE, Elizabeth F. "Mrs. Grundy Adopts Daisy Miller." *NEQ,* XIX (1946), 474–484.

1774 JOHNSON, Lee Ann. "'A Dog in the Manger': James's Depiction of Roger Lawrence in *Watch and Ward.*" *ArQ,* XXIX (1973), 169–176.

1775 KANE, Patricia. "Mutual Perspective: James and Howells as Critics of Each Other's Fiction." *MinnR,* VII (1967), 331–341.

1776 KAYE, Julian B. "*The Awkward Age, The Sacred Fount,* and *The Ambassadors:* Another Figure in the Carpet." *NCF,* XVII (1963), 339–351.

1777 KENNEDY, Ian. "Frederick Winterbourne: The Good Bad Boy in *Daisy Miller.*" *ArQ,* XXIX (1973), 139–150.

1778 KIMBALL, Jean. "The Abyss and the Wings of the Dove: The Image as a Revelation." *NCF,* X (1956), 281–300.

1779 KIMBALL, Jean. "Henry James's Last Portrait of a Lady: Charlotte Stant in *The Golden Bowl.*" *AL,* XXVIII (1957), 449–468.

1780 KIMMEY, John L. "*The Bostonians* and *The Princess Casamassima.*" *TSLL,* IX (1968), 537–546.

1781 KIMMEY, John L. "*The Princess Casamassima* and the Quality of Bewilderment." *NCF,* XXII (1967), 47–62.

1782 KIMMEY, John L. "*The Tragic Muse* and Its Forerunners." *AL,* XLI (1970), 518–531.

1783 KIRBY, David K. "Henry James: Art and Autobiography." *DR,* LII (1972–73), 637–644.

1784 KORNFIELD, Milton. "Villainy and Responsibility in *The Wings of the Dove.*" *TSLL,* XIV (1972), 337–346.

1785 KRAFT, James. "On Reading *The American Scene.*" *Prose,* VI (1973), 115–136.

1786 KRAFT, Quentin G. "The Central Problem of James's Fictional Thought: From *The Scarlet Letter* to *Roderick Hudson.*" *ELH,* XXXVI (1969), 416–439.

1787 KRAUSE, Sydney J. "James's Revisions of the Style of *The Portrait of a Lady.*" *AL,* XXX (1958), 67–88.

1788 KRETSCH, Robert W. "Political Passion in Balzac and Henry James." *NCF*, XIV (1959), 265–270. [On *The Princess Casamassima.*]

1789 LABRIE, Ernest R. "Henry James's Idea of Consciousness." *AL*, XXXIX (1968), 517–529.

1790 LABRIE, Ross. "The Morality of Consciousness in Henry James." *CLQ*, IX (1971), 409–424.

1791 LABRIE, Ross. "The Power of Consciousness in Henry James." *ArQ*, XXIX (1973), 101–114.

1792 LEAVIS, F. R. *The Great Tradition: George Eliot, Henry James, Joseph Conrad.* London: Chatto and Windus, 1948, 126–172.†

1793 LEAVIS, F. R. "The Novel as Dramatic Poem (III): *The Europeans.*" *Scrutiny*, XV (1948), 209–221.

1794 LEE, Brian. "Henry James's 'Divine Consensus': *The Ambassadors, The Wings of the Dove, The Golden Bowl.*" *RMS*, VI (1962), 5–24.

1795 LEVY, Leo B. "Henry James's *Confidence* and the Development of the Idea of the Unconscious." *AL*, XXVIII (1956), 347–358.

1796 LEWIS, R. W. B. "The Vision of Grace: James's 'The Wings of the Dove'." *MFS*, III (1957), 33–40.

1797 LIEBMAN, Sheldon W. "The Light and the Dark: Character Design in *The Portrait of a Lady.*" *PLL*, VI (1970), 163–179.

1798 LIEBMAN, Sheldon W. "Point of View in *The Portrait of A Lady.*" *ES*, LII (1971), 136–147.

1799 LONG, Robert E. "*The Ambassadors* and the Genteel Tradition: James's Correction of Hawthorne and Howells." *NEQ*, XLII (1969), 44–64.

1800 LONG, Robert E. "James's *Washington Square:* The Hawthorne Relation." *NEQ*, XLIV (1973), 573–590.

1801 MCCARTHY, Harold T. "Henry James and the American Aristocracy." *ALR*, IV (1971), 61–71.

1802 MCDONALD, Walter R. "The Inconsistencies in Henry James's Aesthetics." *TSLL*, X (1969), 585–597.

1803 MCELDERRY, B. R., Jr. See **993.**

1804 MACKENZIE, Manfred. "Communities of Knowledge: Secret Society in Henry James." *ELH*, XXXIX (1972), 147–168.

1805 MCLEAN, Robert C. "*The Bostonians:* New England Pastoral." *PLL*, VII (1971), 374–381.

1806 MCLEAN, Robert C. "The Completed Vision: A Study of *Madame de Mauves* and *The Ambassadors.*" *MLQ*, XXVIII (1967), 446–461.

1807 MCLEAN, Robert C. " 'Love by the Doctor's Direction': Disease and Death in *The Wings of the Dove.*" *PLL*, VIII (1972), 128–148.

1808 MCMASTER, Juliet. "The Portrait of Isabel Archer." *AL*, XLV (1973), 50–66.

1809 MCMURRAY, William J. "Pragmatic Realism in *The Bostonians.*" *NCF*, XVI (1962), 329–344.

1810 MACNOUGHTON, W. R. "The First-Person Narrators of Henry James." *SAF*, II (1974), 145–164.

1811 MAGLIN, Nan B. "Fictional Feminists in *The Bostonians* and *The Odd Women.*" In *Images of Women in Fiction: Feminist Perspectives,* edited by Susan K. Cornillon. Bowling Green, Ohio: Bowling Green Univ. Popular Press, 1972, pp. 216–236.

1812 MAROVITZ, Sanford E. "*Roderick Hudson:* James's *Marble Faun.*" *TSLL,* XI (1970), 1427–1443.

1813 MARTIN, W. R. "The Use of the Fairy-Tale: A Note on The Structure of *The Bostonians.*" *ESA,* II (1959), 98–109.

1814 MATTHIESSEN, F. O. "From Hawthorne to James to Eliot." See **43.**

1815 MAYS, Milton A. "Henry James, or, The Beast in the Palace of Art." *AL,* XXXIX (1968), 467–487.

1816 MELLARD, James M. "Modal Counterpoint in James's *The Aspern Papers.*" *PLL,* IV (1968), 299–307.

1817 MERCER, Caroline G. "Adam Verver, Yankee Businessman." *NCF,* XXII (1967), 251–269.

1818 MERRILL, Robert. "What Strether *Sees:* The Ending of *The Ambassadors.*" *BRMMLA,* XXVII (1973), 45–52.

1819 MILLER, Theodore C. "Muddled Politics of Henry James's *The Bostonians.*" *GaR,* XXVI (1972), 336–346.

1820 MORGAN, Alice. "Henry James: Money and Morality." *TSLL,* XII (1970), 75–92.

1821 MORRIS, R. A. "Classical Vision and the American City: Henry James's *The Bostonians.*" *NEQ,* XLVI (1973), 543–557.

1822 MORRISON, Sister Kristin. "James's and Lubbock's Differing Points of View." *NCF,* XVI (1962), 245–255.

1823 MULL, Donald L. "Freedom and Judgment: The Antinomy of Action in *The Portrait of a Lady.*" *ArQ,* XXVII (1971), 124–132.

1824 MULQUEEN, James E. "Perfection of a Pattern: The Structure of *The Ambassadors, The Wings of the Dove,* and *The Golden Bowl.*" *ArQ,* XXVII (1971), 133–142.

1825 NELSON, Carl. "James's Social Criticism: The Voice of the Ringmaster in *The Awkward Age.*" *ArQ,* XXIX (1973), 151–168.

1826 NETTELS, Elsa. "Action and Point of View in *Roderick Hudson.*" *ES,* LIII (1972), 238–247.

1827 NETTLES, Elsa. "*The Ambassadors* and the Sense of the Past." *MLQ,* XXI (1970), 220–235.

1828 NETTELS, Elsa. "James and Conrad on the Art of Fiction." *TSLL,* XIV (1972), 529–543.

1829 NEWLIN, Paul A. "The Development of *Roderick Hudson:* An Evaluation." *ArQ,* XXVII (1971), 101–123.

1830 OLIVER, Clinton. "Henry James as a Social Critic." *AR,* VII (1947), 243–258. [On *The Princess Casamassima.*]

1831 OWEN, Elizabeth. " 'The Given Appearance' of Charlotte Verver." *EIC,* XIII (1963), 364–374. [On *The Golden Bowl.*]

1832 PERLOFF, Marjorie. "Cinderella Becomes the Wicked Stepmother: *The Portrait of a Lady* as Ironic Fairy Tale." *NCF,* XXIII (1969), 413–433.

1833 PERLONGO, Robert A. "*The Sacred Fount:* Labyrinth or Parable?" *KR,* XXII (1960), 635–647.

1834 PIZER, Donald. See **115.**

1835 POIRIER, Richard. "Henry James, *The Portrait of a Lady.*" See **227.**

1836 POWERS, Lyall H. "Henry James and Zola's *Roman Expérimental.*" *UTQ,* XXX (1960), 16–30.

1837 POWERS, Lyall H. "James's *The Tragic Muse*—Ave Atque Vale." *PMLA,* LXXIII (1958), 270–274.

1838 POWERS, Lyall H. "Mr. James's Aesthetic Mr. Nash—Again." *NCF,* XIII (1959), 341–349. [On *The Tragic Muse.*]

1839 POWERS, Lyall H. "*The Portrait of a Lady:* 'The Eternal Mystery of Things'." *NCF,* XIV (1959), 143–155.

1840 RAETH, Claire J. "Henry James's Rejection of *The Sacred Fount.*" *ELH,* XVI (1949), 308–324.

1841 RAHV, Philip. "The Heiress of All the Ages." *PR,* X (1943), 227–247.

1842 RALEIGH, John Henry. "Henry James: The Poetics of Empiricism." *PMLA,* LXVI (1951), 107–123.

1843 RANALD, Ralph A. "*The Sacred Fount*: James's Portrait of the Artist *Manqué.*" *NCF,* XV (1960), 239–248.

1844 RANDALL, John H. "Romeo and Juliet in the New World: A Study in James, Wharton, and Fitzgerald 'Fay ce que vouldras'." *Costerus,* VIII (1973), 109–176.

1845 REED, John Q. "*The Ambassadors:* Henry James's Method." *MQ,* IV (1962), 55–67.

1846 REILLY, Robert J. "Henry James and the Morality of Fiction." *AL,* XXXIX (1967), 1–30.

1847 ROSE, Shirley. "Waymarsh's 'Sombre Glow' and *Der Fliegende Holländer.*" *AL,* XLV (1973), 438–441.

1848 ROURKE, Constance. "The American." See **199.**

1849 ROUSE, H. Blair. "Charles Dickens and Henry James: Two Approaches to the Art of Fiction." *NCF,* V (1950), 151–157.

1850 ROWE, John C. "The Symbolization of Milly Theale: Henry James's *The Wings of the Dove.*" *ELH,* XL (1973), 131–164.

1851 SALZBERG, Joel. "Love, Identity, and Death: James' *The Princess Casamassima* Reconsidered." *BRMMLA,* XXVI (1972), 127–135.

1852 SANDEEN, Ernest. "*The Wings of the Dove* and *The Portrait of a Lady:* A Study of Henry James's Later Phase." *PMLA,* LXIX (1954), 1060–1075.

1853 SCHERTING, John. "*Roderick Hudson:* A Re-evaluation." *ArQ,* XXV (1969), 101–119.

1854 SCHNEIDER, Daniel J. "The Ironic Imagery and Symbolism of James's *The Ambassadors.*" *Criticism,* IX (1967), 174–196.

1855 SCHULZ, Max F. "The Bellegardes' Feud with Christopher Newman: A Study of Henry James's Revision of *The American.*" *AL,* XXVII (1955), 42–55.

1856 SCHULTZ, Elizabeth. "*The Bostonians:* The Contagion of Romantic Illusion." *Genre,* IV (1971), 45–59.

1857 SCOTT, Arthur L. "A Protest Against the James Vogue." *CE,* XIII (1952), 194–201.

1858 SECOR, Robert. "Christopher Newman: How Innocent is James's American?" *SAF,* I (1973), 141–153.

1859 SHORT, R. W. "Henry James's World of Images." *PMLA,* LXVIII (1958), 943–960.

1860 SHORT, R. W. "The Sentence Structure of Henry James." *AL,* XVIII (1946), 71–88.

1861 SHORT, R. W. "Some Critical Terms of Henry James." *PMLA,* (1950), 667–680.

1862 SHUCARD, Alan R. "Diplomacy in Henry James's *The Ambassadors.*" *ArQ,* XXIX (1973), 123–129.

1863 SHULMAN, Robert. "Henry James and the Modern Comedy of Knowledge." *Criticism,* X (1968), 41–53.

1864 SNELL, George. "Henry James: Life Refracted by Temperament." See **99.**

1865 SNOW, Lotus. " 'A Story of Cabinets and Chairs and Tables': Images of Morality in *The Spoils of Poynton* and *The Golden Bowl.*" *ELH,* XXX (1963), 413–435.

1866 SNOW, Lotus. "The Disconcerting Poetry of Mary Temple: A Comparison of Imagery of *The Portrait of a Lady* and *The Wings of the Dove.*" *NEQ,* XXXI (1958), 312–339.

1867 SNOW, Lotus. "The Pattern of Innocence Through Experience in the Character of Henry James." *UTQ,* XXII (1953), 230–236.

1868 SPANOS, Bebe. "The Real Princess Christina." *PQ,* XXXVIII (1959), 488–496. [On *The Princess Casamassima.*]

1869 SPECK, Paul S. "A Structural Analysis of Henry James's *Roderick Hudson.*" *SNNTS,* II (1970), 292–304.

1870 SPENCER, James L. "Symbolism in James's 'The Golden Bowl'." *MFS,* III (1957), 333–344.

1871 SPILKA, Mark. "Henry James and Walter Besant: 'The Art of Fiction' Controversy." *Novel,* VI (1973), 101–119.

1872 STAFFORD, William T. "Henry James the American: Some Views of His Contemporaries." *TCL,* I (1955), 69–76.

1873 STAFFORD, William T. "James Examines Shakespeare: Notes on the Nature of Genius." *PMLA,* LXXIII (1958), 123–128.

1874 STALLMAN, Robert W. " 'The Sacred Rage': The Time-Theme in 'The Ambassadors'." *MFS,* III (1957), 41–56.

1875 STALLMAN, Robert W. "Who Was Gilbert Osmond?" *MFS,* IV (1958), 127–135.

1876 STALLMAN, Robert W. See **765.**

1877 STEIN, William Bysshe. "*The Ambassadors:* The Crucifixion of Sensibility." *CE,* XVII (1956), 289–292.

1878 STEIN, William Bysshe. "*The Aspern Papers:* A Comedy of Masks." *NCF,* XIV (1959), 172–178.

1879 STEIN, William Bysshe. "The Method at the Heart of Madness: *The Spoils of Poynton.*" *MFS,* XIV (1968), 187–202.

1880 STEIN, William Bysshe. "*The Portrait of a Lady: Vis Inertiae.*" *WHR,* XIII (1959), 177–190.

1881 STEIN, William Bysshe. "*The Sacred Fount:* The Poetics of Nothing." *Criticism,* XIV (1972), 373–389.

1882 STOEHR, Taylor. "Words and Deeds in *The Princess Casamassima.*" *ELH,* XXXVII (1970), 95–135.

1883 STONE, Edward. "Henry James's First Novel." *BPLQ,* II (1950), 167–171.

1884 STONE, Edward. "Henry James's Last Novel." *BPLQ,* II (1950), 348–353.

1885 SULLIVAN, Jeremiah J. "Henry James and Hippolyte Taine: The Historical and Scientific Method in Literature." *CLS,* X (1973), 25–50.

1886 TANNER, Tony. "Henry James and Henry Adams." *TriQ,* XI (1968), 91–108.

1887 TANNER, Tony. "The Watcher from the Balcony: Henry James's *The Ambassadors.*" *CritQ,* VIII (1966), 35–52.

1888 THORBERG, Raymond. "*Germaine,* James's *Notebooks,* and *The Wings of the Dove.*" *CL,* XXII (1970), 254–264.

1889 TICK, Stanley. "Henry James's *The American:* Voyons." *SNNTS,* II (1970), 276–291.

1890 TILFORD, John E., Jr. "James the Old Intruder." *MFS,* IV (1958), 157–164. [On *The Ambassadors.*]

1891 TINTNER, Adeline R. "Balzac's 'Madame Firmiani' and James's *The Ambassadors.*" *CL,* XXV (1973), 128–135.

1892 TINTNER, Adeline R. "Keats and James and *The Princess Casamassima.*" *NCF,* XXVIII (1973), 179–193.

1893 TINTNER, Adeline R. "Maggie's Pagoda: Architectural Follies in *The Golden Bowl.*" *MarkhamR,* III (1973), 113–115.

1894 TODASCO, Ruth Taylor. "Theme and Imagery in *The Golden Bowl.*" *TSLL,* IV (1962), 228–240.

1895 TOMPKINS, Jane P. "The Redemption of Time in *Notes on a Son and Brother.*" *TSLL,* XIV (1973), 681–690.

1896 TRASCHEN, Isadore. "An American in Paris." *AL,* XXVI (1954), 67–77. [On *The American.*]

1897 TRASCHEN, Isadore. "Henry James and the Art of Revision." *PQ,* XXXV (1956), 39–47. [On *The American.*]

1898 TRASCHEN, Isadore. "James's Revisions of the Love Affair in *The American.*" *NEQ,* XXIX (1956), 43–62.

1899 VEEDER, William. "Strether and the Transcendence of Language." *MP,* LXIX (1971), 116–132.

1900 VIVAS, Eliseo. "Henry and William (Two Notes)." *KR,* V (1943), 580–594. Reprinted in Vivas' *Creation and Discovery: Essays in Criticism and Aesthetics.* New York: Noonday Press, 1955.

1901 WALLACE, Ronald. "Comic Form in *The Ambassadors.*" *Genre,* V (1972), 31–50.

1902 WALLACE, Ronald. "Gabriel Nash: Henry James's Comic Spirit." *NCF,* XXVIII (1973), 220–224.

1903 WALLACE, Ronald. "Maggie Verver: Comic Heroine." *Genre,* VI (1973), 404–415.

1904 WARD, Joseph A. "*The Ambassadors* as a Conversion Experience." *SoR,* V (1969), 350–374.

1905 WARD, Joseph A. "*The Ambassadors:* Strether's Vision of Evil." *NCF,* XIV (1959), 45–58.

1906 WARD, Joseph A. "James's *The Europeans* and the Structure of Comedy." *NCF,* XIX (1964), 1–16.

1907 WARREN, Austin. "Henry James: Symbolic Imagery in the Later Novels." *Rage for Order: Essays in Criticism.* Chicago: Univ. Of Chicago Press, 1948, pp. 142–161.†

1908 WARREN, Austin. "Myth and Dialectic in the Later Novels." *KR,* V (1943), 551–568.

1909 WARREN, Austin. "The New England Conscience, Henry James, and Ambassador Strether." *MR,* II (1962), 149–161.

1910 WASIOLEK, Edward. "Maisie: Pure or Corrupt?" *CE,* XXII (1960), 167–172. [On *What Maisie Knew.*]

1911 WATANABE, Hisayoshi. "Past Perfect Retrospection in the Style of Henry James." *AL,* XXXIV (1962), 165–181.

1912 WATKINS, Floyd C. "Christopher Newman's Final Instinct." *NCF.* XII (1957), 85–88.

1913 WATT, Ian. "The First Paragraph of *The Ambassadors:* An Explication." *EIC,* X (1960), 250–274.

1914 WEBER, Carl J. "Henry James and His Tiger-Cat." *PMLA,* LXVIII (1953), 672–687.

1915 WEGELIN, Christof. "Henry James's *The Wings of the Dove* as an International Novel." *JA,* III (1958), 151–161.

1916 WEGELIN, Christof. "The 'Internationalism' of *The Golden Bowl.*" *NCF,* XI (1956), 161–181.

1917 WELLEK, René. "Henry James's Literary Theory and Criticism." *AL,* XXX (1958), 293–321.

1918 WILSON, Edmund. "The Ambiguity of Henry James." *The Triple Thinkers: Ten Essays on Literature.* New York: Harcourt, Brace, 1938, pp. 122–164.†

1919 WILSON, Harris W. "What *Did* Maisie Know?" *CE,* XVII (1956), 279–282.

1920 WINNER, Viola H. "Pictorialism in Henry James's Theory of the Novel." *Criticism,* IX (1967), 1–21.

1921 WINTERS, Yvor. "Henry James and the Relation of Morals to Manners." *American Review,* IX (1937), 482–503. Reprinted in *In Defense of Reason.* Denver: Alan Swallow, 1947, 300–343.

1922 WISE, James N. "The Floating World of Lambert Strether." *ArlQ,* II (1969), 80–110.

1923 WOODCOCK, George, "Henry James and the Conspirators." *SR,* LX (1952), 219–229. [On *The Princess Casamassima.*]

1924 WORDEN, Ward S. "A Cut Version of *What Maisie Knew.*" *AL,* XXIV (1953), 493–504.

1925 WORDEN, Ward S. "Henry James's *What Maisie Knew:* A Comparison with the Plans in the Notebooks." *PMLA,* LXVIII (1953), 371–383.

1926 WRIGHT, Nathalia. "Henry James and the Greenough Data." *AQ,* X (1958), 338–343.

1927 WRIGHT, Walter F. "Maggie Verver: Neither Saint Nor Witch." *NCF,* XII (1957), 59–71. [On *The Golden Bowl.*]

1928 ZABEL, Morton Dauwen. "Henry James: The Art of Life." In *Craft and Character: Texts, Methods, and Vocation in Modern Fiction.* New York: Viking Press, 1957, pp. 114–143.

Jewett, Sarah Orne (1849–1909)

Texts

1929 *The Country of the Pointed Firs and Other Stories.* Introduction by Mary Ellen Chase. New York: W. W. Norton, 1968.

1930 *Deephaven and Other Stories.* Introduction by Richard Cary. New Haven: College and University Press, 1966.

Bibliography

1931 CARY, Richard. "Sarah Orne Jewett (1849–1909)." *ALR,* I (1967), 61–66.

1932 CARY, Richard. "Some Bibliographic Ghosts of Sarah Orne Jewett." *CLQ,* VIII (1968), 139–145.

1933 EICHELBERGER, Clayton L. "Sarah Orne Jewett (1849–1909): A Critical Bibliography of Secondary Comment." *ALR,* II (1969), 189–262.

1934 WEBER, Clara Carter, and WEBER, Carl J. *A Bibliography of the Published Writings of Sarah Orne Jewett.* Waterville, Maine: Colby College Library, 1949.

Biographical and Critical Books

1935 BISHOP, Ferman. *The Sense of the Past in Sarah Orne Jewett.* Univ. Of Wichita Bulletin: University Studies, no. 41. Wichita, Kan., 1959.

1936 CARY, Richard. *Sarah Orne Jewett.* New York: Twayne, 1962.†

1937 MATTHIESSEN, F. O. *Sarah Orne Jewett.* Boston: Houghton Mifflin, 1929.

1938 THORP, Margaret F. *Sarah Orne Jewett.* (UMPAW 61.) Minneapolis: Univ. of Minnesota Press, 1966.

Critical Essays

1939 BERTHOFF, Warner. "The Art of Jewett's *Pointed Firs.*" *NEQ,* XXXII (1959), 31–53.

1940 BISHOP, Ferman. "Henry James Criticizes *The Tory Lover.*" *AL,* XXVII (1955), 262–264.

1941 CARY, Richard. "Jewett, Tarkington, and the Maine Line." *CLQ,* Ser. IV (1956), 89–95.

1942 CARY, Richard. "The Other Face of Jewett's Coin." *ALR,* II (1969), 263–270.

1943 CARY, Richard. "The Rise, Decline, and Rise of Sarah Orne Jewett." *CLQ,* IX (1972), 650–663.

1944 CHAPMAN, Edward M. "The New England of Sarah Orne Jewett." *YR,* III (1913), 157–172.

1945 EAKIN, Paul J. "Sarah Orne Jewett and the Meaning of Country Life." *AL,* XXXVIII (1967), 508–531.

1946 HOLLIS, C. Carroll. "Letters of Sarah Orne Jewett to Anna Laurens Davis." *CLQ,* VIII (1968), 97–138.

1947 HORN, Robert L. "The Power of Jewett's *Deephaven.*" *CLQ,* IX (1972), 617–631.

1948 *Jewett Issue. CLQ,* ser. VI, no. X (June, 1964). [Bibliography and essays.]

1949 PARSONS, Helen V. "*The Tory Lover, Oliver Wiswell,* and *Richard Carvel.*" *CLQ,* IX (1970), 220–231.

1950 POOL, Eugene H. "The Child in Sarah Orne Jewett." *CLQ,* VII (1967), 503–509.

1951 RHODE, Robert D. "Sarah Orne Jewett and 'The Palpable Present Intimate'." *CLQ,* VIII (1968), 146–155.

1952 ST. ARMAND, Barton L. "Jewett and Marin: The Inner Vision." *CLQ,* IX (1972), 632–643.

1953 STOUCK, David. "*The Country of the Pointed Firs:* A Pastoral of Innocence." *CLQ,* IX (1970), 213–220.

1954 TOTH, Susan A. "Sarah Orne Jewett and Friends: A Community of Interest." *SSF,* IX (1972), 233–241.

1955 TOTH, Susan A. "The Value of Age in the Fiction of Sarah Orne Jewett." *SSF,* VIII (1971), 433–441.

1956 VELLA, Michael W. "Sarah Orne Jewett: A Reading of *The Country of the Pointed Firs.*" *ESQ,* LXXIII (1973), 275–282.

1957 VOELKER, Paul D. "*The Country of the Pointed Firs:* A Novel by Sarah Orne Jewett." *CLQ,* IX (1970), 201–213.

1958 WAGGONER, Hyatt H. "The Unity of *The Country of the Pointed Firs.*" *TCL,* V (1959), 67–73.

Kennedy, John Pendleton (1795–1870)

Texts

1959 *The Collected Works of John Pendleton Kennedy.* 10 vols. New York: Putnam, 1871. [Contains Tuckerman's *Life.* Standard edition, but long out of print.]

1960 *Horse-Shoe Robinson.* Edited with an introduction, chronology, and bibliography by Ernest E. Leisy. American Fiction Series. New York: American Book Co., 1937. [Very valuable.]†

1961 *Rob of the Bowl: A Legend of St. Inigoe's.* Ed. William S. Osborne. New Haven: College and University Press, 1965.†

1962 *Swallow Barn.* Introduction by Jay B. Hubbell. American Author's Series. New York: Harcourt, Brace, 1929. [Valuable introduction, but edition is out of print.]

1963 *Swallow Barn.* Introduction by William S. Osborne. New York: Hafner, 1962.†

Bibliography

There is no separate bibliography. See **8, 18, 1960, 1964.**

Biographical and Critical Books

1964 BOHNER, Charles H. *John Pendleton Kennedy: Gentleman from Baltimore.* Baltimore: Johns Hopkins Press, 1961.

1965 GWATHNEY, Edward M. *John Pendleton Kennedy.* New York: Thomas Nelson, 1931.

1966 RIDGELY, Joseph V. *John Pendleton Kennedy.* (TUSAS 102.) New York: Twayne, 1966.

1967 TUCKERMAN, Henry T. *The Life of John Pendleton Kennedy.* New York: Putnam, 1871. [The "authorized" biography.]

Critical and Biographical Essays

1968 BOHNER, Charles H. " 'As Much History as . . . Invention': John P. Kennedy's *Rob of the Bowl.*" *WMQ,* XVII (1960), 329–340.

1969 BOHNER, Charles H. "*Swallow Barn:* John P. Kennedy's Chronicle of Virginia Society." *VMHB,* LXVIII (1960), 317–330.

1970 BOHNER, Charles H. "*The Red Book,* 1819–1821, a Satire on Baltimore Society." *MHM,* LI (1956), 175–187.

1971 CAMPBELL, Killis. "The Kennedy Papers." *SR,* XXV (1917), 1–19; 193–208; 348–360.

1972 COOKE, John Esten. "The Author of *Swallow Barn.*" *Appleton's Journal,* X (1873), 205–206.

1973 ELLISON, Rhoda Coleman. "An Interview with Horse-Shoe Robinson." *AL,* XXXI (1959), 329–332.

1974 FORMAN, Henry C. "The Rose Croft in Old St. Mary's." *MHM,* XXXV (1940), 26–31. [On *Rob of the Bowl.*]

1975 GAINES, Francis Pendleton. *The Southern Plantation.* See **171.**

1976 GALLAGHER, F. X. "The Gentleman from Maryland." *Evergreen Q,* V (1948), 48–55.

1977 GRIFFIN, Lloyd W. "The John Pendleton Kennedy Manuscripts." *MHM,* XLVIII (1953), 327–336.

1978 MOORE, John R. "Kennedy's *Horse-Shoe Robinson:* Fact or Fiction?" *AL,* IV (1932), 160–166.

1979 PARRINGTON, Vernon L. Jr. See **44.**

1980 ROSE, Alan H. "The Image of the Negro in the Pre-Civil War Novels of John Pendleton Kennedy and William Gilmore Simms." *JAmS,* IV (1970), 217–226.

1981 UHLER, John Earle. "Kennedy's Novels and His Posthumous Works." *AL,* III (1932), 471–479.

1982 WERMUTH, Paul C. "*Swallow Barn:* A Victorian Idyll." *VC,* IX, i (1959), 30–34.

London, Jack (John Griffith) (1876–1916)

Texts

No standard collection has been made, although one, "The Bodley Head," is in progress. There are many reprinted editions of various titles.

1983 *The Bodley Head Jack London.* Edited with introduction by Arthur Calder-Marshall. London: The Bodley Head, 1963–. [In progress. An admirable edition.]

1984 *Burning Daylight.* Introduction by I. O. Evans. New York: Horizon Press, 1969.

1985 *The Game and The Abysmal Brute.* Introduction by I. O. Evans. New York: Horizon Press, 1969.

1986 *Jack London Reports: War Correspondence, Sports Articles, and Miscellaneous Writings.* Edited with introduction by King Hendricks and Irving Shepard. Garden City, N.Y.: Doubleday, 1970.

1987 *The Jacket.* Introduction by I. O. Evans. New York: Horizon Press, 1969.

Bibliography

See **8, 18, 1999, 2002.**

1988 CHOMET, Otto. "Jack London: Works, Reviews, and Criticism Published in German." *BB,* XIX (1949), 211–215; 239–240.

1989 HAYDOCK, James. "Jack London: A Bibliography of Criticism." *BB,* XXIII (1960), 42–46.

1990 LABOR, Earle. "Jack London: An Addendum." *ALR,* II (1968), 91–93.

1991 WALKER, Dale L., comp. *The Fiction of Jack London: A Chronological Bibliography.* Research and editing by James E. Sisson, III. El Paso: Texas Western Press, 1972.

1992 WALKER, Dale L. "Jack London (1876–1916)." *ALR,* I (1967), 71–78.

1993 WOODBRIDGE, Hensley C.; LONDON, John; and TWENEY, George H., comps. *Jack London: A Bibliography.* Georgetown, Calif.: Talisman Press, 1966.

Biographical and Critical Books

1994 BAMFORD, Georgia L. *The Mystery of Jack London: Some of His Friends, Also a Few Letters—A Reminiscence.* Oakland, Calif.: [the author], 1931.

1995 FEIED, Frederick. *No Pie in the Sky: The Hobo as American Cultural Hero in the Works of Jack London, John Dos Passos, and Jack Kerouac.* New York: Citadel, 1964.†

1996 FONER, Philip S. *Jack London, American Rebel: A Collection of His Social Writings Together with an Extensive Study of the Man and His Times.* New York: Citadel, 1947.†

1997 FRANCHERE, Ruth. *Jack London: The Pursuit of a Dream.* New York: Crowell, 1962.

1998 LABOR, Earle. *Jack London.* (TUSAS 230.) New York: Twayne, 1974.

1999 LONDON, Charmian. *The Book of Jack London.* 2 vols. New York: Century, 1921.

2000 LONDON, Joan. *Jack London and His Times: An Unconventional Biography.* 2d ed. Seattle: Univ. of Washington Press, 1968.†

2001 NOEL, Joseph. *Footloose in Arcadia: A Personal Record of Jack London, George Sterling, Ambrose Bierce.* New York: Carrick & Evans, 1940.

2002 O'CONNOR, Richard. *Jack London: A Biography.* Boston: Little, Brown, 1964. [Most complete and objective.]

2003 STONE, Irving. *Sailor on Horseback: The Biography of Jack London.* Boston: Houghton Mifflin, 1938.†

2004 WALCUTT, Charles C. *Jack London.* (UMPAW 57.) Minneapolis: Univ. of Minnesota Press, 1966.

2005 WALKER, Franklin. *Jack London and the Klondike: The Genesis of an American Writer.* London: Bodley Head; San Marino, Calif.: Huntington Library, 1966.

Critical Essays

2006 ANDERSON, Carl. "Swedish Criticism Before 1920: The Reception of Jack London and Upton Sinclair." *The Swedish Acceptance of American Literature.* Stockholm: Almqvist & Wiksell, 1957, pp. 33–44.

2007 AUSTIN, Mary. "George Sterling at Carmel." *American Mercury,* XI (May, 1927), 68–70.

2008 BASKETT, Sam S. "A Source for *The Iron Heel.*" *AL,* XXVII (1955), 268–270.

2009 BASKETT, Sam S. "Jack London's Heart of Darkness." *AQ,* X (1958), 66–77.

2010 BASKETT, Sam S. "Jack London on the Oakland Waterfront." *AL,* XXVII (1955), 363–371.

2011 BENOIT, Raymond. "Jack London's *The Call of the Wild.*" *AQ,* XX (1968), 246–248.

2012 BLAND, H. M. "Jack London: Traveler, Novelist and Social Reformer," *Craftsman,* IX (1906), 607–619.

2013 BOLL, T. E. M. *"The Divine Fire* (1904) and *Martin Eden* (1909)." *ELT,* XIV (1971), 115–117.

2014 BOWEN, Edwin W. "Jack London's Place in American Literature." *Reformed Church Rev.*, 4th ser., XXIV (1920), 306–315.

2015 CLAYTON, Lawrence. "The Ghost Dog, a Motif in *The Call of the Wild.*" *Jack London Newsletter*, V (1972), 158.

2016 DEANE, Paul. "Jack London: Mirror of His Time." *LHR*, XI (1969), 45–50.

2017 DEANE, Paul. "Jack London: The Paradox of Individualism." *EngRecord*, XIX (1968), 14–19.

2018 DUNN, N. E., and WILSON, Pamela. "The Significance of Upward Mobility in *Martin Eden.*" *Jack London Newsletter*, V (1972), 1–8.

2019 ELLIS, James. "A New Reading of *The Sea Wolf.*" *WAL*, II (1967), 127–134.

2020 FRIEDLAND, L. S. "Jack London as Titan." *Dial*, LXII (Jan. 25, 1917), 49–51.

2021 GEISMAR, Maxwell. "Jack London: The Short Cut." See **102**.

2022 GILES, James R. "Beneficial Atavism in Frank Norris and Jack London." *WAL*, IV (1969), 15–27.

2023 GRATTAN, C. Hartley. "Jack London." *Bookman*, LXVIII (1929), 667–671.

2024 ISANI, Mukhtar A. "Jack London on Norris' *The Octopus.*" *ALR*, VI (1973), 66–69.

2025 KAZIN, Alfred. "Progressivism: The Superman and the Muckrake." See **105**.

2026 LABOR, Earle. "Jack London's Symbolic Wilderness: Four Versions." *NCF*, XVII (1962), 149–161.

2027 LYNN, Kenneth S. "Jack London: The Brain Merchant." See **187**.

2028 MCCLINTOCK, James I. "Jack London's Use of Carl Jung's *Psychology of the Unconscious.*" *AL*, XLII (1970), 336–347.

2029 MENCKEN, H. L. *Prejudices, First Series*. New York: Knopf, 1919, pp. 236–239.

2030 MILLS, Gordon. "Jack London's Quest for Salvation." *AQ*, VII (1955), 3–14.

2031 MILLS, Gordon. See **642**.

2032 MUMFORD, Lewis. "Jack London." *NR*, XXX (1922), 145–147.

2033 PARKAY, Forrest W. "The Influence of Nietzsche's *Thus Spoke Zarathustra* on London's *The Sea-Wolf.*" *Jack London Newsletter*, IV (1971), 16–24.

2034 PETERSON, Clell T. "Jack London's Alaskan Stories." *ABC*, IX, viii (1959), 15–22.

2035 PETERSON, Clell T. "Jack London's Sonoma Novels." *ABC*, IX (October, 1958), 15–20.

2036 SPINNER, Jonathan H. "Jack London's *Martin Eden:* The Development of the Existential Hero." *MichA*, III (1970), 43–48.

2037 VAN DER BEETS, Richard. "Nietzsche of the North: Heredity and Race in London's *The Son of the Wolf.*" *WAL*, II (1967), 229–233.

2038 WALCUTT, Charles C. "Jack London: Blond Beasts and Supermen." See **117**.

2039 WALKER, Franklin. "Ideas and Action in Jack London's Fiction." In *Essays on American Literature in Honor of Jay B. Hubbell*, Edited by Clarence Gohdes, Durham, N.C.: Duke Univ. Press, 1967, pp. 259–272.

2040 WALKER, Franklin. "Jack London's Use of Sinclair Lewis Plots, Together with a Printing of Three of the Plots." *HLQ*, XVII (1953), 59–74.

2041 WHIPPLE, T. K. "Jack London—Wonder Boy." *SRL,* XVIII (Sept. 24, 1938), 3–4, 16–17.

2042 WILCOX, Earle J. "Jack London's Naturalism: The Example of *The Call of the Wild.*" *Jack London Newsletter,* II (1969), 91–101.

2043 WOODWARD, Robert H. "Jack London's Code of Primitivism." *Folio,* XVIII (May, 1953), 39–44.

Melville, Herman (1819–1891)

Texts

There are many available editions of separate titles.

2044 *The Works of Herman Melville.* 16 vols. London: Constable, 1922–1924. [Only collected edition, but out of print. In addition to the "Hendricks House" edition (in progress), a new collected *Works* is in progress by a group for the *MLA.*]

2045 *Complete Works.* "Hendricks House Edition." Chicago and New York: Hendricks House, 1948–   . [Is incomplete and will probably not be completed. Fourteen volumes were projected.]
The following separate volumes are very useful:
The Confidence-Man: His Masquerade. Ed. Elizabeth S. Foster, 1954.
Moby-Dick. Ed. Luther S. Mansfield and Howard P. Vincent, 1952. [Known as the "Centennial Edition," this volume has the greatest amount of useful editorial material available.]
Piazza Tales. Ed. Egbert S. Oliver, 1948.
Pierre; or, The Ambiguities. Ed. Henry A. Murray, 1949.

2046 *Billy Budd, Sailor (An Inside Narrative).* Reading Text and Genetic Text, edited from the manuscript, with introduction and notes by Harrison Hayford and Merton M. Sealts, Jr. Chicago: Univ. of Chicago Press, 1962. [Best of several "edited" versions; the reading text and introduction have been published in paperback form.]†

2047 *The Northwestern-Newberry Edition of the Writings of Herman Melville.* General editors: Harrison Hayford, Hershel Parker, and G. T. Tanselle. Evanston, Ill.: Northwestern Univ. Press, 1968–   .†
Vol. I. *Typee.* Historical note by Leon Howard, 1968.
Vol. II. *Omoo.* Historical note by Gordon Roper, 1968.
Vol. III. *Mardi.* Historical note by Elizabeth S. Foster, 1970.
Vol. IV. *Redburn.* Historical note by Hershel Parker, 1969.
Vol. V. *White-Jacket.* Historical note by Willard Thorp, 1970.
Vol. VI. *Moby-Dick.*
Vol. VII. *Pierre.* Historical note by Leon Howard and Hershel Parker, 1971.

2048 *The Confidence-Man: His Masquerade.* Ed. Hershel Parker. (Norton Critical Ed.) With foreword. New York: Norton, 1971.†

2049 *The Confidence-Man: His Masquerade.* Facsimile of 1st ed. Introduction and bibliography by John Seelye. San Francisco: Chandler, 1968.

2050 *Herman Melville: Representative Selections, with Introduction, Bibliography, and Notes.* Ed. Willard Thorp. New York: American Book Co., 1938.

2051 DAVIS, Merrill R., and GILMAN, William H., eds. *The Letters of Herman Melville.* New Haven: Yale Univ. Press, 1960.

Bibliography

See **1, 3, 8, 18, 2045.**

2052 BOWMAN, David H., and BOHAN, Ruth L. "Herman Melville's *Mardi, and a Voyage Thither:* An Annotated Checklist of Criticism." *RALS,* III (1973), 27–72.

2053 CAHOON, Herbert. "Herman Melville: A Checklist of Books and Manuscripts in the Collections of the New York Public Library." *BNYPL,* LV (1951), 263–275; 325–338.

2054 MINNIGERODE, Meade. *Some Personal Letters of Herman Melville and a Bibliography.* New York: The Brick Row Book Shop, 1922.

2055 MYERSON, Joel A., and MILLER, Arthur H., Jr. *Melville Dissertations: An Annotated Directory.* Philadelphia: Melville Society of America, 1972.

2056 SADLIER, Michael. "Herman Melville." *Excursions in Victorian Bibliography.* London: Cox, 1922, 217–234.

2057 SHERMAN, Stuart B.; BIRSS, John H.; and ROPER, Gordon, comps. *Melville Bibliography, 1952–1957.* Including published works and research completed or in progress during the years 1952–1957 about Herman Melville. Providence: Providence Public Library, 1959.

2058 STERN, Milton R. "A Checklist of Melville Studies." *The Fine Hammered Steel of Herman Melville.* Urbana: Univ. of Illinois Press, 1957, pp. 252–291.

2059 VANN, J. Don., ed. "A Checklist of Melville Criticism, 1958–1968." *SNNTS,* I (1969), 507–530.

2060 VINCENT, Howard P. *Checklist of Herman Melville.* (Merrill Checklists.) Columbus, Ohio: Charles E. Merrill, 1969.

2061 VINCENT, Howard P. *Guide to Herman Melville.* (Merrill Guides.) Columbus, Ohio: Charles E. Merrill, 1969.

2062 WRIGHT, Nathalia, See **22,** pp. 173–224.

Biographical and Critical Books

2063 ALLEN, Gay Wilson. *Melville and His World.* New York: Viking, 1971.

2064 ANDERSON, Charles Roberts. *Melville in the South Seas.* New York: Columbia Univ. Press, 1939. [A basic work of historical criticism.]†

2065 ARVIN, Newton. *Herman Melville.* New York: Sloane, 1950. [Best single, one-volume, critical-biographical study.]†

2066 AUDEN, W. H. *The Enchafèd Flood: Or the Romantic Iconography of the Sea.* New York: Random House, 1950.†

2067 BAIRD, James. *Ishmael: The Art of Melville in the Contexts of International Primitivism.* Baltimore: Johns Hopkins Press, 1956.†

2068 BERNSTEIN, John. *Pacifism and Rebellion in the Writings of Herman Melville.* The Hague: Mouton, 1964.

2069 BERTHOFF, Warner. *The Example of Melville.* Princeton: Princeton Univ. Press, 1962.†

2070 BOWEN, Merlin. *The Long Encounter: Self and Experience in the Writings of Herman Melville.* Chicago: Univ. of Chicago Press, 1960.†

2071 BRASWELL, William. *Melville's Religious Thought: An Essay in Interpretation.* New York: Pageant Book Co., 1959. [Originally published in 1943.]

2072 BREDAHL, A. Carl, Jr. *Melville's Angles of Vision.* Gainesville: Univ. of Florida Press, 1972.

2073 BRODTKORB, Paul, Jr. *Ishmael's White World: A Phenomenological Reading of Moby-Dick.* New Haven: Yale Univ. Press, 1965.

2074 BROWNE, Ray B. *Melville's Drive to Humanism.* Lafayette, Ind.: Purdue University Studies, 1971.

2075 CANADAY, Nicholas, Jr. *Melville and Authority.* Gainesville: Univ. of Florida Press, 1968.

2076 CHASE, Owen. *Narrative of the Most Extraordinary and Distressing Shipwreck of the Whaleship ESSEX. Supplementary Accounts of Survivors and Herman Melville's Notes.* Introduction by B. R. McElderry, Jr. New York: Corinth Books, 1963. [A source for *Moby Dick.*]†

2077 CHASE, Richard. *Herman Melville: A Critical Study.* New York: Macmillan, 1949.

2078 DAVIS, Merrell R. *Melville's Mardi: A Chartless Voyage.* New Haven: Yale Univ. Press, 1952.

2079 DILLINGHAM, William B. *An Artist in the Rigging: The Early Work of Herman Melville.* Athens: Univ. of Georgia Press, 1972.

2080 DRYDEN, Edgar A. *Melville's Thematics of Form: The Great Art of Telling the Truth.* Baltimore: Johns Hopkins, 1968.

2081 FINKELSTEIN, Dorothee M. *Melville's Orienda.* New Haven: Yale Univ. Press, 1961. [Melville's knowledge and use of the Near East.]

2082 FRANKLIN, H. Bruce. *The Wake of the Gods: Melville's Mythology.* Stanford: Stanford Univ. Press, 1963.†

2083 FREEMAN, John. *Herman Melville.* English Men of Letters Series. New York: Macmillan, 1926.

2084 FRIEDMAN, Maurice. *Problematic Rebel: Melville, Dostoievsky, Kafka, Camus.* Rev. ed. Chicago: Univ. of Chicago Press, 1970.†

2085 FRIEDRICH, Gerhard. *In Pursuit of Moby Dick: Melville's Image of Man.* Wallingford. Penn.: Pendle Hill, 1958. [Pamphlet.]

2086 GALE, Robert L. *Plots and Characters in the Fiction and Narrative Poetry of Herman Melville.* Foreword by Harrison Hayford. Hamden, Conn.: Archon, 1969.†

2087 GILMAN, William H. *Melville's Early Life and Redburn.* New York: New York Univ. Press, 1951.

2088 GLEIM, William S. *The Meaning of Moby Dick.* New York: Edmond Byrne Hackett, 1938. [Pamphlet.]

2089 GUETTI, James. *The Limits of Metaphor: A Study of Melville, Conrad, and Faulkner.* Ithaca, N.Y.: Cornell Univ. Press, 1967.

2090 HETHERINGTON, Hugh W. *Melville's Reviewers, British and American, 1846–1891.* Chapel Hill: Univ. of North Carolina Press, 1961.

2091 HILLWAY, Tyrus. *Herman Melville.* New York: Twayne, 1963.†

2092 HILLWAY, Tyrus. *Melville and the Whale.* Stonington, Conn.: [the author], 1950.

2093 HOWARD, Leon. *Herman Melville: A Biography.* Berkeley, Univ. of California Press, 1951. [A biography based on Leyda's *Melville Log.*]†

2094 HOWARD, Leon. *Heman Melville.* University of Minnesota Pamphlets on American Writers, no. 13. Minneapolis: Univ. of Minnesota Press, 1961.

2095 HUMPHREYS, Arthur R. *Herman Melville.* Edinburgh: Oliver and Boyd; New York: Grove Press, 1962.†

2096 JAMES, C. L. R. *Mariners, Renegades and Castaways.* New York: C. L. R. James, 1953.

2097 KEYSSAR, Alexander. *Melville's 'Israel Potter': Reflections on the American Dream.* LeBaron Russell Briggs Prize Honors Essays in English. Cambridge: Harvard Univ. Press, 1969.

2098 KULKARNI, H. B. *'Moby-Dick': A Hindu Avatar: A Study of Hindu Myth and Thought in 'Moby-Dick'.* Logan: Utah State Univ. Press, 1970.

2099 LEBOWITZ, Alan. *Progress into Silence: A Study of Melville's Heroes.* Bloomington: Indiana Univ. Press, 1970.

2100 LEYDA, Jay. *The Melville Log: A Documentary Life of Herman Melville.* 2 vols. New York: Harcourt, Brace, 1951.

2101 *Life and Remarkable Adventures of Israel Potter.* Introduction by Leonard Kriegel. New York: Corinth Books, 1962. [Source of Melville's *Israel Potter.*]†

2102 MASON, Ronald. *The Spirit Above the Dust: A Study of Herman Melville.* London: John Lehmann, 1951.

2103 MAXWELL, D. E. S. *Herman Melville.* London: Routledge & K. Paul, 1968.†

2104 MAY, John R. See **191.**

2105 MAYOUX, Jean-Jacques. *Melville.* New York: Grove Press, 1960. [Biographical-critical study.]†

2106 METCALF, Eleanor Melville. *Herman Melville: Cycle and Epicycle.* Cambridge: Harvard Univ. Press, 1953. [Many letters and primary documents are interwoven into this portrait.]

2107 MILLER, James E., Jr. *A Reader's Guide to Herman Melville.* New York: Farrar, Straus, Cudahy, 1962.†

2108 MUMFORD, Lewis. *Herman Melville: A Study of His Life and Vision.* Rev. ed. New York: Harcourt, Brace and World, 1962.†

2109 OLSON, Charles. *Call Me Ishmael.* New York: Reynal and Hitchcock, 1947. [Eccentric in style, invaluable in content.]†

2110 PERCIVAL, M. O. *A Reading of Moby-Dick.* Chicago: Univ. of Chicago Press, 1950.

2111 POMMER, Henry F. *Milton and Melville.* Pittsburgh: Univ. of Pittsburgh Press, 1950.

2112 RAMPERSAD, Arnold. *Melville's 'Israel Potter': A Pilgrimage and Progress.* Bowling Green, Ohio: Bowling Green Univ. Popular Press, 1969.

2113 ROSENBERRY, Edward H. *Melville and the Comic Spirit.* Cambridge: Harvard Univ. Press, 1955.

2114 RYSTEN, Felix S. A. *False Prophets in the Fiction of Camus, Dostoevsky, Melville, and Others.* Coral Gables: Univ. of Miami Press, 1972.

2115 SEALTS, Merton M., Jr. *Melville's Reading: A Checklist of Books Owned and Borrowed.* Cambridge: Harvard Univ. Press, 1950. [This material is also available in Sealts' "Melville's Reading: A Checklist of Books Owned and Borrowed." *HLB,* II (1948), 141–163, 378–392; III (1949), 119–130, 268–277, 407–421; IV (1950), 98–109; VI (1952), 239–247.]

2116 SEDGWICK, William Ellery. *Herman Melville: The Tragedy of Mind.* Cambridge: Harvard Univ. Press, 1944.

2117 SEELYE, John. *Melville: The Ironic Diagram.* Evanston, Ill.: Northwestern Univ. Press, 1970.

2118 SELTZER, Leon F. *The Vision of Melville and Conrad: A Comparative Study.* Athens: Ohio Univ. Press, 1970.

2119 STANONIK, Janez. *Moby Dick, The Myth and the Symbol: A Study in Folklore and Literature.* Ljubljana, Yugoslavia: Ljubljana Univ. Press, 1962.

2120 STERN, Milton R. *The Fine Hammered Steel of Herman Melville.* Urbana: Univ. of Illinois Press, 1957. [Has an excellent bibliography of studies of Melville.]

2121 STONE, Geoffrey. *Melville.* New York: Sheed & Ward, 1949.

2122 THOMPSON, Lawrance. *Melville's Quarrel With God.* Princeton: Princeton Univ. Press, 1952.

2123 VINCENT, Howard P. *Melville and Hawthorne in the Berkshires.* Kent, Ohio: Kent State Univ. Press, 1968.

2124 VINCENT, Howard P. *The Tailoring of Melville's 'White Jacket'.* Evanston, Ill.: Northwestern Univ. Press, 1970.

2125 VINCENT, Howard P. *The Trying-Out of Moby Dick.* Boston: Houghton Mifflin, 1949.†

2126 WEAVER, Raymond M. *Herman Melville, Mariner and Mystic.* New York: Doran, 1921. [Although outdated and inaccurate, still the major landmark in Melville studies.]

2127 WIDMER, Kingsley. *The Ways of Nihilism: A Study of Herman Melville's Short Novels.* Los Angeles: The Ward Ritchie Press for the California State Colleges, 1970.

2128 WRIGHT, Nathalia. *Melville's Use of the Bible.* Durham, N.C.: Duke Univ. Press, 1949.

2129 ZOELLNER, Robert H. *The Salt-Sea Mastodon: A Reading of 'Moby-Dick.'* Berkeley and Los Angeles: Univ. of California Press, 1973.

Critical Essays

The first eleven entries are book-length collections of critical materials, followed by a listing of individual essays.

2130 BOWEN, James K., and VAN DER BEETS, Richard. *A Critical Guide to Herman Melville: Abstracts of Forty Years of Criticism.* Glenview, Ill.: Scott, Foresman, 1971.

2131 CHASE, Richard, ed. *Melville: A Collection of Critical Essays.* Englewood Cliffs, N.J.: Prentice-Hall, 1962.†

2132 *Moby-Dick.* Eds. Harrison Hayford and Hershel Parker. New York: Norton, 1967.†

2133 HILLWAY, Tyrus, and MANSFIELD, Luther S., eds. *Moby-Dick Centennial Essays.* Dallas: So. Methodist Univ. Press, 1953. [An important volume of original essays.]

2134 PARKER, Hershel, ed. *The Recognition of Herman Melville: Selected Criticism Since 1846.* Ann Arbor: Univ. of Michigan Press, 1967.†

2135 PARKER, Hershel, and HAYFORD, Harrison, eds. *Moby-Dick as Doubloon: Essays and Extracts (1851–1970).* With foreword. New York: Norton, 1970. [Contains "An Annotated Bibliography," pp. 367–388.]†

2136 ROUNTREE, Thomas J., ed. *Critics on Melville.* With introduction. Coral Gables: Univ. of Miami Press, 1972.

2137 STAFFORD, William T., ed. *Melville's 'Billy Budd' and the Critics.* 2d ed. Belmont, Calif.: Wadsworth, 1968. [Contains checklist of *Billy Budd* studies.]

2138 STERN, Milton R., ed. *Discussions of Moby-Dick.* Boston: Heath, 1960. [A selection of essays.]†

2139 VINCENT, Howard P., ed. *Merrill Studies in 'Moby-Dick'.* (Merrill Studies.) Columbus, Ohio: Charles E. Merrill, 1969.

2140 VINCENT, Howard P., ed. *Twentieth Century Interpretations of 'Billy Budd'.* With introduction. Englewood Cliffs, N.J.: Prentice-Hall, 1971.†

2141 AARON, Daniel. "An English Enemy of Melville." *NEQ,* VIII (1935), 561–567.

2142 AARON, Daniel. "Melville and the Missionaries." *NEQ,* VIII (1935), 404–408.

2143 ADLER, Joyce S. "The Imagination and Melville's Endless Probe for Relation." *ATQ,* XIX (1973), 37–42.

2144 ALBRECHT, Robert C. "White Jacket's Intentional Fall." *SNNTS,* IV (1972), 17–26.

2145 ALLEN, Priscilla. "*White-Jacket* and the Man-of-War Microcosm." *AQ,* XXV (1973), 32–47.

2146 AMENT, William S. "Bowdler and the Whale: Some Notes on the First English and American Editions of *Moby-Dick.*" *AL,* IV (1932), 39–46.

2147 ANDERSON, Charles Roberts. "A Reply to Herman Melville's *White Jacket* by Rear Admiral Thomas O. Selfridge, Sr." *AL,* VII (1935), 123–144.

2148 ANDERSON, Marilyn. "Melville's Jackets: *Redburn* and *White-Jacket.*" *ArQ,* XXVI (1970), 173–181.

2149 ARVIN, Newton. "Melville and the Gothic Novel." *NEQ,* XXII (1949), 33–48.

2150 ARVIN, Newton. "Melville's *Mardi.*" *AQ,* II (1950), 71–81.

2151 ASPIZ, Harold. "Phrenologizing the Whale." *NCF,* XXIII (1968), 18–27.

2152 ASQUINO, Mark L. "Hawthorne's Village Uncle and Melville's Moby Dick." *SSF,* X (1973), 413–414.

2153 BABIN, James L. "Melville and the Deformation of Being: From Typee to Leviathan." *SoR,* VII (1971), 89–114.

2154 BACH, Bert C. "Narrative Technique and Structure in *Pierre.*" *ATQ,* VII (1970), 5–8.

2155 BALL, Roland C. See **596.**

2156 BANTA, Martha. "The Man of History and the Mythy Man in Melville." *ATQ,* X (1971), 3–11.

2157 BEACH, Joseph Warren. "Hart Crane and Moby Dick." *WR,* XX (1956), 183–196.

2158 BELGION, Montgomery. "Heterodoxy on *Moby-Dick.*" *SR,* LV (1947), 108–125.

2159 BELL, Michael D. "The Glendinning Heritage: Melville's Literary Borrowings in *Pierre.*" *SIR,* XII (1973), 741–762.

2160 BELL, Michael D. "Melville's *Redburn:* Initiation and Authority." *NEQ,* XLVI (1973), 558–572.

2161 BELL, Millicent. "Pierre Bayle and *Moby Dick.*" *PMLA,* LXVI (1951), 626–648.

2162 BERCOVITCH, Sacvan. "Melville's Search for National Identity: Son and Father in *Redburn, Pierre,* and *Billy Budd.*" *CLAJ,* X (1967), 217–228.

2163 BERGLER, Edmund. "A Note on Herman Melville." *AI,* XI (1954), 385–397.

2164 BERGMANN, Johannes D. "The Original Confidence Man." *AQ,* XXI (1969), 560–577.

2165 BERKELEY, David S. "Figure Futurarum in *Moby-Dick.*" *BuR,* XXI (1973), 108–123.

2166 BERTHOFF, Warner. "Herman Melville: *The Confidence-Man.*" See **243,** pp. 121–133.

2167 BEWLEY, Marius. "A Truce of God for Melville." *SR,* LXI (1953), 682–700.

2168 BEWLEY, Marius. "Melville." See **156.**

2169 BEZANSON, Walter E. "Melville's Reading of Arnold's Poetry." *PMLA,* LXIX (1954), 365–391.

2170 BLACKMUR, Richard P. "The Craft of Herman Melville: A Putative Statement." *The Lion and the Honeycomb.* New York: Harcourt, Brace, 1955, pp. 124–144.†

2171 BOND, William H. "Melville and *Two Years Before the Mast.*" *HLB,* VII (1953), 362–365.

2172 BOOTH, Thornton Y. "*Moby-Dick:* Standing Up to God." *NCF,* XVII (1962), 33–43.

2173 BOUDREAU, Gordon V. "Of Pale Ushers and Gothic Piles: Melville's Architectural Symbology." *ESQ,* LXVII (1972), 67–82. [Rock symbolism in *Moby-Dick.*]

2174 BRANCH, Watson G. "The Genesis, Composition, and Structure of *The Confidence-Man.*" *NCF,* XXVII (1973), 424–448.

2175 BRASHERS, H. C. "Ishmael's Tattoos." *SR,* LXX (1962), 137–154.

2176 BRASWELL, William. "Melville's Use of Seneca." *AL,* XIII (1940), 98–104.

2177 BRASWELL, William. "A Note on 'The Anatomy of Melville's Fame'." *AL,* V (1934), 360–364.

2178 BRASWELL, William. "The Satirical Temper of Melville's *Pierre.*" *AL,* VII (1936), 424–438.

2179 BROOKS, Van Wyck. "Notes on Herman Melville." *Emerson and Others.* New York: Dutton, 1927, pp. 171–205.

2180 BROWNE, Ray B. *"Israel Potter:* Metamorphosis of Superman." In *Frontiers of American Culture,* edited by Ray B. Browne, Richard H. Crowder, Virgil L. Lokke, and William T. Stafford. Lafayette, Ind.: Purdue Univ., 1968, pp. 88–98.

2181 CAMBON, Glanco. "Ishmael and the Problem of Formal Discontinuities in *Moby Dick.*" *MLN,* LXXVI (1961), 516–523.

2182 CAROTHERS, Robert L., and MARSH, John L. "The Whale and the Panorama." *NCF,* XXVI (1971), 319–328.

2183 CARPENTER, Frederic I. "Melville: The World in a Man-of-War." *UKCR,* XIX (1953), 257–264.

2184 CARPENTER, Frederic I. "Puritans Preferred Blondes: The Heroines of Melville and Hawthorne." *NEQ,* IX (1936), 253–272.

2185 CAWELTI, John G. "Some Notes on the Structure of *The Confidence Man.*" *AL,* XXIX (1957), 278–288.

2186 CHARVAT, William. "Melville and the Common Reader." *SB,* XII (1959), 41–57.

2187 CHASE, Richard. "Melville's *Confidence-Man.*" *KR,* XI (1949), 122–140.

2188 CHITTICK, V. L. O. "The Way Back to Melville—Sea-Chart of a Literary Revival." *SWR,* XL (1955), 238–248.

2189 COOK, Charles H., Jr. "Ahab's 'Intolerable Allegory'." *BUSE,* I (1955), 45–52.

2190 COWAN, S. A. "In Praise of Self-Reliance: The Role of Bulkington in *Moby-Dick.*" *AL,* XXXVIII (1967), 547–556.

2191 DAHL, Curtis. "Moby Dick's Cousin Behemoth." *AL,* XXXI (1959), 21–29.

2192 DAHLBERG, Edward. *"Moby Dick*—An Hamitic Dream." *LitR,* IV (1960), 87–118.

2193 DALE, T. R. "Melville and Aristotle: The Conclusion of *Moby-Dick* as a Classical Tragedy." *BUSE,* III (1957), 45–50.

2194 DAMON, S. Foster. "Why Ishmael Went to Sea." *AL,* II (1930), 281–283.

2195 DAVIS, Merrell R. "The Flower Symbolism in *Mardi.*" *MLQ,* II (1941), 625–638.

2196 DEW, Marjorie. "The Prudent Captain Vere." *ATQ,* VII (1970), 81–85.

2197 DILLINGHAM, William B. "The Narrator of *Moby Dick.*" *ES,* XLIX (1968), 20–29.

2198 DONALDSON, Scott. "Damned Dollars and a Blessed Company: Financial Imagery in *Moby-Dick.*" *NEQ,* XLVI (1973), 279–283.

2199 DONOW, Herbert S. "Herman Melville and the Craft of Fiction." *MLQ,* XXV (1964), 181–186.

2200 DUBLER, Walter. "Theme and Structure in Melville's *The Confidence Man.*" *AL,* XXXIII (1961), 307–319.

2201 DUERKSON, Roland A. "The Deep Quandary in *Billy Budd.*" *NEQ,* XLI (1968), 51–66.

2202 EIGNER, Edwin M. "The Romantic Unity of Melville's *Omoo.*" *PQ,* XLVI (1967), 95–108.

2203 ELDRIDGE, Herbert G. " 'Careful Disorder': The Structure of *Moby Dick.* " *AL,* XXXIX (1967), 145–162.

2204 FARNSWORTH, Robert M. "Ishmael to the Royal Masthead." *UKCR,* XXVIII (1962), 183–190.

2205 FIESS, Edward. "Melville as a Reader and Student of Byron." *AL,* XXIV (1952), 186–194.

2206 FISKE, John C. "Herman Melville in Soviet Criticism." *CL,* V (1953), 30–39.

2207 FITE, Olive L. "Billy Budd, Claggart, and Schopenhauer." *NCF,* XXIII (1968), 336–343.

2208 FOSTER, Charles H. "Something in Emblems: A Reinterpretation of *Moby-Dick.* " *NEQ,* XXXIV (1961), 3–35.

2209 FOSTER, Elizabeth S. "Another Note on Melville and Geology." *AL,* XXII (1951), 479–487.

2210 FULWILER, Toby. "The Death of the Handsome Sailor: A Study of *Billy Budd* and *The Red Badge of Courage.* " *ArQ,* XXVI (1970), 101–112.

2211 GALLOWAY, David D. "Herman Melville's *Benito Cereno:* An Anatomy." *TSLL,* XI (1967), 239–252.

2212 GEIGER, Don. "Demonism in *Moby Dick:* A Study of Twelve Chapters." *Per,* VI (1953), 111–124.

2213 GEIGER, Don. "Melville's Black God: Contrary Evidence in 'The Town-Ho's Story'." *AL,* XXV (1954), 464–471.

2214 GEORGE, J. L. "*Israel Potter:* The Height of Patriotism." *ATQ,* VII (1970), 53–56.

2215 GLASSER, William. "*Moby-Dick.* " *SR,* LXXVII (1969), 462–486.

2216 GLEASON, Philip. "*Moby-Dick:* Meditation for Democracy." *Person,* XLIV (1963), 499–517.

2217 GLEIM, William S. "A Theory of *Moby Dick.* " *NEQ,* II (1929), 402–419.

2218 GOLEMBA, Henry L. "The Shape of *Moby-Dick.* " *SNNTS,* V (1973), 197–210.

2219 GRAHAM, Philip. "The Riddle of Melville's *Mardi:* A Re-Interpretation." *TexSE,* XXXVI (1957), 93–99.

2220 GRDSELOFF, Dorothee. "A Note on the Origin of Fedallah in *Moby-Dick.* " *AL,* XXVII (1955), 396–403.

2221 GROSS, John J. "Melville's *The Confidence Man:* The Problem of Source and Meaning." *NM,* LX (1959), 299–310.

2222 GROSS, John J. "The Rehearsal of Ishmael: Melville's 'Redburn'." *VQR,* XXVII (1951), 581–600.

2223 GROSS, Theodore L. "Herman Melville: The Nature of Authority." *ColQ,* XVI (1968), 397–412.

2224 GUIDO, John F. "Melville's *Mardi:* Bentley's Blunder?" *PBSA,* LXII (1968), 361–371.

2225 HABERSTROH, Charles. "*Redburn:* The Psychological Pattern." *SAF,* II (1974), 133–144.

2226 HART, James D. "Melville and Dana." *AL,* IX (1937), 49–55.

2227 HAYFORD, Harrison. "Hawthorne, Melville, and the Sea." *NEQ*, XIX (1946), 435–452.

2228 HAYFORD, Harrison. "Melville's *Usable* or *Visible Truth.*" *MLN*, LXXIV (1959), 702–705.

2229 HAYFORD, Harrison. "Poe in *The Confidence-Man.*" *NCF*, XIV (1959), 207–218.

2230 HAYFORD, Harrison. "The Significance of Melville's 'Agatha' Letters." *ELH*, XIII (1946), 299–310.

2231 HAYFORD, Harrison. "Two New Letters of Herman Melville." *ELH*, XI (1944), 76–83.

2232 HERBERT, T. Walter, Jr. "Calvinism and Cosmic Evil in *Moby-Dick.*" *PMLA*, LXXXIV (1969), 1613–1619.

2233 Herman Melville Special Number. *MFS*, VIII, iii (1962). [Essays and a bibliographical checklist.]

2234 Herman Melville Special Number. *SNNTS*, I (1969).

2235 HETHERINGTON, Hugh W. "A Tribute to the Late Hiram Melville." *MLQ*, XVI (1955), 325–331.

2236 HICKS, Granville. "On Re-Reading *Moby-Dick.*" See **225.**

2237 HIGGINS, Brian. "Plinlimmon and the Pamphlet Again." *SNNTS*, IV (1972), 27–38. [On *Pierre.*]

2238 HILLWAY, Tyrus. "Melville and the Spirit of Science." *SAQ*, XLVIII (1949), 77–88.

2239 HILLWAY, Tyrus. "Melville as Amateur Zoologist." *MLQ*, XII (1951), 159–164.

2240 HILLWAY, Tyrus. "Melville as Critic of Science." *MLN*, LXV (1950), 411–414.

2241 HILLWAY, Tyrus. "Melville's Art: One Aspect." *MLN*, LXII (1947), 477–480.

2242 HILLWAY, Tyrus. "Melville's Geological Knowledge." *AL*, XXI (1949), 232–237.

2243 HILLWAY, Tyrus. "Pierre, the Fool of Virtue." *AL*, XXI (1949), 201–211.

2244 HILLWAY, Tyrus. "Taji's Quest for Certainty." *AL*, XVIII (1946), 27–34.

2245 HIRSCH, David H. "The Dilemma of the Liberal Imagination: Melville's Ishmael." *TSLL*, V (1963), 169–188.

2246 HOFFMAN, Daniel G. "Moby-Dick: Jonah's Whale or Job's?" *SR*, LXIX (1961), 205–224.

2247 HOFFMAN, Michael J. "The Anti-Transcendentalism of *Moby-Dick.*" *GaR*, XXIII (1969), 3–16.

2248 HOLDER, Alan. "Style and Tone in Melville's *Pierre.*" *ESQ*, LX (1970), 76–86.

2249 HOLMAN, C. Hugh. "The Reconciliation of Ishmael: *Moby-Dick* and the Book of Job." *SAQ*, LVII (1958), 477–490.

2250 HOMANS, George C. "The Dark Angel: The Tragedy of Herman Melville." *NEQ*, V (1932), 699–730.

2251 HORSFORD, Howard C. "Evidence of Melville's Plans for a Sequel to *The Confidence-Man.*" *AL*, XXIV (1952), 85–89.

2252 HOWARD, Leon. "Herman Melville, *Moby-Dick.*" See **227.**

111

2253 HOWARD, Leon. "Melville's Struggle with the Angel." *MLQ,* I (1940), 195–206.

2254 HUNTRESS, Keith. "Melville's Use of a Source for *White-Jacket.*" *AL,* XVII (1945), 66–74.

2255 HYMAN, Stanley Edgar. "Melville the Scrivener." *NMQ,* XXIII (1953), 381–415.

2256 ISANI, Mukhtar A. "Zoroastrianism and the Fire Symbolism in *Moby Dick.*" *AL,* XLIV (1972), 385–397.

2257 JAFFÉ, David. "The Captain Who Sat for the Portrait of Ahab." *BUSE,* IV (1960), 1–22.

2258 JAFFÉ, David. "Some Origins of *Moby-Dick:* New Finds in an Old Source." *AL,* XXIX (1957), 263–277.

2259 JAFFÉ, David. "Some Sources of Melville's *Mardi.*" *AL,* IX (1937), 56–69.

2260 JASTER, Frank. "Melville's Cosmopolitan: The Experience of Life in *The Confidence-Man: His Masquerade.*" *SoQ,* VIII (1970), 201–210.

2261 JERMAN, Bernard R. " 'With Real Admiration': More Correspondence between Melville and Bentley." *AL,* XXV (1953), 307–313.

2262 JONES, Joseph. "Humor in *Moby Dick.*" *TexSE,* XXV (1945–1946), 51–71.

2263 KARCHER, Carolyn Lury. "The Story of Charlemont: A Dramatization of Melville's Concepts of Fiction in *The Confidence-Man: His Masquerade.*" *NCF,* XXI (1966), 73–84.

2264 KAZIN, Alfred. "Ishmael and Ahab." *Atl,* CXCVIII (November, 1956), 81–85.

2265 KAZIN, Alfred. "On Melville as Scripture." *PR,* XVII (1950), 67–75.

2266 KEARNS, Edward A. "Omniscient Ambiguity: The Narrators of *Moby-Dick* and *Billy Budd.*" *ESQ,* LVIII (1970), 117–120.

2267 KENNY, Vincent S. "Melville's Problem of Detachment and Engagement." *ATQ,* XIX (1973), 30–37.

2268 KEYSER, Elizabeth. " 'Quite an Original': The Cosmopolitan in *The Confidence-Man.*" *TSLL,* XV (1973), 279–300.

2269 KISSANE, James. "Imagery, Myth, and Melville's *Pierre.*" *AL,* XXVI (1955), 564–572.

2270 KLINGERMAN, Charles. "The Psychology of Herman Melville." *Psychoanalytic Review,* XL (1953), 125–143.

2271 LACY, Patricia. "The Agatha Theme in Melville's Stories." *TexSE,* XXXV (1956), 96–105.

2272 LEWIS, R. W. B. "Melville on Homer." *AL,* XXII (1950), 166–176.

2273 LEYDA, Jay. "Another Friendly Critic for Melville." *NEQ,* XXVII (1954), 243–249.

2274 LEYDA, Jay. "Herman Melville, 1972." See **216,** pp. 163–171.

2275 LEYDA, Jay. "Ishmael Melville: Remarks on Board of Ship *Amazon.*" *BPLQ,* I (1949), 119–134.

2276 LISH, Terrence G. "Melville's *Redburn:* A Study in Dualism." *ELN,* V (1967), 113–120.

2277 LUCAS, Thomas E. "Herman Melville: The Purpose of the Novel." *TSLL,* XIII (1972), 641–661.

2278 LUCID, Robert F. "The Influence of *Two Years Before the Mast* on Herman Melville." *AL,* XXXI (1959), 243–256.

2279 LUTWACK, Leonard. "Herman Melville and *Atlantic Monthly* Critics." *HLQ,* XIII (1950), 414–416.

2280 MCCARTHY, Harold T. "Melville's *Redburn* and the City." *MQ,* XII (1971), 395–410.

2281 MCCARTHY, Paul. "Affirmative Elements in *The Confidence-Man.*" *ATQ,* VII (1970), 56–61.

2282 MCCARTHY, Paul. "City and Town in Melville's Fiction." *RS,* XXXVIII (1970), 214–229.

2283 MCCARTHY, Paul. "Symbolic Elements in *White Jacket.*" *MQ,* VII (1966), 309–325.

2284 MCCUTCHEON, Roger P. "The Technique of Melville's *Israel Potter.*" *SAQ,* XXVII (1928), 161–174.

2285 MACDONALD, Allan. "A Sailor Among the Transcendentalists." *NEQ,* VIII (1935), 307–319.

2286 MCMILLAN, Grant. "Ishmael's Dilemma—The Significance of the Fiery Hunt." *CentR,* XV (1971), 204–217.

2287 MACSHANE, Frank. "Conrad on Melville." *AL,* XXIX (1958), 463–464.

2288 MAGAW, Malcolm O. "*The Confidence-Man* and Christian Diety: Melville's Imagery of Ambiguity." In *Explorations of Literature* edited by Rima D. Reck. Baton Rouge: Louisiana State Univ. Press, 1966, pp. 81–99.

2289 MERRILL, Robert. "The Narrative Voice in *Billy Budd.*" *MLQ,* XXXIV (1973), 283–291.

2290 MILLER, James E., Jr. "Hawthorne and Melville: The Unpardonable Sin." *PMLA,* LXX (1955), 91–114.

2291 MILLER, Paul W. "Sun and Fire in Melville's *Moby Dick.*" *NCF,* XIII (1958), 139–144.

2292 MILLER, Perry. "Melville and Transcendentalism." *VQR,* XXIX (1953), 556–575.

2293 MILLS, Gordon H. "The Castaway in *Moby-Dick.*" *TexSE,* XXIX (1950), 231–248.

2294 MITCHELL, Charles. "Melville and the Spurious Truth of Legalism." *CentR,* XII (1968), 110–126.

2295 MITCHELL, Edward. "From Action to Essence: Some Notes on the Structure of Melville's *The Confidence-Man.*" *AL,* XL (1968), 27–37.

2296 MOORMAN, Charles. "Melville's *Pierre* and the Fortunate Fall." *AL,* XXV (1953), 13–30.

2297 MORRIS, Wright. "The High Seas." *The Territory Ahead: Critical Interpretations of American Literature.* New York: Harcourt, Brace, 1958, pp. 66–77.†

2298 MOWDER, William. "Volition in *Moby Dick.*" *ELUD,* I (1973), 18–30.

2299 MURRAY, Henry A. "In Nomine Diaboli." *NEQ,* XXIV (1951), 435–452. [On *Moby-Dick.*]

2300 MYERS, Henry Alonzo. "Captain Ahab's Discovery: The Tragic Meaning of *Moby Dick.*" *NEQ,* XV (1942), 15–34.

2301 NICHOL, John W. "Melville and the Midwest." *PMLA,* LXVI (1951), 613–625.

2302 OATES, J. C. "Melville and the Manichean Illusion." *TSLL,* IV (1962), 117–129.

2303 O'CONNOR, William Van. "Melville on the Nature of Hope." *UKCR,* XXII (1955), 123–130.

2304 OLIVER, Egbert S. "Melville's Goneril and Fanny Kemble." *NEQ,* XVIII (1945), 489–506. [On *The Confidence Man.*]

2305 OLIVER, Egbert S. "Melville's Picture of Emerson and Thoreau in *The Confidence Man.*" *CE,* VIII (1946), 61–72.

2306 PARKE, John. "Seven Moby-Dicks." *NEQ,* XXVIII (1955), 319–338.

2307 PARKER, Hershel. "The Metaphysics of Indian-Hating." *NCF,* XVIII (1963), 165–173. [On *The Confidence Man.*]

2308 PARKES, Henry Bramford. "Poe, Hawthorne, Melville: An Essay in Sociological Criticism." *PR,* XVI (1949), 157–165.

2309 PAUL, Sherman. "Melville's 'The Town-Ho's Story'." *AL,* XXI (1949), 212–221.

2310 PEARCE, Roy Harvey. "Melville's Indian Hater: A Note on the Meaning of *The Confidence Man.*" *PMLA,* LXVII (1952), 942–948.

2311 PERRY, Robert L. "*Billy Budd:* Melville's *Paradise Lost.*" *MQ,* X (1969), 173–185.

2312 PHILBRICK, Thomas L. "Another Source for *White-Jacket.*" *AL,* XXIX (1958), 431–439.

2313 PHILBRICK, Thomas L. "Melville's 'Best Authorities'." *NCF,* XV (1960), 171–179. [Sources for *White-Jacket.*]

2314 PHILLIPS, Barry. " 'The Good Captain': A Reading of 'Benito Cereno'." *TSLL,* IV (1962), 188–197.

2315 POLK, James. "Melville and the Idea of the City." *UTQ,* XLI (1972), 227–292.

2316 POMMER, Henry F. "Herman Melville and the Wake of *The Essex.*" *AL,* XX (1948), 290–304.

2317 PROCTER, Page S., Jr. "A Source for the Flogging Incident in *White Jacket.*" *AL,* XXII (1950), 176–182.

2318 PUTZEL, Max. "The Source and the Symbols of Melville's 'Benito Cereno'." *AL,* XXIV (1962), 191–206.

2319 REYNOLDS, Michael S. "The Prototype for Melville's Confidence-Man." *PMLA,* LXXXVI (1971), 1009–1013.

2320 RICE, Julian C. "The Ship as Cosmic Symbol in *Moby Dick* and *Benito Cereno.*" *CentR,* XVI (1972), 138–154.

2321 RITCHIE, Mary C. "Herman Melville." *QQ,* XXXVII (1930), 36–61.

2322 ROCKWELL, Frederick S. "DeQuincey and the Ending of *Moby-Dick.*" *NCF,* IX (1954), 161–168.

2323 ROSE, Edward J. "Annihilation and Ambiguity: *Moby-Dick* and 'The Town-ho's Story'." *NEQ,* XLV (1972), 541–558.

2324 ROSENHEIM, Frederick. "Flight from Home: Some Episodes in the Life of Herman Melville." *AI,* I (1939–1940), 1–30.

2325 ROTHFORK, John. "The Sailing of the *Pequod:* An Existential Voyage." *ArQ,* XXVIII (1972), 55–60.

2326 RULAND, Richard, "Melville and the Fortunate Fall: Typee as Eden." *NCF,* XXIII (1968), 312–323.

2327 SCHLESS, Howard H. "*Moby-Dick* and Dante: A Critique and Time Scheme." *BNYPL,* LXV (1961), 289–312.

2328 SCHROETER, James. "*Redburn* and the Failure of Mythic Criticism." *AL,* XXXIX (1967), 279–297.

2329 SCHWENDINGER, Robert J. "The Language of the Sea: Relationships Between the Language of Herman Melville and Sea Shanties of the 19th Century." *SFQ,* XXXVII (1973), 53–73.

2330 SCOTT, Sumner W. D. "Some Implications of the Typhoon Scenes in *Moby-Dick.*" *AL,* XII (1940), 91–98.

2331 SEALTS, Merton M., Jr. "Melville and the Shakers." *SB,* II (1949–1950), 105–114.

2332 SHERWOOD, John C. "Vere as Collingwood: A Key to *Billy Budd.*" *AL,* XXXV (1964), 476–484.

2333 SHORT, R. W. "Melville As Symbolist." *UKCR,* XV (1948), 38–46.

2334 SHROEDER, John W. "Sources and Symbols for Melville's *Confidence-Man.*" *PMLA,* LXVI (1951), 363–380.

2335 SHULMAN, Robert. "Melville's Thomas Fuller: An Outline for Starbuck and an Instance of the Creator as Critic." *MLQ,* XXIII (1962), 337–352.

2336 SHULMAN, Robert. "The Serious Functions of Melville's Phallic Jokes." *AL,* XXXIII (1961), 179–194.

2337 SIMPSON, Eleanor E. "Melville and the Negro: From *Typee* to 'Benito Cereno'." *AL,* XLI (1969), 19–38.

2338 SLOCHOWER, Harry. "*Moby Dick:* The Myth of Democratic Expectancy." *AQ,* II (1950), 259–269.

2339 SMITH, Paul. "*The Confidence Man* and the Literary World of New York." *NCF,* XVI (1962), 329–337.

2340 SPOFFORD, William K. "Melville's Ambiguities: A Re-evaluation of 'The Town-Ho's Story'." *AL,* XLI (1969), 264–270.

2341 STARK, John. " 'The Cassock' Chapter in *Moby-Dick* and the Theme of Literary Creativity." *SAF,* I (1973), 105–111.

2342 STAVROU, C. N. "Ahab and Dick Again." *TSLL,* III (1961), 309–320.

2343 STEIN, William Bysshe. "Melville Roasts Thoreau's Cock." *MLN,* LXXIV (1959), 218–219.

2344 STERN, Milton R. "Melville's Tragic Imagination: The Hero Without a Home." See **538**, pp. 39–52.

2345 STERN, Milton R. "*Moby Dick,* Millennial Attitudes, and Politics." *ESQ,* LIV (1969), 51–60.

2346 STERN, Milton R. "Some Techniques of Melville's Perception." *PMLA,* LXXIII (1958), 251–259.

2347 STEWART, George R. "The Two Moby-Dicks." *AL,* XXV (1954), 417–448.

2348 STEWART, Randall. "Melville and Hawthorne." *SAQ*, LI (1952), 436–446.

2349 STITT, Peter A. "Herman Melville's *Billy Budd:* Sympathy and Rebellion." *ArQ*, XXVIII (1972), 39–54.

2350 STONE, Geoffrey. "Loyalty to the Heart." In *American Classics Reconsidered: A Christian Appraisal,* edited by Harold C. Gardiner, S. J. New York: Scribner's, 1958, pp. 210–228.

2351 STOUT, Janis. "Melville's Use of the Book of Job." *NCF*, XXV (1970), 69–83.

2352 SUMNER, D. Nathan. "The American West in Melville's *Mardi* and *The Confidence-Man.*" *RS*, XXXVI (1968), 37–49.

2353 THORP, Willard. "Redburn's Prosy Old Guidebook." *PMLA*, LIII (1938), 1146–1156.

2354 TICHI, Cecelia. "Melville's Craft and Theme of Language Debased in *The Confidence-Man.*" *ELH*, XXXIX (1972), 639–658.

2355 TRACHTENBERG, Stanley. " 'A Sensible Way to Play the Fool': Melville's *The Confidence Man.*" *GaR*, XXVI (1972), 38–52.

2356 TRIMPI, Helen P. "Conventions of Romance in *Moby-Dick.*" *SoR*, VII (1971), 115–129.

2357 TRIMPI, Helen P. "Harlequin-Confidence-Man: The Satirical Tradition of Commedia dell'Arte and Pantomime in Melville's *The Confidence-Man.*" *TSLL*, XVI (1974), 147–193.

2358 TURNAGE, Maxine. "Melville's Concern with the Arts in *Billy Budd.*" *ArQ*, XXVIII (1972), 74–82.

2359 TUVESON, Ernest. "The Creed of the Confidence-Man." *ELH*, XXXIII (1966), 247–270.

2360 VARGISH, Thomas. "Gnostic *Mythos* in *Moby-Dick.*" *PMLA*, LXXXI (1966), 272–277.

2361 VINCENT, Howard P. "*White-Jacket:* An Essay in Interpretation." *NEQ*, XXII (1949), 304–315.

2362 VOGEL, Dan. "The Dramatic Chapters in *Moby-Dick.*" *NCF*, XIII (1958), 239–247.

2363 WADLINGTON, Warwick. "Ishmael's Godly Gamesomeness: Selftaste and Rhetoric in *Moby Dick.*" *ELH*, XXXIX (1972), 309–331.

2364 WALCUTT, Charles C. "The Fire Symbolism in *Moby Dick.*" *MLN*, LIX (1944), 304–310.

2365 WALCUTT, Charles C. "The Soundings of *Moby-Dick.*" *ArQ*, XXIV (1968), 101–116.

2366 WARD, Joseph A. "The Function of the Cetological Chapters in *Moby-Dick.*" *AL*, XXVIII (1956), 164–183.

2367 WATKINS, Floyd C. "Melville's Plotinus Plinlimmon and Pierre." *Myth and Reality.* See **1063,** pp. 39–51.

2368 WATSON, Charles N., Jr. "Melville and the Theme of Timonism: From *Pierre* to *The Confidence Man.*" *AL*, XLIV (1972), 398–413.

2369 WATSON, E. L. Grant. "Melville's *Pierre.*" *NEQ*, III (1930), 195–234.

2370 WATTERS, R. E. "Melville's 'Isolatoes'." *PMLA*, LX (1945), 1138–1148.

2371 WATTERS, R. E. "Melville's Metaphysics of Evil." *UTQ*, IX (1940), 170–182.

2372 WATTERS, R. E. "Melville's 'Sociality'." *AL*, XVII (1945), 33–49.

2373 WATTERS, R. E. "The Meaning of the White Whale." *UTQ*, XX (1951), 155–168.

2374 WEAKS, Mabel. "Long Ago and 'Faraway'." *BNYPL*, LII (1948), 362–369.

2375 WEATHERS, Willie T. "*Moby Dick* and the Nineteenth-Century Scene." *TSLL*, I (1960), 477–501.

2376 WEBER, Walter. "Some Characteristic Symbols in Herman Melville's Works." *ES*, XXX (1949), 217–224.

2377 WEEKS, Donald. "Two Uses of *Moby Dick.*" *AQ*, II (1950), 155–164.

2378 WEST, Ray B., Jr. "Primitivism in Melville." *PrS*, XXX (1956), 369–385.

2379 WIDMER, Kingsley. "The Learned Try-Works: A Review of Recent Scholarly Criticism of Melville." *SNNTS*, V (1973), 117–124.

2380 WILLETT, Maurita. "The Silences of Herman Melville." *ATQ*, VII (1970), 85–92.

2381 WILLIAMS, Mentor L. "Some Notices and Reviews of Melville's Novels in American Religious Periodicals, 1846–1849." *AL*, XXII (1950), 119–127.

2382 WILLIAMS, Stanley T. "Spanish Influences in American Fiction: Melville and Others." *NMQ*, XXII (1952), 5–14.

2383 WINTERS, Yvor. "Herman Melville and the Problems of Moral Navigation." *In Defense of Reason*. Denver, Colo.: Alan Swallow, 1947, pp. 200–233.

2384 WITHERINGTON, Paul. "The Art of Melville's *Typee.*" *ArQ*, XXVI (1970), 136–150.

2385 WOODSON, Thomas. "Ahab's Greatness: Prometheus as Narcissus." *ELH*, XXXIII (1966), 351–369.

2386 WRIGHT, Nathalia. "The Head and the Heart in Melville's *Mardi.*" *PMLA*, LXVI (1951), 351–362.

2387 WRIGHT, Nathalia. "*Mosses from an Old Manse* and *Moby-Dick:* The Shock of Discovery." *MLN*, LXVII (1952), 387–392.

2388 WRIGHT, Nathalia. "*Pierre:* Herman Melville's *Inferno.*" *AL*, XXXII (1960), 167–181.

2389 YOUNG, James Dean. "The Nine Gams of the *Pequod.*" *AL*, XXV (1954), 449–463.

2390 ZIRKER, Priscilla Allen. "Evidence of the Slavery Dilemma in *White-Jacket.*" *AQ*, XVIII (1966), 477–492.

Norris, Frank (1870–1902)

Texts

2391 *The Complete Works of Frank Norris.* 10 vols. Garden City, N.Y.: Doubleday, 1928. [The standard collected edition. There are numerous reprint editions of various novels. The following editions have useful editorial materials.]

2392 *The Letters of Frank Norris.* Ed. Franklin Walker. San Francisco: Book Club of California, 1956.

2393 *The Literary Criticism of Frank Norris.* Ed. Donald Pizer. Austin: Univ. of Texas Press, 1964. [Uncollected criticism, 1895–1903.]

2394 *The Octopus: A Story of California.* Introduction by Kenneth S. Lynn. Boston: Houghton Mifflin, 1958. [Excellent introduction.]†

Bibliography

See **8** and **18**.

2395 FRENCH, Warren. "Frank Norris (1870–1902)." *ALR,* I (1967), 84–89.

2396 GAER, Joseph, ed. *Frank Norris: Bibliography and Biographical Data.* California Literary Research Project, Monograph no. 3, 1934.

2397 HILL, John S. *Checklist of Frank Norris.* (Merrill Checklists.) Columbus, Ohio: Charles E. Merrill, 1970.

2398 LOHF, Kenneth A., and SHEEHY, Eugene P. *Frank Norris: A Bibliography.* Los Gatos, Calif.: Talisman Press, 1959.

2399 WHITE, William. "Frank Norris: Bibliographical Addenda." *BB,* XXII (1959), 227–228.

Biographical and Critical Books

2400 ÅHNEBRINK, Lars. *The Influence of Emile Zola on Frank Norris.* Cambridge: Harvard Univ. Press, 1947.

2401 BIENCOURT, Marius. *Une Influence du Naturalisme Francais en Amérique.* Paris, 1933.

2402 DILLINGHAM, William B. *Frank Norris: Instinct and Art.* Boston: Houghton Mifflin, 1969.†

2403 FRENCH, Warren. *Frank Norris.* New York: Twayne, 1962.†

2404 MARCHAND, Ernest C. *Frank Norris: A Study.* Stanford: Stanford Univ. Press, 1942.

2405 PIZER, Donald. *The Novels of Frank Norris.* Bloomington: Indiana Univ. Press, 1966.

2406 WALKER, Franklin. *Frank Norris: A Biography.* New York: Doubleday, Doran, 1932.

Critical Essays

2407 DAVIDSON, Richard A., ed. *Studies in 'The Octopus'.* (Merrill Studies.) Columbus, Ohio: Charles E. Merrill, 1969. [A collection of critical essays.]

2408 BIXLER, Paul H. "Frank Norris's Literary Reputation." *AL,* VI (1934), 107–121.

2409 BURNS, Stuart L. "The Rapist in Frank Norris's *The Octopus.*" *AL,* XLII (1971), 567–569.

2410 CASSADY, Edward E. "Muckraking in the Gilded Age." *AL,* XIII (1941), 134–141.

2411 COOPERMAN, Stanley. "Frank Norris and the Werewolf of Guilt." *MLQ*, XX (1959), 252–258.

2412 DILLINGHAM, William B. "Frank Norris and the Genteel Tradition." *TSL*, V (1960), 15–24.

2413 DOBIE, Charles Caldwell. "Frank Norris or Up from Culture." *American Mercury*, XIII (1928), 412–424.

2414 EDWARDS, Herbert W. "Zola and the American Critics." *AL*, IV (1932), 114–129.

2415 FOLSOM, James K. "Social Darwinism or Social Protest? The 'Philosophy' of *The Octopus.*" *MFS*, VIII (1963), 393–400.

2416 FRANCIS, Herbert E., Jr. "A Reconsideration of Frank Norris." *EUQ*, XV (1959), 110–118.

2417 GOLDMAN, Suzy B. "*McTeague:* The Imagistic Network." *WAL*, VII (1972), 83–99.

2418 GRAHAM, D. B. "Studio Art in *The Octopus.*" *AL*, XLIV (1973), 657–666.

2419 HILL, John S. "The Influence of Cesare Lombroso on Frank Norris's Early Fiction." *AL*, XLII (1970), 89–91.

2420 HOFFMAN, Charles G. "Norris and the Responsibility of the Novelist." *SAQ*, LIV (1955), 508–515.

2421 JOHNSON, George W. "Frank Norris and Romance." *AL*, XXXIII (1961), 52–63.

2422 JOHNSON, George W. "The Frontier Behind Frank Norris' *McTeague.*" *HLQ*, XXVI (1962), 91–104.

2423 KAPLAN, Charles. "Fact into Fiction in *McTeague.*" *HLB*, VIII (1954), 381–385.

2424 KAPLAN, Charles. "Norris's Use of Sources in *The Pit.*" *AL*, XXV (1953), 75–84.

2425 KATZ, Joseph. "The Manuscript of Frank Norris' *McTeague:* A Preliminary Census of Pages." *RALS*, II (1972), 91–97.

2426 KWIAT, Joseph J. "Frank Norris: The Novelist as Social Critic and Literary Theorist." *ArQ*, XVIII (1962), 319–328.

2427 KWIAT, Joseph J. "The Newspaper Experience: Crane, Norris, and Dreiser." *NCF*, VIII (1953), 99–117.

2428 LABRIE, Rodrigue E. "The Howells-Norris Relationship and the Growth of Naturalism." *Discourse*, XI (1968), 363–371.

2429 LYNN, Kenneth S. "Frank Norris: Mama's Boy." See **187.**

2430 MCKEE, Irving. "Notable Memorials to Mussel Slough." *PHR*, XVII (Jan., 1948), 19–27.

2431 MARTIN, Willard E., Jr. "Frank Norris's Reading at Harvard College." *AL*, VII (1935), 203–204.

2432 MEYER, George Wilbur. "A New Interpretation of *The Octopus.*" *CE*, IV (1943), 351–359.

2433 MORGAN, H. Wayne. "Frank Norris: The Romantic as Naturalist." See **223.**

2434 PIPER, Henry Dan. "Frank Norris and Scott Fitzgerald." *HLQ*, XIX (1956), 393–400.

2435 PIZER, Donald. "Another Look at *The Octopus.*" *NCF*, X (1955), 217–224.

2436 PIZER, Donald. "Evolutionary Ethical Dualism in Frank Norris' *Vandover and the Brute* and *McTeague.*" *PMLA*, LXXVI (1961), 552–560.

2437 PIZER, Donald. "Frank Norris' Definition of Naturalism." *MFS*, VIII (1963), 408–410.

2438 PIZER, Donald. "The Concept of Nature in Frank Norris' *The Octopus.*" *AQ*, XIV (1962), 73–80.

2439 PIZER, Donald. "The Masculine-Feminine Ethic in Frank Norris' Popular Novels." *TSLL*, VI (1964), 84–91.

2440 PIZER, Donald. "Romantic Individualism in Garland, Norris, and Crane." *AQ*, X (1958), 463–475.

2441 PIZER, Donald. "Synthetic Criticism and Frank Norris; or, Mr. Marx, Mr. Taylor, and *The Octopus.*" *AL*, XXXIV (1963), 532–541.

2442 RENINGER, H. Willard. "Norris Explains *The Octopus:* A Correlation of His Theory and Practice." *AL*, XII (1940), 218–227.

2443 SHERWOOD, John C. "Norris and the *Jeannette.*" *PQ*, XXXVII (1958), 245–252. [On *Blix.*]

2444 STRONKS, James B. "Frank Norris's *McTeague:* A Possible Source in H. C. Bunner." *NCF*, XXV (1971), 474–478.

2445 TODD, Edgeley W. "The Frontier Epic: Frank Norris and John G. Neilhardt." *WHR*, XIII (1959), 40–45.

2446 VANCE, William L. "Romance in *The Octopus.*" *Genre*, III (1970), 111–136.

2447 WALCUTT, Charles C. "Frank Norris and the Search for Form." *UKCR*, XIV (1947), 126–136.

2448 WALCUTT, Charles C. "Frank Norris on Realism and Naturalism." *AL*, XIII (1941), 61–63.

2449 WALKER, Don D. "The Western Naturalism of Frank Norris." *WAL*, II (1967), 14–29.

2450 WOODWARD, Robert H. "Frank Norris and Frederic: A Source for *McTeague.*" *Frederic Herald*, II (1968), 2.

2451 WYATT, Bryant N. "Naturalism as Expediency in the Novels of Frank Norris." *MarkhamR*, II (1971), 83–87.

Poe, Edgar Allan (1809–1849)

Texts

Poe's only novel is *The Narrative of Arthur Gordon Pym.* See **3, 8, 18, 22, 184.**

2452 AUDEN, W. H., ed. *Edgar Allan Poe: Selected Prose and Poetry.* With introduction. New York: Rinehart, 1950.

2453 KAPLAN, Sidney, ed. *The Narrative of Arthur Gordon Pym.* With introduction. New York: Hill and Wang, 1960.†

2454 KRUTCH, Joseph W. "Introduction." *The Narrative of Arthur Gordon Pym.* New York: Heritage, 1930, vii-xvi.

2455 SEELYE, John. "Introduction." *Arthur Gordon Pym, Benito Cereno, and Related Writings.* New York: J. B. Lippincott, 1967, pp. 1–13.

Bibliography

2456 DAMERON, J. Lasley, and CAUTHEN, Irby B., Jr. *Edgar Allan Poe: A Bibliography of Criticism 1827–1967.* Charlottesville: Univ. Press of Virginia, 1974.

2457 HUBBELL, Jay B. "Edgar Allan Poe." See **22**, pp. 3–36.

Biographical and Critical Books

2458 BONAPARTE, Marie. *The Life and Works of Edgar Allan Poe: A Psychoanalytic Interpretation.* London: Imago, 1949, pp. 290–352.

2459 DAVIDSON, Edward H. *Poe: A Critical Study.* Cambridge: Harvard Univ. Press, 1957, pp. 156–180.

2460 GALE, Robert L. *Plots and Characters in the Fiction and Poetry of Edgar Allan Poe.* Hamden, Conn.: Archon, 1970.

2461 HALLIBURTON, David. *Edgar Allan Poe: A Phenomenological View.* Princeton: Princeton Univ. Press, 1973.

2462 KESTERSON, David B., ed. *Critics on Poe.* (RLitC 22.) Coral Gables: Univ. of Miami Press, 1973.

2463 QUINN, Arthur Hobson. *Edgar Allan Poe: A Critical Biography.* New York: Appleton-Century, 1941. [The standard biography.]

2464 WAGENKNECHT, Edward. *Edgar Allan Poe: The Man Behind the Legend.* New York: Oxford Univ. Press, 1963. [A brief, graceful, sensible, and accurate study.]

Critical Essays

2465 BAILEY, J. O. "Sources of Poe's *Arthur Gordon Pym,* 'Hans Pfaal,' and Other Pieces." *PMLA,* LVII (1942), 513–535. [The primary source is Symmes' *Symzonia,* available as "Captain Adam Seaborn" (John C. Symmes). *Symzonia: A Voyage of Discovery.* Introduction by J. O. Bailey. Gainesville: Scholar's Facsimiles, 1965.)

2466 BEZANSON, Walter E. "The Troubled Sleep of Arthur Gordon Pym." In *Essays in Literary History Presented to Milton French,* edited by Rudolf Kirk and C. F. Main. New Brunswick, N.J.: Rutgers Univ. Press, 1960, pp. 149–175.

2467 CARRINGER, Robert L. "Circumscription of Space and Form of Poe's *Arthur Gordon Pym.*" *PMLA,* LXXXIX (1974), 506–515.

2468 CECIL, L. Moffitt, "Poe's Tsalal and the Virginia Springs." *NCF,* XIX (March 1965), 398–402.

2469 CECIL, L. Moffitt. "The Two Narratives of Arthur Gordon Pym." *TSLL,* V (Summer 1963), 232–241.

2470 COVICI, Pascal, Jr. "Toward a Reading of Poe's *Narrative of A. Gordon Pym.*" *MissQ,* XXI (1968), 111–118.

2471 COWIE, Alexander. See **97,** pp. 300–306.

2472 FIEDLER, Leslie A. "Blackness of Darkness: E. A. Poe and the Development of the Gothic." See **168,** pp. 370–414.

2473 HALMS, Randel. "Another Source for Poe's *Arthur Gordon Pym.*" *AL,* XLI (1970), 572–575.

2474 HINZ, Evelyn J. " 'Tekeli-li': *The Narrative of Arthur Gordon Pym* as Satire." *Genre,* III (1970), 379–399.

2475 HUNTRESS, Keith. "Another Source of Poe's *Narrative of Arthur Gordon Pym.*" *AL,* XVI (1944), 19–25.

2476 HUSSEY, John P. " 'Mr. Pym' and 'Mr. Poe': The Two Narrators of *Arthur Gordon Pym.*" *SAB,* XXXIX (1974), 22–32.

2477 KENNEDY, J. Gerald. "The Preface as a Key to the Satire in *Pym.*" *SNNTS,* V (1973), 191–196.

2478 LEE, Grace F. "The Quest of Arthur Gordon Pym." *SLJ,* IV (1972), 22–33.

2479 LEE, Helen. "Possibilities of *Pym.*" *EJ,* LV (December 1966), 1149–1154.

2480 MCKEITHAN, D. M. "Two Sources of Poe's *Narrative of Arthur Gordon Pym.*" *TexSE,* XIII (1933), 116–137.

2481 MOLDENHAUER, Joseph J. "Imagination and Perversity in *The Narrative of Arthur Gordon Pym.*" *TSLL,* XIII (1971), 267–280.

2482 MOSS, Sidney P. "*Arthur Gordon Pym,* or the Fallacy of Thematic Interpretation." *UR,* XXXIII (1967), 299–306.

2483 O'DONNELL, Charles. "From Earth to Ether: Poe's Flight into Space." *PMLA,* LXXVII (1962), 85–91.

2484 PEDEN, William. "Prologue to a Dark Journey: The 'Opening' of Poe's *Pym.*" In *Papers on Poe: Essays in Honor of John Ward Ostrom,* edited by Richard P. Veler. Springfield, Ohio: Chantry Music Press at Wittenberg Univ., 1972, pp. 84–91.

2485 POLLIN, Burton. "Poe's *Narrative of Arthur Gordon Pym* and the Contemporary Reviewers." *SAF,* II (1974), 37–56.

2486 QUINN, Patrick F. "Poe's Imaginary Voyage." *The French Face of Edgar Poe.* Carbondale: So. Illinois Univ. Press, 1957, pp. 169–215.

2487 RHEA, Robert Lee. "Some Observations on Poe's Origins." *UTSE,* no. 10 (1930), 135–146.

2488 RIDGELY, Joseph V., and HAVERSTICK, Iola S. "Chartless Voyage: The Many Narratives of Arthur Gordon Pym." *TSLL,* VII (1966), 63–80.

2489 RIDGELY, Joseph V. "The End of Pym and the Ending of *Pym.*" See **2484,** pp. 104–112.

2490 STROUPE, John H. "Poe's Imaginary Voyage: Pym as Hero." *SSF,* IV (1967), 315–321.

Simms, William Gilmore (1806–1870)

Texts

2491 *The Works of William Gilmore Simms.* 20 vols. New York: J. S. Redfield, 1853–1859. [The plates of this edition were used for 15 other editions by various printers, the last being Atlanta, Ga.: Martin & Hoyt Co., 1901.]

2492 *The Writings of William Gilmore Simms.* General editor: John C. Guilds. Columbia: Univ. of South Carolina Press, 1969:
Vol. I. *Voltmeier or The Mountain Men.* Introduction and explanatory notes by Donald Davidson and Mary C. Simms Oliphant. Text established by James B. Meriwether, 1969.
Vol. III. *As Good as a Comedy, or the Tennessean's Story* and *Paddy McGann, or the Demon of the Stump.* Introduction and notes by Robert Bush. Text established by James B. Meriwether, 1969.

2493 HETHERINGTON, Hugh W., ed. *Cavalier of Old South Carolina: William Gilmore Simms's Captain Porgy.* With introduction. Chapel Hill: Univ. of North Carolina Press, 1967.

2494 *The Letters of William Gilmore Simms.* Eds. Mary C. Simms Oliphant, Alfred Taylor Odell, and T. C. Duncan Eaves. 5 Vols. Columbia: Univ. of South Carolina Press, 1952–1956.

2495 *Views and Reviews in American Literature, History and Fiction, First Series.* Edited with introduction by C. Hugh Holman. Cambridge: Harvard Univ. Press, 1962.†

2496 *The Yemassee: A Romance of Carolina.* Edited with an introduction and notes by C. Hugh Holman. Boston: Houghton Mifflin, 1961. [Much editorial data.]†

2497 *The Yemassee.* Edited with an introduction, chronology, and bibliography by Alexander Cowie, New York: American Book Co., 1937. [Excellent editorial material.]†

Bibliography

See **8, 18,** and **2503.**

2498 SALLEY, Alexander S. *Catalogue of the Salley Collection of the Works of Wm. Gilmore Simms.* Columbia, S. C.: [the author], 1943. [The most useful and fullest bibliographical tool for Simms.]

2499 HOLMAN, C. Hugh. "William G. Simms (1806–1870)." *A Bibliographical Guide to the Study of Southern Literature.* Ed. Louis D. Rubin, Jr. Baton Rouge: Louisiana State Univ. Press, 1969, pp. 284–288.

2500 WATSON, Charles S. "William Gilmore Simms: An Essay in Bibliography." *RALS,* III (1973), 3–26.

2501 WEGELIN, Oscar. *A Bibliography of the Separate Writings of William Gilmore Simms, 1806–1870.* 3d ed. Hattiesburg, Miss.: [the author], 1941.

Biographical and Critical Books

2502 PARKS, Edd Winfield. *William Gilmore Simms as Literary Critic.* Athens: Univ. of Georgia Press, 1961.†

123

2503 RIDGELY, Joseph V. *William Gilmore Simms.* New York: Twayne, 1962.†

2504 TRENT, William P. *William Gilmore Simms.* American Men of Letters Series. Boston: Houghton Mifflin, 1892. [Although inaccurate in some respects and marred by outdated critical judgments, Trent is still the best biographer of Simms.]

2505 WAKELYN, Jon L. *The Politics of a Literary Man: William Gilmore Simms.* Westport, Conn.: Greenwood, 1973.

Critical Essays

2506 BARBOUR, Frances M. "William Gilmore Simms and the Brutus Legend." *MWF,* VII (1957), 159–162.

2507 BUSH, Lewis M. "Werther on the Alabama Frontier: A Reinterpretation of Simms's *Confession." MissQ,* XXI (1968), 119–130.

2508 CECIL, L. Moffitt. "Functional Imagery in Simms' *The Partisan." Studies in Medieval, Renaissance, [and] American Literature: A Festschrift,* edited by Betsy F. Colquitt. Fort Worth: Texas Christian Univ. Press, 1971, pp. 155–164.

2509 CECIL, L. Moffitt. "Symbolic Pattern in *The Yemassee." AL,* XXXV (1964), 510–514.

2510 CULLEN, Maurice R., Jr. "William Gilmore Simms, Southern Journalist." *JQ,* XXXVIII (1961), 298–302, 412.

2511 DEEN, Floyd H. "The Genesis of Martin Faber in Caleb Williams." *MLN,* LIX (1944), 315–317.

2512 DOXEY, William S. "Dogs and Dates in Simms' *The Yemassee." ATQ,* I (1969), 41–43.

2513 DUVALL, S. P. C. "W. G. Simms's Review of Mrs. Stowe." *AL,* XXX (1958), 107–117. [In the *Southern Quarterly Review;* attribution to Simms is questionable.]

2514 EATON, Clement. "The Romantic Mind: William Gilmore Simms." *The Mind of the Old South.* Baton Rouge: Louisiana State Univ. Press, 1964, pp. 181–201.

2515 ERSKINE, John. "William Gilmore Simms." See **217.**

2516 GATES, W. B. "William Gilmore Simms and the Kentucky Tragedy." *AL,* XXXII (1960), 158–166.

2517 GRIFFIN, Max L. "Bryant and the South." *TSE,* I (1949), 53–80. [Much on Simms who was a friend of Bryant.]

2518 GUILDS, John C. "The Literary Criticism of William Gilmore Simms." *SCR,* II (1970), 49–56.

2519 GUILDS, John C. "Simms's Views on National and Sectional Literature, 1825–1845." *NCHR,* XXXIV (1957), 393–405.

2520 HAYWARD, Edward F. "Some Romances of the Revolution." *Atl,* LXIV (1889), 627–636. [Detailed criticism of Simms's "Revolutionary Romances."]

2521 HIGHAM, John W. "The Changing Loyalties of William Gilmore Simms." *JSH,* IX (1943), 210–223.

2522 HOLMAN, C. Hugh. "Simms and the British Dramatists." *PMLA,* LXV (1950), 346–359. Reprinted in Holman, *The Roots of Southern Writing: Essays on the Literature of the American South.* Athens: Univ. of Georgia Press, 1972, pp. 61–74.

2523 HOLMAN, C. Hugh. "The *Hiawatha* Meter in *The Yemassee.*" *MLN,* LXVII (1952), 418–419.

2524 HOLMAN, C. Hugh. "The Influence of Scott and Cooper on Simms." *AL,* XXIII (1951), 203–218. Reprinted in **2522,** pp. 50–60.

2525 HOLMAN, C. Hugh. "The Status of Simms." *AQ,* X (1958), 181–185.

2526 HOLMAN, C. Hugh. "William Gilmore Simms and the American Renaissance." *MissQ,* XV (1962), 126–137. Reprinted in **2522,** pp. 75–86.

2527 HOLMAN, C. Hugh. "William Gilmore Simms' Picture of the Revolution as a Civil Conflict." *JSH,* XV (1949), 441–462. Reprinted in **2522,** pp. 35–49.

2528 HOOLE, William Stanley. "Alabama and W. Gilmore Simms." *AlaR,* XVI (1963), 83–107, 185–199.

2529 HOWELL, Elmo. "The Concept of Character in Simms' Border Romances." *MissQ,* XXII (1969), 303–312.

2530 HUBERT, Thomas. "Simms's Use of Milton and Wordsworth in *The Yemassee:* An Aspect of Symbolism in the Novel." *SCR,* VI (1973), 58–65.

2531 JARRELL, Hampton M. "Falstaff and Simms's Porgy." *AL,* III (1931), 204–212.

2532 KEISER, Albert. "Simms' Romantic Naturalism." *The Indian in American Literature.* New York: Oxford Univ. Press, 1933, pp. 154–174.

2533 KOLODNY, Annette. "The Unchanging Landscape: The Pastoral Impulse in Simms' Revolutionary War Romances." *SLJ,* V (1972), 46–67. Reprinted in **580,** pp. 115–132.

2534 MCDAVID, Raven I., Jr. "*Ivanhoe* and Simms' *Vasconselos.*" *MLN,* LVI (1941), 294–297.

2535 MCHANEY, Thomas L. "William Gilmore Simms." See **216,** pp. 175–190.

2536 MORRIS, J. Allen. "Gullah in the Stories and Novels of William Gilmore Simms." *ASp,* XXII (1947), 46–53.

2537 PARKS, Edd Winfield. "Simms: A Candid Self-Portrait." *GaR,* XII (1958), 94–103.

2538 RIDGELY, Joseph V. "Simms's Concept of Style in the Historical Romance." *ESQ,* LX (1970), 16–23.

2539 RIDGELY, Joseph V. "*Woodcraft:* Simms's First Answer to *Uncle Tom's Cabin.*" *AL,* XXXI (1960), 421–433.

2540 SHELTON, Austin J. "African Realistic Commentary on Culture Hierarchy and Racistic Sentimentalism in *The Yemassee.*" *Phylon,* XXV (1964), 72–78.

2541 SHILLINGSBURG, Miriam J. "From Notes to Novel: Simms' Creative Method." *SLJ,* V (1972), 89–107.

2542 STONE, Edward. " 'Caleb Williams' and 'Martin Faber': A Contrast." *MLN,* LXII (1947), 480–483.

2543 TAYLOR, William R. "Revolution in South Carolina." *Cavalier and Yankee: The Old South and American National Character.* New York: George Braziller, 1961.†

2544 THOMAS, J. Wesley. "The German Sources of William Gilmore Simms." In *Anglo-German and American-German Crosscurrents, Volume One,* edited by Philip Allison Shelley; Arthur O. Lewis, Jr.; and William W. Betts, Jr. Chapel Hill: Univ. of North Carolina Press, 1957, pp. 127–153.

2545 TURNER, Arlin. "Poe and Simms: Friendly Critics, Sometimes Friends." See **2484,** pp. 140–160.

2546 TURNER, Arlin. "William Gilmore Simms in His Letters." *SAQ,* LIII (1954), 404–415.

2547 VANDIVER, Edward P., Jr. "Simms' Porgy and Cooper." *MLN,* LXX (1955), 272–274.

2548 VAUTHIER, Simone. "Of Time and the South: The Fiction of William Gilmore Simms." *SLJ,* V (1972), 3–45.

2549 WATSON, Charles S. "A New Approach to Simms: Imagery and Meaning in *The Yemassee.*" *MissQ,* XXVI (1973), 155–164.

2550 WELSH, John R. "William Gilmore Simms: Critic of the South." *JSH,* XXVI (1960), 201–214.

2551 WHALEY, Grace Wine. "A Note on Simms's Novels." *AL,* II (1930), 173–174.

2552 WILLIAMS, Stanley T. "Spanish Influences on the Fiction of William Gilmore Simms." *HR,* XXI (1953), 221–228.

2553 WIMSATT, Mary Ann. "Simms and Irving." *MissQ,* XX (1968), 25–37.

2554 WIMSATT, Mary Ann. "Simms as Novelist of Manners: *Katherine Walton.*" *SLJ,* V (1972), 68–88.

Stowe, Harriet Beecher (1811–1896)

Texts

2555 *The Writings of Harriet Beecher Stowe.* 16 vols. Boston: Houghton Mifflin, 1896. [The only collected edition.]

2556 LYNN, Kenneth S., ed. *Uncle Tom's Cabin.* Cambridge: Harvard Univ. Press, 1962.

Bibliography

See **8, 18,** and **2561.**

2557 ADAMS, John R. "Harriet Beecher Stowe (1811–1896)." *ALR,* II (1969), 160–164.

2558 KIRKHAM, E. Bruce. "The First Editions of *Uncle Tom's Cabin:* A Bibliographical Study." *PBSA,* LXV (1971), 365–382.

2559 RANDALL, David A., and WINTERICH, John T. "One Hundred Good Novels: Stowe, Harriet Beecher: *Uncle Tom's Cabin.*" *PW,* CXXXVII (1940), 1931–1932. [A collection of editions.]

2560 TALBOT, William. "*Uncle Tom's Cabin:* First English Editions." *ABC,* III (1933), 292–297.

Biographical and Critical Books

2561 ADAMS, John R. *Harriet Beecher Stowe*. New York: Twayne, 1963.†

2562 CROZIER, Alice C. *The Novels of Harriet Beecher Stowe*. New York: Oxford Univ. Press, 1969.

2563 FOSTER, Charles H. *The Rungless Ladder: Harriet Beecher Stowe and New England Puritanism*. Durham, N.C.: Duke Univ. Press, 1956.

2564 FURNAS, J. C. *Goodbye to Uncle Tom*. New York: Sloane, 1956. [On the novel and its effect; not friendly.]†

2565 WILSON, Forrest. *Crusader in Crinoline: The Life of Harriet Beecher Stowe*. Philadelphia: Lippincott, 1941.

Critical Essays

2566 ANONYMOUS. "Uncle Tom: That Enduring Old Image." *AH*, XXIII (1971), 50–57.

2567 BANNING, Margaret C. "*Uncle Tom's Cabin* by Harriet Beecher Stowe." *GaR*, IX (1955), 461–465.

2568 BEATTY, Lillian. "The Natural Man Versus the Puritan." *Person*, XL (1959), 22–30.

2569 BRADFORD, Gamaliel. "Portraits of American Women: Harriet Beecher Stowe." *Atl*, CXXII (1918), 84–94. Reprinted in Bradford's *Portraits of American Women*. Boston: Houghton Mifflin, 1919.

2570 BURNS, Wayne, and SUTCLIFFE, Emerson Grant. "Uncle Tom and Charles Reade." *AL*, XVII (1946), 334–347.

2571 CASSARA, Ernest. "The Rehabilitation of Uncle Tom: Significant Themes in Mrs. Stowe's Antislavery Novel." *CLAJ*, XVII (1973), 230–240.

2572 DAVIS, Richard B. "Mrs. Stowe's Characters-in-Situations and a Southern Literary Tradition." See **2039**, pp. 108–125.

2573 DOWNS, Robert B. "Uncle Tom's Cabin." *Books that Changed the World*. New York: New American Library, 1956, pp. 76–85.†

2574 DUVALL, S. P. C. "*Uncle Tom's Cabin:* The Sinister Side of the Patriarchy." *NEQ*, XXXVI (1963), 3–22.

2575 DUVALL, S. P. C. "W. G. Simms's Review of Mrs. Stowe." *AL*, XXX (1958), 107–117. [In the *Southern Quarterly Review*. The attribution to Simms, although likely, is still subject to question.]

2576 FLETCHER, Edward G. "Illustrations for Uncle Tom." *TQ*, I (1958), 166–180.

2577 FOSTER, Charles H. "The Genesis of Harriet Beecher Stowe's 'The Minister's Wooing'." *NEQ*, XXI (1948), 493–517.

2578 GRAHAM, Thomas. "Harriet Beecher Stowe and the Question of Race." *NEQ*, XLVI (1973), 614–622.

2579 HALE, Nancy. "What God Was Writing." *TQ*, I (1958), ii, 35–40. [On Mrs. Stowe's conviction that God wrote *Uncle Tom's Cabin*.]

2580 HUDSON, Benjamin F. "Another View of 'Uncle Tom'." *Phylon*, XXIV (1963), 79–87.

2581 JACKSON, Frederick H. "*Uncle Tom's Cabin* in Italy." *Symposium,* VII (1953), 323–332.

2582 JONES, Michael O. " 'Ye Must Contrive Allers to Keep Jest the Happy Medium Between Truth and Falsehood': Folklore and the Folk in Mrs. Stowe's Fiction." *NYFQ,* XXVII (1971), 357–369.

2583 LEVIN, David. "American Fiction as Historical Evidence: Reflections on *Uncle Tom's Cabin.*" *NALF,* V (1971), 132–136, 154.

2584 MCDOWELL, Tremaine. "The Use of Negro Dialect by Harriet Beecher Stowe." *ASp,* VI (1931), 322–326.

2585 MAXFIELD, E. K. " 'Goody Goody' Literature and Mrs. Stowe." *ASp,* IV (1929), 189–202.

2586 NICHOLAS, Herbert G. "*Uncle Tom's Cabin,* 1852–1952." *GaR,* VIII (1954), 140–148.

2587 NICHOLS, Charles. "The Origins of *Uncle Tom's Cabin.*" *Phylon,* XIX (1958), 328–334.

2588 PICKENS, Donald K. "Uncle Tom Becomes Nat Turner: A Commentary on Two American Heroes." *NALF,* III (1969), 45–48.

2589 ROPPOLO, Joseph P. "Harriet Beecher Stowe and New Orleans: A Study in Hate." *NEQ,* XXX (1957), 346–362.

2590 ROSSI, Joseph. "*Uncle Tom's Cabin* and Protestantism." *AQ,* XI (1959), 416–424.

2591 STEELE, Thomas J., S. J. "Tom and Eva: Mrs. Stowe's Two Dying Christs." *NALF,* VI (1972), 85–90.

2592 STONE, Harry. "Charles Dickens and Harriet Beecher Stowe." *NCF,* XII (1957), 188–202.

2593 STROUT, Cushing. "*Uncle Tom's Cabin* and the Portent of Millennium." *YR,* LVII (1968), 375–385.

2594 WARD, John William. "*Uncle Tom's Cabin,* As a Matter of Historical Fact." *CUF,* IX (1966), 42–47.

2595 WILSON, Edmund. "Harriet Beecher Stowe." In *Patriotic Gore: Studies in the Literature of the American Civil War.* New York: Oxford Univ. Press, 1962, pp. 3–58.

2596 WYMAN, Margaret. "Harriet Beecher Stowe's Topical Novel on Woman Suffrage." *NEQ,* XXV (1952), 383–391. [On *My Wife and I.*]

Wharton, Edith (1862–1937)

Texts

There is no collected edition of her works. The following works and editions have value for the student.

2597 *A Backward Glance.* New York: Appleton-Century, 1934. [A reticent but useful autobiography.]

2598 *The Age of Innocence.* Introduction by R. W. B. Lewis. New York: Charles Scribner's, 1968.†

2599 *An Edith Wharton Treasury.* Edited with an introduction by Arthur Hobson Quinn. New York: Appleton-Century, 1950.

2600 *The Custom of the Country.* Introduction by Blake Nevius. New York: Scribner's, 1956.†

2601 *The Edith Wharton Reader.* Edited with an introduction by Louis Auchincloss. New York: Scribner's, 1965.†

2602 *The Reef.* Introduction by Louis Auchincloss. New York: Scribner's, 1965.†

Bibliography

See **8, 18, 2610,** and **2616.**

2603 BRENNI, Vito J. *Edith Wharton: A Bibliography.* Morgantown: West Virginia Univ. Library, 1966.

2604 DAVIS, Lavinia R. *Bibliography of the Writings of Edith Wharton.* Portland, Me.: Southworth Press, 1933.

2605 MELISH, L. McC. *A Bibliography of the Collected Writings of Edith Wharton.* New York: Brick Row Book Shop, 1927.

2606 TUTTLETON, James W. "Edith Wharton: An Essay in Bibliography." *RALS,* III (1973), 163–202.

Biographical and Critical Books

2607 AUCHINCLOSS, Louis. *Edith Wharton.* University of Minnesota Pamphlets on American Writers Series, no. 12. Minneapolis: Univ. of Minnesota Press, 1961. [Reprinted in revised form in **214.**]

2608 AUCHINCLOSS, Louis. *Edith Wharton: A Woman in Her time.* New York: Viking, 1971.

2609 BELL, Millicent. *Edith Wharton and Henry James.* See **1558.**

2610 BROWN, E. K. *Edith Wharton: Étude Critique.* Paris: Librairie E. Droz, 1935.

2611 COOLIDGE, Olivia. *Edith Wharton, 1862–1937.* New York: Scribner's, 1965.†

2612 KELLOGG, Grace. *The Two Lives of Edith Wharton.* New York: Appleton-Century-Crofts, 1965.

2613 LOVETT, Robert Morss. *Edith Wharton.* New York: McBride, 1925.

2614 LUBBOCK, Percy. *Portrait of Edith Wharton.* New York: Appleton-Century, 1947.

2615 LYDE, Marilyn J. *Edith Wharton: Convention and Morality in the Work of a Novelist.* Norman: Univ. of Oklahoma Press, 1959.

2616 NEVIUS, Blake. *Edith Wharton: A Study of Her Fiction.* Berkeley, Univ. of California Press, 1953.†

2617 WALTON, Geoffrey. *Edith Wharton: A Critical Interpretation.* Rutherford, N.J.: Fairleigh Dickinson Univ. Press, 1970.

Critical Essays

The first two titles are collections of the best criticism of Mrs. Wharton'w work. Individual essays follow.

2618 HOWE, Irving, ed. *Edith Wharton: A Collection of Critical Essays,* Englewood Cliffs, N.J.: Prentice-Hall, 1962.†

2619 NEVIUS, Blake, ed. *Edith Wharton's 'Ethan Frome': The Story With Sources and Commentary.* With introduction. New York: Charles Scribner's, 1968.

2620 ANDERSON, Hilton. "Edith Wharton and the Vulgar American." *SoQ,* VII (1968), 17–22.

2621 ANDERSON, Hilton. "Edith Wharton as Fictional Heroine." *SAQ,* LXIX (1970), 118–123.

2622 AUCHINCLOSS, Louis. "Edith Wharton and Her New Yorks." See **134.**

2623 BERNARD, Kenneth. "Imagery and Symbolism in *Ethan Frome.*" *CE,* XXIII (1961), 178–184.

2624 BRENNAN, Joseph X. "*Ethan Frome:* Structure and Metaphor." *MFS,* XII (1961), 347–356.

2625 BRISTOL, Marie. "Life Among the Ungentle Genteel: Edith Wharton's *The House of Mirth.*" *WHR,* XVI (1962), 371–374.

2626 BROWN, E. K. "Edith Wharton." *EA,* II (1938), 16–26.

2627 BUCHAN, Alexander M. "Edith Wharton and 'The Elusive Bright-Winged Thing'." *NEQ,* XXXVII (1964), 343–362. [On *Hudson River Bracketed.*]

2628 CARGAS, Harry J. "Seeing, But not Living: Two Characters from James and Wharton." *NLauR,* I (1972), 5–7.

2629 CLOUGH, David. "Edith Wharton's War Novels: A Reappraisal." *TCL,* XIX (1973), 1–14.

2630 DOOLEY, R. B. "A Footnote to Edith Wharton." *AL,* XXVI (1954), 78–85.

2631 DOYLE, Charles C. "Emblems of Innocence: Imagery Patterns in Wharton's *The Age of Innocence.*" *XUS,* X (1971), 19–25.

2632 FRIMAN, Anne. "Determinism and Point of View in *The House of Mirth.*" *PLL,* II (1966), 175–178.

2633 GARGANO, James W. "*The House of Mirth:* Social Futility and Faith." *AL,* LXIV (1972), 137–143.

2634 GELFANT, Blanche Housman. "The Destructive Element in 'Fashionable New York'." See **174.**

2635 GRUMBACH, Doris. "Reconsideration: Edith Wharton." *New Republic,* CLXVIII (1973), 29–30.

2636 HARVEY, John. "Contrasting Worlds: A Study in the Novels of Edith Wharton." *EA,* VII (1954), 190–198.

2637 HOFFMAN, Frederick J. "Points of Moral Reference: A Comparative Study of Edith Wharton and F. Scott Fitzgerald." In *English Institute Essays, 1949.* New York: Columbia Univ. Press, 1950, pp. 147–176.

2638 HOPKINS, Viola. "The Ordering Style of *The Age of Innocence.*" *AL,* XXX (1958), 345–357.

2639 JACOBSON, Irving. "Perception, Communication, and Growth as Correlative Theme in Edith Wharton's *The Age of Innocence.*" *Agora,* II (1973), 68–82.

2640 JESSUP, Josephine Lurie. *The Faith of Our Feminists; A Study in the Novels of Edith Wharton, Ellen Glasgow, Willa Cather.* New York: Richard R. Smith, 1950.

2641 KAZIN, Alfred. "Two Educations: Edith Wharton and Theodore Dreiser." See **105.**

2642 LAGUARDIA, Eric. "Edith Wharton on Critics and Criticism." *MLN,* LXXIII (1958), 587–589.

2643 LAMAR, Lillie B. "Edith Wharton's Foreknowledge in *The Age of Innocence.*" *TSLL,* VIII (1966), 385–389.

2644 LEACH, Nancy R. "Edith Wharton's Unpublished Novel." *AL,* XXV (1953), 334–353.

2645 LEACH, Nancy R. "New England in the Stories of Edith Wharton." *NEQ,* XXX (1957), 90–98.

2646 LEAVIS, Q. D. "Henry James's Heiress: The Importance of Edith Wharton." *Scrutiny,* VII (1938), 261–276.

2647 LONEY, G. M. "Edith Wharton and *The House of Mirth:* The Novelist Writes for the Theater." *MD,* IV (1961), 152–163.

2648 LYNSKEY, Winifred. "The 'Heroes' of Edith Wharton." *UTQ,* XXIII (1954), 354–361.

2649 MCMANIS, Jo A. "Edith Wharton's Hymns to Respectability." *SoR,* VII (1971), 986–993.

2650 MONROE, N. Elizabeth. "Moral Situation in Edith Wharton." See **1054.**

2651 MOSELEY, Edwin M. "*The Age of Innocence:* Edith Wharton's Weak Faust." *CE,* XXI (1959), 156–160.

2652 MURPHY, John J. "The Satiric Structure of Wharton's *The Age of Innocence.*" *MarkhamR,* II (1970), 1–4.

2653 NEVIUS, Blake. " 'Ethan Frome' and the Themes of Edith Wharton's Fiction." *NEQ,* XXIV (1951), 197–207.

2654 PHELPS, Donald. "Edith Wharton and the Invisible." *Prose,* VII (1973), 227–245.

2655 POIRIER, Richard. "Edith Wharton: *The House of Mirth.*" See **227.**

2656 RIDEOUT, Walter B. "Edith Wharton's *The House of Mirth.*" See **226.**

2657 RUSSELL, Frances Theresa. "Melodramatic Mrs. Wharton." *SR,* XL (1932), 425–437.

2658 STEELE, Erskine. "Fiction and Social Ethics." *SAQ,* V (1906), 254–263. [On *The House of Mirth.*]

2659 THOMAS, J. D. "Marginalia on *Ethan Frome.*" *AL,* XXVII (1955), 405–409.

2660 TRILLING, Diana. "*The House of Mirth* Revisited." *ASch,* XXXII (1963), 113–128.

2661 TRILLING, Lionel. "The Morality of Inertia." In *Great Moral Dilemmas,* edited by Robert MacIver. New York: Harper, 1956.

2662 TUTTLETON, James W. "Edith Wharton: Form and the Epistemology of Artistic Creation." *Criticism,* X (1968), 334–351.

2663 TUTTLETON, James W. "Edith Wharton: The Archaeological Motive." *YR*, LXI (1972), 562–574.

2664 TUTTLETON, James W. "Leisure, Wealth and Luxury: Edith Wharton's Old New York." *MQ*, VII (1966), 337–352.

2665 VALDIVA, Olga A. de. "Edith Wharton." *Andean Quarterly*, V (1944), 8–21, 39–58; VI (1944), 56–73.

2666 VELLA, Michael W. "Technique and Theme in *The House of Mirth.*" *MarkhamR*, II (1970), 17–20.

2667 WEGELIN, Christof. "Edith Wharton and the Twilight of the International Novel." *SoR*, V (1969), 398–418.

2668 WILSON, Edmund. "Justice to Edith Wharton." In *The Wound and the Bow. Seven Studies in Literature.* Boston: Houghton Mifflin, 1941.†

2669 VINNER, Viola H. "Convention and Prediction in Edith Wharton's *Fast and Loose.*" *AL*, XLII (1970), 50–69.

Lesser American Novelists

[In this section are presented 14 writers of novels of a lesser order than those of the 24 major novelists. In several cases, major writers, of whose work only a minor portion is novels, are included. These writers have been given relatively brief treatment in this section. Their chief novels are listed.]

Adams, Henry (1838–1918)

Novels: *Democracy* (1879); *Esther* (1884). See **3, 8, 18, 152.**

2670 AUCHINCLOSS, Louis. *Henry Adams* (UMPAW 93.) Minnapolis: Univ. of Minnesota Press, 1971.

2671 BARBER, David S. "Henry Adams' Esther: The Nature of Individuality and Immortality." *NEQ*, XLV (1972), 227–240.

2672 BEATTY, Richmond C. "Henry Adams and American Democracy." *GaR*, IV (1950), 147–156.

2673 BLACKMUR, Richard P. "The Novels of Henry Adams." *SR*, LI (1943), 281–304.

2674 COLACURCIO, Michael J. "*Democracy* and *Esther:* Henry Adams' Flirtation with Pragmatism." *AQ*, XIX (1967), 53–70.

2675 CONDER, John J. *A Formula of His Own: Henry Adams's Literary Experiment.* Chicago: Univ. of Chicago Press, 1970.

2676 EDENBAUM, Robert I. "The Novels of Henry Adams: Why Man Failed." *TSLL*, VIII (1966), 245–255.

2677 HARBERT, Earl N. "Henry Adams." See **572**, pp. 3–36.

2678 LEVENSON, J. C. *The Mind and Art of Henry Adams.* Boston: Houghton Mifflin, 1957.†

2679 LYON, Melvin. *Symbol and Idea in Henry Adams.* Lincoln: Univ. of Nebraska Press, 1970.

2680 RULE, Henry B. "Henry Adams' Satire on Human Intelligence: Its Method and Purpose." *CentR,* XV (1971), 430–444.

2681 SAMUELS, Ernest. *Henry Adams.* 3 vols. Cambridge: Harvard Univ. Press, 1948, 1958, 1964. [Standard and authoritative.]

2682 SAVETH, Edward H. "The Heroines of Henry Adams." *AQ,* VIII (1956), 231–242.

2683 SCHEYER, Ernest. *The Circle of Henry Adams: Art and Artist.* Detroit: Wayne State Univ. Press, 1970.

2684 SCHMITZ, Neil. "The Difficult Art of American Political Fiction: Henry Adams' *Democracy* as Tragical Satire." *WHR,* XXV (1971), 147–162.

2685 SKLAR, Robert. "Henry Adams and Democratic Society." *KAL,* XIV (1972), 30–33.

2686 STEVENSON, Elizabeth. *Henry Adams: A Biography.* New York: Macmillan, 1955.†

2687 STROUT, Cushing. "Personality and Cultural History in the Novel: Two American Examples." *NLH,* I (1970), 423–437. [Deals with Adams' *Esther* and Cahan's *The Rise of David Levinsky.*]

2688 TAYLOR, Gordon O. "Astigmatic Images: The 'American Novels' of Henry Adams." In *The Interpretation of Narrative: Theory and Practice,* edited by Morton W. Bloomfield. Cambridge: Harvard Univ. Press, 1970, pp. 171–187.

2689 VANDERSEE, Charles. "Henry Adams (1838–1918)." *ALR,* II (1969), 89–120.

2690 VANDERSEE, Charles. "The Pursuit of Culture in Adams' *Democracy.*" *AQ,* XIX (1967), 239–248.

2691 WAGNER, Vern. *The Suspension of Henry Adams: A Study of Manner and Matter.* Detroit: Wayne State Univ. Press, 1969.

2692 WASSER, Henry. "Science and Religion in Henry Adams's *Esther.*" *MarkhamR,* II (1970), 4–6.

Alger, Horatio, Jr. (1834–1899)

Many popular, "cheap book," "success" novels, such as *Risen from the Ranks, Jed, the Poor House Boy, From Rags to Riches,* and *Pluck and Luck.* See **8** and **187.**

2693 GARDNER, Ralph D. *Horatio Alger, or The American Hero Era.* Mendota, Ill.: Wayside Press, 1964. [Biography and bibliography of Alger's works. Admitted by its author to be largely fiction.]

2694 COYLE, William, ed. *Adrift in New York and The World Before Him.* With introduction. New York: Odyssey, 1966.

2695 COAD, Bruce E. "The Alger Hero: Humanitarian or Hustler?" Proceedings of Conference of College Teachers of English of Texas, XXXVII (1972), 21–24.

2696 GARDNER, Ralph D. *Road to Success: The Bibliography of the Works of Horatio Alger.* Mendota, Ill.: Wayside Press, 1973.

2697 HOLLAND, Norman N. "Hobbling with Horatio, or The Uses of Literature." *HudR,* XII (1959), 549–557.

2698 MAYES, Herbert R. *Alger: A Biography Without a Hero.* New York: Macy-Masius, 1928.

2699 TEBBEL, John. *From Rags to Riches: Horatio Alger, Jr., and the American Dream.* New York: Macmillan, 1963.

2700 WIMBERLEY, Lowry C. "Hemingway and Horatio Alger, Jr." *PrS,* X (1936), 208–211.

2701 ZUCKERMAN, Michael. "The Nursery Tales of Horatio Alger." *AQ,* XXIV (1972), 191–209.

Bird, Robert Montgomery (1806–1894)

Best-Known Novels: *Calavar* (1834), *The Infidel* (1835), *The Hawks of Hawk-Hollow,* and *Nick of the Woods* (1837). See **3, 8, 18, 181, 185.**

2702 BIRD, Robert Montgomery. *Nick of the Woods; or, The Jibbenainosay: A Tale of Kentucky.* Edited with an introduction, bibliography, and chronology by Cecil B. Williams. New York: American Book Co., 1939. [Introduction is best treatment of Bird as a novelist.]

2703 BRONSON, Daniel R. "A Note on Robert Montgomery Bird's *Oralloossa.*' *ELN,* IX (1971), 46–49.

2704 BRYANT, James C. "The Fallen World in *Nick of the Woods.*" *AL,* XXXVIII (1966), 352–364.

2705 DAHL, Curtis. *Robert Montgomery Bird.* New York: Twayne, 1963.†

2706 WILLIAMS, Cecil B. "R. M. Bird's Plans for Novels of the Frontier." *AL,* XXI (1949), 321–324.

Brackenridge, Hugh Henry (1748–1816)

Novel: *Modern Chivalry* (1792, 1793, 1797, 1805, 1815). [Published in parts, revised, and collected.] See **3, 8,** and **18.**

2707 BRACKENRIDGE, Hugh Henry. *Modern Chivalry.* Edited with an introduction, chronology, and bibliography by Claude M. Newlin. New York: American Book Co., 1937. [The editorial aids are very useful.]

2708 BUSH, Sargent, Jr. "*Modern Chivalry* and 'Young's Magazine'." *AL,* XLIV (1972), 292–299.

2709 HARKEY, Joseph H. "The *Don Quixote* of the Frontier: Brackenridge's *Modern Chivalry.*" *EAL,* VIII (1973), 193–203.

2710 KENNEDY, W. Benjamin. "Hugh Henry Brackenridge: Thoughts and Acts of a Modern Democrat." *WGCR,* II (1970), 26–38.

2711 MARDER, Daniel. *Hugh Henry Brackenridge.* (TUSAS 114.) New York: Twayne, 1967.

2712 MARTIN, Wendy. "On the Road with the Philosopher and Profiteer: A Study of Hugh Henry Brackenridge's *Modern Chivalry.*" *ECS,* IV (1971), 241–256.

2713 MARTIN, Wendy. "The Rogue and the Rational Man: Hugh Henry Brackenridge's Study of a Con Man in *Modern Chivalry.*" *EAL,* VIII (1973), 179–192.

2714 NANCE, William L. "Satiric Elements in Brackenridge's *Modern Chivalry.*" *TSLL,* IX (1967), 381–389.

2715 NEWLIN, Claude M. *The Life and Writings of Hugh Henry Brackenridge.* Princeton: Princeton Univ. Press, 1932.

2716 WHITTLE, Amberys R. "*Modern Chivalry:* The Frontier as Crucible." *EAL,* VI (1971), 263–270.

Brown, William Hill (1765–1793)

Novels: *The Power of Sympathy* (1789), *Ira and Isabella* (1807). See **8, 11, 168.**

2717 ARNER, Robert D. "Sentiment and Sensibility: The Role of Emotion and William Hill Brown's *The Power of Sympathy.*" *SAF,* I (1973), 121–132.

2718 BROWN, William Hill. *The Power of Sympathy.* Edited with an introduction by Herbert Ross Brown. Boston: New Frontiers Press, 1961.

2719 BROWN, William Hill. *The Power of Sympathy.* Edited by William S. Kable. Columbus: Ohio State Univ. Press, 1969.

2720 BYERS, John R., Jr. "Further Verification of the Authorship of *The Power of Sympathy.*" *AL,* XLIII (1971), 421–427.

2721 ELLIS, Milton. "The Author of the First American Novel." *AL,* IV (1933), 359–368.

2722 MCDOWELL, Tremaine. "The First American Novel." *Amer. Rev.* II (1933), 73–81.

2723 MARTIN, Terence. "William Hill Brown's *Ira and Isabella.*" *NEQ,* XXXII (1959), 238–242.

2724 WALSER, Richard. "More About the First American Novel." *AL,* XXIV (1952), 352–357.

Brown, William Wells (1816–1884)

Novel: *Clotel; or, The President's Daughter* (1853).

2725 BROWN, William Wells. *Clotel, or the President's Daughter.* Preface by Jean F. Yellin. New York: Arno Press, 1969.

2726 FARRISON, W. Edward. "Clotel, Thomas Jefferson, and Sally Hemings." *CLAJ,* XVII (1973), 147–174.

2727 FARRISON, William E. *William Wells Brown: Author & Reformer.* Chicago: Univ. of Chicago Press, 1969.

2728 HEERMANCE, J. Noel. *William Wells Brown and 'Clotelle': A Portrait of the Artist in the First Negro Novel.* Hamden, Conn.: Archon, 1969.

Eggleston, Edward (1837–1902)

Best-Known Novels: *The Hoosier School-Master* (1871), *The Circuit Rider* (1874), *Roxy* (1878), *The Graysons* (1888). See **8, 18,** and **114.**

2729 BENSON, Ronald M. "Ignoble Savage: Edward Eggleston and the American Indian." *Ill. Quart.*, XXXV (1973), 41–51.

2730 EGGLESTON, Edward. *The Circuit Rider: A Tale of the Heroic Age.* Introduction by Holman Hamilton. Lexington: Univ. Press of Kentucky, 1970.†

2731 EGGLESTON, Edward. *The Circuit Rider: A Tale of the Heroic Age.* Edited by William P. Randel. New Haven: College and University Press, 1966.†

2732 FLANAGAN, John T. "The Novels of Edward Eggleston." *CE,* V (1944), 250–254.

2733 JOHANNSEN, Robert W. "Literature and History: The Early Novels of Edward Eggleston." *IMH,* XLVIII (1952), 37–54.

2734 KAY, Donald. "Infant Realism in Eggleston's *The Hoosier Schoolmaster.*" *MarkhamR,* II (1971), 81–83.

2735 RANDEL, William Peirce. "Edward Eggleston (1837–1902)." *ALR,* I (1967), 36–38. [Bibliography.]

2736 RANDEL, William Peirce. *Edward Eggleston.* New York: Twayne, 1963.†

2737 RANDEL, William Peirce. *Edward Eggleston: Author of 'The Hoosier School-Master'.* New York: King's Crown Press, 1946.

2738 RANDEL, William Peirce. "Edward Eggleston's Minnesota Fiction." *MH,* XXXIII (1953), 189–193.

2739 SPENCER, Benjamin T. "The New Realism and a National Literature." *PMLA,* LVI (1941), 1116–1132.

2740 WILSON, Jack H. "Eggleston's Indebtedness to George Eliot in *Roxy.*" *AL,* XLII (1970), 38–49.

Fuller, Henry B. (1857–1929)

Best-Known Novels: *The Cliff-Dwellers* (1892), *With the Procession* (1895), and *From the Other Side* (1898). See **8.**

2741 ABEL, Darrel. "Expatriation and Realism in American Fiction in the 1880's: Henry Blake Fuller." *ALR,* III (1970), 245–257.

2742 BOWRON, Bernard R. *Henry B. Fuller of Chicago.* Contributions in American Studies, no. 11. Westport, Conn.: Greenwood Press, 1974.

2743 CHESHIRE, David, and BRADBURY, Malcolm. "American Realism and the Romance of Europe: Fuller, Frederic, Garland." *Perspectives in American History.* vol. IV. Cambridge: Charles Warren Center for Studies in American History, Harvard Univ., 1970, pp. 285–310.

2744 DUFFEY, Bernard. "Henry Fuller." *The Chicago Renaissance in American Letters.* East Lansing: Michigan State College Press, 1954, pp. 27–50.

2745 FULLER, Henry B. *With the Procession.* Introduction by Mark Harris. Chicago: Univ. of Chicago Press, 1965.†

2746 MURRAY, Donald M. "Henry B. Fuller: Friend of Howells." *SAQ*, LII (1953), 431–444.

2747 PILKINGTON, John. "Aftermath of a Novelist." *UMSE*, X (1968), 1–23.

2748 PILKINGTON, John. "Fuller and 'The Americanization of Europe's Youth'." *UMSE*, VIII (1967), 31–42.

2749 PILKINGTON, John. "Fuller, Garland, Taft, and the Art of the West." *PLL*, VIII (1972), 39–56.

2750 PILKINGTON, John. *Henry Blake Fuller*. (TUSAS 175.) New York: Twayne, 1971.

2751 PILKINGTON, John. "Henry Blake Fuller's Satire on Hamlin Garland." *UMSE*, VIII (1967), 1–6.

2752 SZUBERLA, Guy. "Making the Sublime Mechanical: Henry Blake Fuller's Chicago." *AmerS*, XIV (1973), 83–93.

2753 WILLIAMS, Kenny J. "Henry Blake Fuller (1857–1919)." *ALR*, III (1968), 9–13.

2754 WILSON, Edmund. "Two Neglected American Novelists: I—Henry B. Fuller: The Art of Making It Flat." *NY*, XLVI (May 23, 1970), 112–139.

Holmes, Oliver Wendell (1809–1894)

Novels: *Elsie Venner* (1861), *The Guardian Angel* (1867), *A Mortal Antipathy* (1885). See **3, 8, 18.**

2755 *The Psychiatric Novels of Oliver Wendell Holmes.* Ed. Clarence P. Oberndorf. New York: Columbia Univ. Press, 1944. Rev. ed., 1946. [Abridgements that emphasize the medical and psychiatric aspects of the novels.]

2756 *The Works of Oliver Wendell Holmes.* 13 vols. Boston: Houghton Mifflin, 1892. [Standard.]

2757 BOEWE, Charles. "Reflex Action in the Novels of Oliver Wendell Holmes." *AL*, XXVI (1954), 303–319.

2758 BROOKS, Van Wyck. "Dr. Holmes: Forerunner of the Moderns." *SRL*, XIV (June 27, 1936), 3–4, 13–15.

2759 KERN, Alexander C. "Dr. Oliver Wendall Holmes Today." *UKCR*, XIV (1948), 191–199.

2760 MENIKOFF, Barry. "Oliver Wendell Holmes." See **572**, pp. 207–228.

2761 RODITI, Edouard. "Oliver Wendell Holmes as Novelist." *ArQ*, I (1945), 23–33.

2762 SMALL, Miriam R. *Oliver Wendell Holmes.* New York: Twayne, 1962.†

2763 TILTON, Eleanor M. *Amiable Autocrat: A Biography of Dr. Oliver Wendell Holmes.* New York: H. Schuman, 1947.

2764 TILTON, Eleanor M., and CURRIER, Thomas Franklin. *Bibliography of Oliver Wendell Holmes.* New York: New York Univ. Press, 1953.

Kirkland, Joseph (1830–1894)

Best-Known Novels: Zury: The Meanest Man in Spring County (1887), The McVeys (1888), The Captain of Company K (1891). See 8.

2765 EICHELBERGER, Clayton L. "Edgar Watson Howe and Joseph Kirkland: More Critical Comment." ALR, IV (1971), 279–290. [Annotated checklists.]

2766 FLANAGAN, John T. "Joseph Kirkland, Pioneer Realist." AL, XI (1939), 273–284.

2767 HENSON, Clyde E. "Joseph Kirkland (1830–1894)." ALR, I (1967), 67–70. [Bibliography.]

2768 HENSON, Clyde E. Joseph Kirkland. New York: Twayne, 1962.†

2769 HENSON, Clyde E. "Joseph Kirkland's Influence on Hamlin Garland." AL, XXIII (1952), 458–463.

2770 HOLADAY, Clayton A. "Kirkland's Captain of Company K: A Twice-Told Tale." AL, XXV (1953), 62–68.

2771 KIRKLAND, Joseph. Zury: The Meanest Man in Spring County. Edited with an introduction by John T. Flanagan. Urbana: Univ. of Illinois Press, 1956.

2772 LA BUDDE, Kenneth J. "A Note on the Text of Joseph Kirkland's Zury." AL, XX (1949), 452–455.

2773 LEASE, Benjamin. "Realism and Joseph Kirkland's Zury." AL, XXIII (1952), 464–466.

2774 ROBERTS, Audrey J. "Two Additions to the Joseph Kirkland Canon." ALR, VI (1973), 252–254.

Paulding, James Kirke (1778–1860)

Best-Known Novels: Koningsmarke, the Long Finne (1823), The Dutchman's Fireside (1831), The Puritan and His Daughters (1849), Westward Ho! (1832). See 8.

2775 ADERMAN, Ralph M. "James Kirke Paulding on Literature and the West." AL, XXVII (1955), 97–101.

2776 ADERMAN, Ralph M., ed. The Letters of James Kirke Paulding. Madison: Univ. of Wisconsin Press, 1962.

2777 DAVIDSON, Frank. "Paulding's Treatment of The Angel of Hadley." AL, VII (1935), 330–332.

2778 DONDORE, Dorothy. "The Debt of Two Dyed-in-the-Wool Americans to Mrs. Grant's Memoirs: Cooper's Satanstoe, Paulding's The Dutchman's Fireside." AL, XII (1940), 52–58.

2779 GERBER, Gerald E. "James Kirke Paulding and the Image of the Machine." AQ, XXII (1970), 736–741.

2780 HEROLD, Amos L. James Kirke Paulding: Versatile American. New York: Columbia Univ. Press, 1926.

2781 PAULDING, James Kirke. The Dutchman's Fireside. Ed. Thomas F. O'Donnell. With introduction. New Haven: College and University Press, 1966.†

2782 TURNER, Arlin. "James K. Paulding and Timothy Flint." *MVHR*, XXXIV (1947), 105–111.

2783 WATKINS, Floyd C. "James Kirke Paulding and the South." *AQ*, V (1953), 219–230.

2784 WATKINS, Floyd C. "James Kirke Paulding's Creole Tale." *LHQ*, XXXIII (1950), 364–379.

Sinclair, Upton (1878–1968)

Best-Known Novels: *The Jungle* (1906), *Manassas* (1904), *The Money Changers* (1908), *The Brass Check* (1919), *Oil!* (1927), the "Lanny Budd" novels (1940–1953). See **8, 18, 105, 146, 198.**

2785 ALLATT, Edward. "Jack London and Upton Sinclair." *Jack London Newsletter,* I (1968), 22–27.

2786 *The Autobiography of Upton Sinclair.* New York: Harcourt, Brace, and World, 1962.

2787 BECKER, George J. "Upton Sinclair: Quixote in a Flivver." *CE*, XXI (1959), 133–140.

2788 BROOKS, Van Wyck. "The Novels of Upton Sinclair." *Emerson and Others.* New York: E. P. Dutton, 1927, pp. 209–217.

2789 DELL, Floyd. *Upton Sinclair: A Study in Social Protest.* New York: Doran, 1927.

2790 GOTTESMAN, Ronald. *Upton Sinclair: An Annotated Checklist.* Serif Series in Bibliography 24. With introduction. Kent, Ohio: Kent State Univ. Press, 1973.

2791 GOTTESMAN, Ronald, and SILET, Charles L. P. *The Literary Manuscripts of Upton Sinclair.* Columbus: Ohio State Univ. Press, 1972.

2792 GRENIER, Judson A. "Upton Sinclair: A Remembrance." *CHSQ*, XLVIII (1969), 165–169.

2793 GRENIER, Judson A. "Upton Sinclair and the Press: *The Brass Check* Reconsidered." *JQ*, XLIX (1972), 427–436.

2794 HICKS, Granville. "The Survival of Upton Sinclair." *CE*, IV (1943), 213–220.

2795 HITCHCOCK, Curtice N. "*The Brass Check.* . . ." *Journal of Political Economy, XXIX* (1921), 336–348.

2796 KOERNER, J. D. "The Last of the Muckrake Men." *SAQ*, LV (1956), 221–232.

2797 LIPPMANN, Walter. "Upton Sinclair." *SRL*, IV (1928), 641–643.

2798 QUINT, Howard H. "Upton Sinclair's Quest for Artistic Independence—1909." *AL*, XXIX (1957), 194–202.

2799 SODERBERGH, Peter A. "Upton Sinclair and Hollywood." *MQ*, XI (1970), 173–191.

Tourgée, Albion W. (1838–1905)

Best-Known Novels: *A Fool's Errand* (1879), *Bricks Without Straw* (1880), *Hot Plowshares* (1883). See **8, 18, 130, 146.**

2800 BECKER, George J. "Albion W. Tourgée: Pioneer in Social Criticism." *AL*, XIX (1947), 59–72.

2801 DIBBLE, Roy Floyd. *Albion W. Tourgée*. New York: Lemcke & Buechner, 1921.

2802 FRANKLIN, John Hope, ed. *A Fool's Errand*. Cambridge: Harvard Univ. Press, 1961.

2803 GROSS, Theodroe L. *Albion W. Tourgée*. New York: Twayne, 1963.†

2804 MAGDOL, Edward. "A Note of Authenticity: Eliab Hill and Nimbus Ware in *Bricks Without Straw*." *AQ*, XXII (1970), 907–911.

2805 OLSEN, Otto H. *Carpetbagger's Crusade: The Life of Albion Winegar Tourgée*. Baltimore: Johns Hopkins Press, 1965.

2806 TOURGÉE, Albion W. *A Fool's Errand*. Introduction by George M. Frederickson. New York: Harper & Row, 1966.†

2807 TOURGÉE, ALBION W. *Bricks Without Straw*. Introduction by Otto H. Olsen. Baton Rouge: Louisiana State Univ. Press, 1969.

Woolson, Constance Fenimore (1840–1894)

Best-Known Novels: *Anne* (1883), *East Angels* (1886), *Horace Chase* (1894). See **8**.

2808 BROOKS, Van Wyck. "The South: Constance Fenimore Woolson." See **35**.

2809 HELMICK, Evelyn T. "Constance Fenimore Woolson: First Novelist of Florida." *Carrell*, X (1969), 8–18.

2810 KERN, John Dwight. *Constance Fenimore Woolson, Literary Pioneer*. Philadelphia: Univ. of Pennsylvania Press, 1934.

2811 MOORE, Rayburn S. "Constance Fenimore Woolson (1840–1894)." *ALR*, III (1968), 36–38. [Bibliography.]

2812 MOORE, Rayburn S. *Constance Fenimore Woolson*. New York: Twayne, 1963†

2813 MOORE, Rayburn S., ed. *For the Major and Selected Short Stories*. With introduction. New Haven: College and University Press, 1967.†

2814 PATTEE, Fred Lewis. "Constance Fenimore Woolson and the South." *SAQ*, XXXVI (1939), 130–141.

2815 RICHARDSON, Lyon N. "Constance Fenimore Woolson, 'Novelist Laureate' of America." *SAQ*, XXXIX (1940), 18–36.

2816 SIMMS, L. Moody, Jr. "Constance Fenimore Woolson on Southern Literary Taste." *MissQ*, XXII (1969), 362–366.

SUPPLEMENT

The following material is supplementary to the bibliography proper. It brings the bibliography through 1976 for books and into 1976 for articles. It is arranged in the same general pattern as the bibliography proper and is numbered consecutively with it. All items in this supplement are included in the index.

Bibliographies

2817 EICHELBERGER, Clayton L., comp. *A Guide to Critical Reviews of United States Fiction, 1870–1910: Volume II.* Metuchen, N.J.: Scarecrow, 1974.

2818 GOHDES, Clarence. *Bibliographical Guide to the Study of the Literature of the U.S.A.* 4th ed. Durham, N.C.: Duke Univ. Press, 1976.

2819 KIRBY, David K. *American Fiction to 1900: A Guide to Information Sources.* Detroit: Gale Research, 1975.

2820 KOLB, Harold H., Jr. *A Field Guide to the Study of American Literature.* Charlottesville: Univ. Press of Va., 1976.

2821 LEARY, Lewis. with AUCHARD, John. *American Literature: A Study and Research Guide.* New York: St. Martin's Press, 1976.

Special Studies of the American Novel

2822 CAMERON, Kenneth Walter. "Defining the American Transcendental Novel." *ATQ,* XX supp. (1973), 114–122.

2823 DOUBLEDAY, Neal Frank. *Variety of Attempt: British and American Fiction in the Early Nineteenth Century.* Lincoln: Univ. of Nebraska Press, 1976.

2824 DUUS, Louise. "Neither Saint Nor Sinner: Women in Late Nineteenth-Century Fiction." *ALR,* VII (1974), 276–278.

2825 FRYER, Judith. *The Faces of Eve: Women in the Nineteenth Century American Novel.* New York: Oxford Univ. Press, 1976.

2826 HENDERSON, Harry B., III. *Versions of the Past: The Historical Imagination in American Fiction.* New York: Oxford Univ. Press, 1974.

2827 SMITH, Henry Nash. "The Scribbling Women and the Cosmic Success Story." *CritI,* I (1974), 47–70.

2828 STOUT, Janis P. *Sodoms in Eden: The City in American Fiction Before 1860.* Westport, Conn.: Greenwood Press, 1976.

2829 TANNER, Tony. "Problems and Roles of the American Artist as Portrayed by the American Novelist." *PBA,* LVII (1971), 159–179.

Major American Novelists

For each author, entries are arranged in the following order: Texts, Bibliography, Biographical and Critical Books, Critical Essays.

Bellamy, Edward

2830 CORNET, Robert J. "Rhetorical Strategies in *Looking Backward.*" *MarkhamR,* IV (1974), 53–58.

Brown, Charles Brockden

2831 *The Novels and Related Works of Charles Brockden Brown.* Vol. I: *Wieland* and "Memoirs of Carwin." Ed. Sydney J. Krause. Kent, Ohio: Kent State Univ. Press, 1977.

2832 WITHERINGTON, Paul. "Charles Brockden Brown: A Bibliographical Essay." *EAL,* IX (1974), 164–187.

2833 ALDERSON, Evan. "To Reconcile with Common Maxims: Edgar Huntley's Ruses." *PCP,* X (1975), 5–9.

2834 BELL, Michael D. " 'The Double-Tongued Deceiver': Sincerity and Duplicity in the Novels of Charles Brockden Brown." *EAL,* IX (1974), 143–163.

2835 CLEMAN, John. "Ambiguous Evil: A Study of Villains and Heroes in Charles Brockden Brown's Major Novels." *EAL,* X (1975), 190–219.

2836 FRANKLIN, Wayne. "Tragedy and Comedy in Brown's *Wieland.*" *Novel,* VIII (1975), 147–163.

2837 HEDGES, William L. "Charles Brockden Brown and the Culture of Contradictions." *EAL,* IX (1974), 107–142.

2838 NELSON, Carl. "A Method for Madness: The Symbolic Patterns in *Arthur Mervyn.*" *WVUPP,* XXII (1975), 29–50.

2839 REID, S. W. "Brockden Brown in England: Notes on Henry Colburn's 1822 Editions of His Novels." *EAL,* IX (1974), 188–195.

2840 RODGERS, Paul C., Jr. "Brown's *Ormond:* The Fruits of Improvisation." *AQ,* XXVI (1974), 4–22.

2841 SOLDATI, Joseph A. "The Americanization of Faust: A Study of Charles Brockden Brown's *Wieland.*" *ESQ,* LXXIV (1974), 1–14.

2842 WEIDMAN, Bette S. "White Men's Red Man: A Penitential Reading of Four American Novels." *MLS,* IV (1974), 14–26.

2843 WITHERINGTON, Paul. "Charles Brown's Other Novels: *Clara Howard* and *Jane Talbot. NCF,* XXIX (1974), 257–272.

Cable, George Washington

2844 CAMPBELL, Michael L. "The Negro in Cable's *The Grandissimes." MissQ,* XXVII (1974), 165–178.

2845 CLEMAN, John. "The Art of Local Color in George W. Cable's *The Grandissimes." AL,* XLVII (1975), 396–410.

2846 EATON, Richard Bozman. "George W. Cable and the Historical Romance." *SLJ,* VIII (1975), 84–94.

2847 EVANS, William. "French-English Literary Dialect in *The Grandissimes." AS,* XLVI (1971), 210–222.

2848 RUBIN, Louis D., Jr. "Politics and the Novel: George W. Cable and the Genteel Tradition." *William Elliott Shoots a Bear: Essays on the Southern Literary Imagination.* Baton Rouge: Louisiana State Univ. Press, 1975, pp. 61–81.

Chesnutt, Charles Waddell

2849 SEDLACK, Robert P. "The Evolution of Charles Chesnutt's *The House Behind the Cedars." CLAJ,* XIX (1975), 125–135.

Clemens, Samuel L. ("Mark Twain")

2850 GALE, Robert L. *Plots and Characters in the Works of Mark Twain.* 2 vols. Hamden, Conn.: Archon, 1973.

2851 GEISMAR, Maxwell. *Mark Twain: An American Prophet.* Edited and abridged by Maxwell Geismar. New York: McGraw-Hill, 1973.

2852 GIBSON, William M. *The Art of Mark Twain.* New York: Oxford Univ. Press, 1976.

2853 KAPLAN, Justin. *Mark Twain and His World.* New York: Simon and Schuster, 1974.

2854 PETTIT, Arthur G. *Mark Twain and the South.* Lexington: Univ. Press of Kentucky, 1974.

2855 BEAVER, Harold. "Run, Nigger, Run: *Adventures of Huckleberry Finn* as a Fugitive Slave Narrative." *JAmS,* VIII (1974), 339–361.

2856 BURG, David F. "Another View of *Huckleberry Finn." NCF,* XXIX (1974), 299–319.

2857 COLLINS, Billy G. "Huckleberry Finn: A Mississippi Moses." *JNT,* V (1975), 86–104.

2858 DAVID, Beverly R. "The Pictorial *Huck Finn:* Mark Twain and His Illustrator, E. W. Kemble." *AQ,* XXVI (1974), 331–351.

2859 DOUGLAS, Ann. "Art and Advertising in *A Connecticut Yankee:* The 'Robber Baron' Revisited." *CRevAS,* VI (1975), 182–195.

2860 DURAM, James C. "Mark Twain and the Middle Ages." *Wichita State Univ. Bull.,* XLVII (1971), 3–16.

2861 GARGANO, James W. *"Pudd'nhead Wilson:* Mark Twain as Genial Satan." *SAQ,* LXXIV (1975), 365–375.

2862 GASTON, Georg Meri-Akri. "The Function of Tom Sawyer in *Huckleberry Finn.* " *MissQ,* XXVII (1973–74), 33–39.

2863 GRIFFITH, Clark. "Merlin's Grin: From 'Tom' to 'Huck' in *A Connecticut Yankee.* " *NEQ,* XLVIII (1975), 28–46.

2864 HARRELL, Don W. "Mark Twain's *Joan of Arc:* Fact or Fiction?" *MarkhamR,* IV (1975), 95–97.

2865 KLASS, Philip. "An Innocent in Time: Mark Twain in King Arthur's Court." *Extrapolation,* XVI (1974), 17–32.

2866 MANN, Karen B. "Pudd'nhead Wilson: One Man or Two?" *RS,* XLII (1974), 175–181.

2867 SAWEY, Orlan. "The Consistency of the Character of Nigger Jim in *Huckleberry Finn.* " *TAIUS* (Texas A&I), IV (1971), 35–41.

2868 TOWERS, Tom H. " 'I Never Thought We Might Want to Come Back': Strategies of Transcendence in *Tom Sawyer.* " *MFS,* XXI (1975), 509–520.

2869 WADLINGTON, Warwick. *The Confidence Game in American Literature.* Princeton: Princeton Univ. Press, 1975.

Cooper, James Fenimore

2870 DEKKER, George, and MCWILLIAMS, John P., eds. *Fenimore Cooper: The Critical Heritage.* London: Routledge & K. Paul, 1973.

2871 NEVIUS, Blake. *Cooper's Landscapes: An Essay on the Picturesque Vision.* Berkeley: Univ. of Calif. Press, 1976.

2872 COSGROVE, William E. "Family Lineage and Narrative Pattern in Cooper's Littlepage Trilogy." *ForumH,* XII (1974), 2–8.

2873 FINK, Robert A. "Harvey Birch: The Yankee Peddler as an American Hero." *NYFQ,* XXX (1974), 137–152.

2874 KLIGERMAN, Jack. "Style and Form in James Fenimore Cooper's *Homeward Bound* and *Home as Found.* " *JNT,* IV (1974), 45–61.

2875 RINGE, Donald A. "Cooper's *Lionel Lincoln:* The Problem of Genre." *ATQ,* XXIV (1974), 24–30.

2876 ROSS, Morton L. "Cooper's *The Pioneers* and the Ethnographic Impulse." *AmerS,* XVI (1975), 29–39.

2877 TANNER, James. "A Possible Source for *The Prairie.* " *AL,* XLVII (1975), 102–104.

2878 VANCE, William L. " 'Man and Beast': The Meaning of Cooper's *The Prairie.*" *PMLA,* LXXXIX (1974), 323–331.

2879 WEIDMAN, Bette S. "White Men's Red Man: A Penitential Reading of Four American Novels." See **2842.**

Crane, Stephen

2880 COPPA, Joseph. "Stephen Crane Bibliography." *Thoth,* XIII (1974), 45–46.

2881 LAFRANCE, Marston. "Stephen Crane Scholarship Today and Tomorrow." *ALR,* VII (1974), 125–135.

2882 BERGON, Frank. *Stephen Crane's Artistry.* New York: Columbia Univ. Press, 1975.

2883 BURHANS, Clinton S., Jr. "Judging Henry Judging: Point of View in *The Red Badge of Courage.*" *BSUF,* XV (1974), 38–48.

2884 BURHANS, Clinton S., Jr. "Twin Lights on Henry Fleming: Structural Parallels in *The Red Badge of Courage.*" *ArQ,* XXX (1974), 149–159.

2885 FINE, David M. "Abraham Cahan, Stephen Crane, and the Romantic Tenement Tale of the Nineties." *AmerS,* XIV (1974), 95–107.

2886 GOLLIN, Rita K. " 'Little Souls Who Thirst for Fight' in *The Red Badge of Courage.*" *ArQ,* XXX (1974), 111–118.

2887 KARLEN, Arno. "The Craft of Stephen Crane." *GaR,* XXVIII (1974), 470–484.

2888 MAYNARD, Reid. "Red as Leitmotiv in *The Red Badge of Courage.*" *ArQ,* XXX (1974), 135–141.

2889 RECHNITZ, Robert M. "Depersonalization and the Dream in *The Red Badge of Courage.*" *SNNTS,* VI (1974), 76–87.

2890 SIMONEAUX, Katherine G. "Color Imagery in Crane's *Maggie: A Girl of the Streets.*" *CLAJ,* XVIII (1974), 91–100.

2891 VAN METER, Jan. "Sex and War in *The Red Badge of Courage:* Cultural Themes and Literary Criticism." *Genre,* VII (1974), 71–90.

2892 ZAMBRANO, Ana Laura. "The Role of Nature in *The Red Badge of Courage.*" *ArQ,* XXX (1974), 164–166.

Frederic, Harold

2893 O'DONNELL, Thomas F., GARNER, Stanton, and WOODWARD, Robert H., comps. *A Bibliography of Writings by and about Harold Frederic.* Boston: Hall, 1975.

2894 DONALDSON, Scott. "The Seduction of Theron Ware." *NCF,* XXIX (1975), 441–452.

2895 LECLAIR, Thomas. "The Ascendant Eye: A Reading of *The Damnation of Theron Ware.*" *SAF,* III (1975), 95–102.

2896 LUEDTKE, Luther S. "Harold Frederic's Satanic Soulsby: Interpretation and Sources." *NCF,* XXX (1975), 82–104.

2897 O'DONNELL, Thomas F. "Theron Ware, the Irish Picnic, and *Comus.*" *AL,* XLVI (1975), 528–537.

2898 REES, John O. "Dead Men's Bones, Dead Men's Beliefs: Ideas of Antiquity in Upstate New York and *Theron Ware.*" *AmerS,* XVI (1975), 77–87.

2899 SPANGLER, George M. "Theron Ware and the Perils of Relativism." *CRevAS,* V (1974), 36–46.

Glasgow, Ellen

2900 INGE, M. Thomas, ed. *Ellen Glasgow: Centennial Essays.* Charlottesville: Univ. Press of Virginia, 1976. [Essays by Howard Mumford Jones, Edgar E. Mac-Donald, Dorothy Scura, F. P. W. McDowell, C. Hugh Holman, Blair Rouse, and Monique Parent Frazee.]

2901 DUNN, N. E. "Ellen Glasgow: The Great Tradition and the New Morality." *CLQ,* XI (1975), 98–115.

2902 HOLMAN, C. Hugh. "Ellen Glasgow and History: *The Battleground.*" *Prospects: An Annual of American Cultural Studies,* Vol. II. Ed. Jack Salzman. New York: Burt Franklin, 1976, pp. 385–398.

2903 MACDONALD, Edgar E. "Glasgow, Cabell, and Richmond." *MissQ,* XXVII (1974), 393–413.

2904 MURR, Judy Smith. "History in *Barren Ground* and *Vein of Iron:* Theory, Structure, and Symbol." *SLJ,* VIII (1975), 39–54.

2905 PAYNE, Ladell. "Ellen Glasgow's Vein of Iron: Vanity, Irony, Idiocy." In *Inter-culture: A Collection of Essays and Creative Writing Commemorating the Twen-tieth Anniversary of the Fulbright Program at the Institute of Translation and Interpretation, Univ. of Vienna (1955–1974),* edited by Sy Kahn and Martha Raetz. Vienna: Braumüller, 1974, pp. 260–267.

2906 RAPER, J. R. "Glasgow's Psychology of Deceptions and *The Sheltered Life.*" *SLJ,* VIII (1975), 27–38.

2907 STEELE, Oliver. "Ellen Glasgow's *Virginia:* Preliminary Notes." *SB,* XXVII (1974), 265–289.

Hawthorne, Nathaniel

2908 AXELSSON, Arne. *The Links in the Chain: Isolation and Interdependence in Nathaniel Hawthorne's Fictional Characters.* (AUUSAU 17.) Uppsala: Univer-sitetsbiblioteket, 1974.

2909 BAYM, Nina. *The Shape of Hawthorne's Career.* Ithaca, N.Y.: Cornell Univ. Press, 1976.

2910 ABRAHAMSSON, Hans. "The Main Characters of Hawthorne's *The Scarlet Letter* and Their Interrelationships." *MSpr,* LXVIII (1974), 337–348.

2911 BABIIHA, Thaddeo Kitasimbwa. "James's *Washington Square:* More on the Hawthorne Relation." *NHJ* 1974, 270–272.

2912 BALES, Kent. "The Allegory and the Radical Romantic Ethic of *The Blithedale Romance.*" *AL,* XLVI (1974), 41–53.

2913 BAYM, Nina. "Hawthorne's Gothic Discards: *Fanshawe* and 'Alice Doane'." *NHJ* 1974, 105–115.

2914 BERTHOLD, Dennis. "Hawthorne, Ruskin, and the Gothic Revival: Transcendent Gothic in *The Marble Faun.*" *ESQ*, LXXIV (1974), 15–32.

2915 BRUMM, Ursula. "Hawthorne's 'The Custom House' and the Problem of Point of View in Historical Fiction." *Anglia*, XCIII (1975), 391–412.

2916 BYERS, John R., Jr. "*The House of the Seven Gables* and 'The Daughters of Dr. Byles': A Probable Source." *PMLA*, LXXXIX (1974), 174–177.

2917 COX, James M. "*The Scarlet Letter:* Through the Old Manse and the Custom House." *VQR*, LI (1975), 432–447.

2918 CURRAN, Ronald T. "The Reluctant Yankee in Hawthorne's Abortive Gothic Romances." *NHJ* 1974, pp. 179–194.

2919 DAMERON, J. Lasley. "Hawthorne and the *Edinburgh Review* on the Prose Romance." *NHJ* 1975, pp. 170–176.

2920 DOHERTY, Joseph F. "Hawthorne's Communal Paradigm: The American Novel Reconsidered." *Genre*, VII (1974), 30–53.

2921 EAKIN, Paul John. *The New England Girl: Cultural Ideals in Hawthorne, Stowe, Howells, and James.* Athens: Univ. of Georgia Press, 1976.

2922 EHRENPREIS, Anne H. "Elizabeth Gaskell and Nathaniel Hawthorne." *NHJ* 1973, pp. 89–119.

2923 ESTRIN, Mark W. " 'Triumphant Ignominy': *The Scarlet Letter* on Screen." *LFQ*, II (1974), 110–122.

2924 FLECK, Richard F. "Industrial Imagery in *The House of the Seven Gables.*" *NHJ* 1974, pp. 273–276.

2925 GOLLIN, Rita K. "Painting and Character in *The Marble Faun.*" *ESQ*, XXI (1975), 1–10.

2926 GREENWOOD, Douglas. "The Heraldic Device in *The Scarlet Letter:* Hawthorne's Symbolic Use of the Past." *AL*, XLVI (1974), 207–210.

2927 HANSEN, Elaine Tuttle. "Ambiguity and the Narrator in *The Scarlet Letter.*" *JNT*, V (1975), 147–163.

2928 JANSSEN, James G. "Pride and Prophecy: The Final Irony of *The Scarlet Letter.*" *NHJ* 1975, pp. 241–247.

2929 JARRETT, David W. "Hawthorne and Hardy as Modern Romancers." *NCF*, XXVIII (1974), 458–471.

2930 JOYNER, Nancy. "Bondage in Blithedale." *NHJ* 1975, pp. 227–231.

2931 JUSTUS, James H. "Hawthorne's Coverdale: Character and Art in *The Blithedale Romance.*" *AL*, XLVII (1975), 21–36.

2932 KEHLER, Joel R. "*The House of the Seven Gables:* House, Home, and Hawthorne's Psychology of Habitation." *ESQ*, XXI (1975), 142–153.

2933 LEVY, Leo B. "The Notebook Source and the 18th Century Context of Hawthorne's Theory of Romance." *NHJ* 1973, pp. 120–129.

2934 MAGRETTA, Joan. "The Coverdale Translation: *Blithedale* and the Bible." *NHJ* 1974, pp. 250–256.

2935 MANN, Charles W. "D. H. Lawrence: Notes on Reading Hawthorne's *The Scarlet Letter.*" *NHJ* 1973, pp. 8–25.

2936 MAY, Charles E. "Pearl as Christ and Antichrist." *ATQ*, XXIV supp. 1 (1974), pp. 8–11.

2937 MOSS, Sidney P. "Hawthorne and Melville: An Inquiry into Their Art and the Mystery of Their Friendship." *LMonog*, VII (1975), 45–84.

2938 OWENS, Louis. "Paulding's 'The Dumb Girl,' a Source of *The Scarlet Letter.*" *NHJ* 1974, pp. 240–249.

2939 ST. ARMAND, Barton L. "The Golden Stain of Time: Ruskinian Aesthetics and the Ending of Hawthorne's *The House of the Seven Gables.*" *NHJ* 1973, pp. 143–153.

2940 SANDERLIN, Reed. "Hawthorne's *Scarlet Letter:* A Study of the Meaning of Meaning." *SHR*, IX (1975), 145–157.

2941 SATTELMEYER, Robert. "The Aesthetic Background of Hawthorne's *Fanshawe.*" *NHJ* 1975, pp. 200–209.

2942 STERNE, Richard Clark. "Hawthorne's Politics in *The House of the Seven Gables.*" *CRevAS*, VI (1975), 74–83.

2943 STONE, Edward. "Hawthorne's House of Pyncheon: A Theory of American Drama." In *Artful Thunder: Versions of the Romantic Tradition in American Literature in Honor of Howard P. Vincent*, edited by Robert J. DeMott and Sanford E. Marovitz. Kent: Kent State Univ. Press, 1975, pp. 69–84.

2944 WARD, Joseph A. "Self-Revelation in *The Scarlet Letter.*" *RUS*, LXI (1975), 141–150.

2945 WHEELER, Otis B. "Love Among the Ruins: Hawthorne's Surrogate Religion." *SoR*, X (1974), 535–565.

2946 WHITFORD, Kathryn. *"The Blithedale Romance:* Hawthorne's *Reveries of a Bachelor."* *Thoth*, XV (1974–75), 19–28.

2947 YODER, R. A. "Transcendental Conservatism and *The House of the Seven Gables.*" *GaR*, XXVIII (1974), 33–51.

Howells, William Dean

2948 VANDERBILT, Kermit. "Howells Studies: Past, or Passing, or to Come." *ALR*, VII (1974), 143–153.

2949 CADY, Edwin H., ed. *W. D. Howells as Critic.* London: Routledge & K. Paul, 1973.

2950 CROW, Charles L. "Howells and William James: 'A Case of Metaphantasmia' Solved." *AQ*, XXVII (1975), 169–177.

2951 CROWLEY, John W. "Howells' *Questionable Shapes:* From Psychologism to Psychic Romance." *ESQ*, XXI (1975), 169–178.

2952 EAKIN, Paul John. *The New England Girl: Cultural Ideals in Hawthorne, Stowe, Howells, and James.* See **2921.**

2953 ESCHHOLZ, Paul A. "The Landlord at Lion's Head: William Dean Howells' Use of the Vermont Scene." *Vermont History*, XLII (1974), 44–47.

2954 HILTON, Earl. "Howells's *The Shadow of a Dream* and Shakespeare." *AL*, XLVI (1974), 220–222.

2955 KAZIN, Alfred. "Howells the Bostonian." *ClioW*, III (1974), 219–234.

2956 PERKINS, George. "*A Modern Instance:* Howells' Transition to Artistic Maturity." *NEQ,* XLVII (1974), 427–439.

2957 SEE, Fred G. "The Demystification of Style: Metaphoric and Metonymic Language in *A Modern Instance.*" *NCF,* XXVIII (1974), 379–403.

2958 TOTH, Susan Allen. "Character and Focus in *The Landlord at Lion's Head.*" *CLQ,* XI (1975), 116–128.

2959 WELLS, Gerald K. "The Phoenix Symbol in *The Rise of Silas Lapham.*" *SAB,* XL (1975), 10–14.

James, Henry

2960 *The Letters of Henry James: Vol. II, 1875–1883.* Ed. Leon Edel. Cambridge: Harvard Univ. Press, 1976.

2961 RICKS, Beatrice. *Henry James: A Bibliography of Secondary Works.* Metuchen, N.J.: Scarecrow, 1975.

2962 LEEMING, Glenda. *Who's Who in Henry James.* New York: Taplinger Pub., 1976.

2963 AUCHINCLOSS, Louis. *Reading Henry James.* Minneapolis: Univ. of Minnesota Press, 1975.

2964 BROOKS, Peter. *The Melodramatic Imagination: Balzac, Henry James, Melodrama and the Mode of Excess.* New Haven: Yale Univ. Press, 1976.

2965 GRAHAM, Kenneth. *Henry James: The Drama of Fulfilment: An Approach to the Novels.* New York: Oxford Univ. Press, 1975.

2966 GROVER, Philip. *Henry James and the French Novel: A Study in Inspiration.* New York: Barnes & Noble, 1973.

2967 JONES, Granville. *Henry James's Psychology of Experience: Innocence, Responsibility, and Renunciation in the Fiction of Henry James.* The Hague: Mouton, 1975.

2968 MACKENZIE, Manfred. *Communities of Honor and Love in Henry James.* Cambridge: Harvard Univ. Press, 1976.

2969 MOORE, Harry T. *Henry James and His World.* New York: Viking, 1974.

2970 ROWE, John Carlos. *Henry Adams and Henry James: The Emergence of a Modern Consciousness.* Ithaca, N.Y.: Cornell Univ. Press, 1976.

2971 SCHNEIDER, Daniel J. *Symbolism: The Manichean Vision: A Study in the Art of James, Conrad, Woolf, & Stevens.* Lincoln: Univ. of Nebraska Press, 1975.

2972 VEEDER, William. *Henry James—the Lessons of the Master: Popular Fiction and Personal Style in the Nineteenth Century.* Chicago: Univ. of Chicago Press, 1975.

2973 WALLACE, Ronald. *Henry James and the Comic Form.* Ann Arbor: Univ. of Michigan Press, 1975.

2974 YEAZELL, Ruth Bernard. *Language and Knowledge in the Late Novels of Henry James.* Chicago: Univ. of Chicago Press, 1976.

2975 BABIIHA, Thaddeo Kitasimbwa. "James's *Washington Square:* More on the Hawthorne Relation." See **2911.**

2976 BAŠIĆ, Sonja. "Love and Politics in *The Bostonians:* A Note on Motivation." *SRAZ,* XXXIII-XXXVI (1972–73), 293–303.

2977 BELLRINGER, Alan W. *"The Sacred Fount:* The Scientific Method." *EIC,* XXII (1972), 244–264.

2978 BIRJE-PATIL, J. *"The Beast in the Jungle* and *Portrait of a Lady."* *LCrit,* XI (1975), 45–52.

2979 BOARDMAN, Arthur. "Mrs. Grose's Reading of *The Turn of the Screw."* *SEL,* XIV (1974), 619–635.

2980 COHEN, Sarah B. *"The Ambassadors:* A Comedy of Musing and Manners." *Studies in American Humor.* I (1974), 79–90.

2981 CROWLEY, Francis E. "Henry James' *The Beast in the Jungle* and *The Ambassadors."* *PsyR,* LXII (1975), 154–163.

2982 DONOGHUE, Denis. "The American Style of Failure." *SR,* LXXXII (1974), 407–432.

2983 EAKIN, Paul John. *The New England Girl: Cultural Ideals in Hawthorne, Stowe, Howells, and James.* See **2921.**

2984 FLETCHER, Pauline. "The Sense of Society in *The Ambassadors."* *ESA,* XVII (1974), 79–88.

2985 GIRLING, Harry K. "On Editing a Paragraph of *The Princess Casamassima."* *Lang&S,* VIII (1975), 243–263.

2986 GUSTAFSON, Judith A. *"The Wings of the Dove:* Or, A Gathering of Pigeons." *GyS,* III (1975), 13–19.

2987 HARRIS, Josephine. *"The Sacred Fount:* The Geometry in the Jungle." *MQR,* XIII (1974), 57–73.

2988 HARTSOCK, Mildred E. "Time for Comedy: The Late Novels of Henry James." *ES,* LVI (1975), 114–128.

2989 HARTSOCK, Mildred E. "Unintentional Fallacy: Critics and *The Golden Bowl."* *MLQ,* XXXV (1974), 272–288.

2990 HOILE, Christopher. "Lambert Strether and the Boaters—Tonio Kröger and the Dancers: Confrontation and Self-Acceptance." *CRCL,* II (1975), 243–261.

2991 JACOBSON, Marcia. "Literary Convention and Social Criticism in Henry James's *The Awkward Age."* *PQ,* LIV (1975), 633–646.

2992 JOHANNSEN, Robert R. "Two Sides of *Washington Square."* *SCR,* VI (1974), 60–65.

2993 JOHNSON, Lee Ann. "The Psychology of Characterization: James's Portraits of Verena Tarrant and Olive Chancellor." *SNNTS,* VI (1974), 295–303.

2994 KING, Mary J. "The Touch of the Earth: A Word and a Theme in *The Portrait of a Lady."* *NCF,* XXIX (1974), 345–347.

2995 KIRSCHKE, James J. "Henry James's Use of Impressionist Painting Techniques in *The Sacred Fount* and *The Ambassadors."* *Studies in the Twentieth Century,* XIII (1974), 83–116.

2996 KROOK, Dorothea. "Intentions and Intentions: The Problem of Intention and Henry James's *The Turn of the Screw."* *The Theory of the Novel: New Essays.* Ed. John Halperin. New York: Oxford Univ. Press, 1974, pp. 353–372.

2997 LING, Amy. "The Pagoda Image in Henry James's *The Golden Bowl."* *AL,* XLVI (1974), 383–388.

2998 LOHMANN, Christoph K. "Jamesian Irony and the American Sense of Mission." *TSLL,* XVI (1974), 329–347.

2999 MACKENZIE, Manfred. "A Theory of Henry James's Psychology." *YR,* LXIII (1974), 347–371.

3000 MACNAUGHTON, W. R. "The Narrator in Henry James's *The Sacred Fount.*" In *Literature and Ideas in America: Essays in Memory of Harry Hayden Clark,* edited by Robert Falk. Athens: Ohio Univ. Press, 1975, pp. 155–181.

3001 MACNAUGHTON, W. R. "Turning the Screw of Ordinary Human Virtue: The Governess and the First-Person Narrators." *CRevAS,* V (1974), 18–25.

3002 MARKS, Sita P. "A Silent Morality: Non-Verbal Expression in *The Ambassadors.*" *SAB,* XXXIX (1974), 102–106.

3003 MINNICK, Thomas L. " 'The Light of Deepening Experience' in the Major Novels of Henry James." *Rendezvous,* X (1975), 37–51.

3004 NETTELS, Elsa. "*The Portrait of a Lady* and the Gothic Romance." *SAB,* XXXIX (1974), 73–82.

3005 NETTELS, Elsa. "The Scapegoats and Martyrs of Henry James." *CLQ,* X (1974), 413–427.

3006 NETTELS, Elsa. "Vision and Knowledge in *The Ambassadors* and *Lord Jim.*" *ELT,* XVIII (1975), 181–193.

3007 NIEMTZOW, Annette. "Marriage and the New Woman in *The Portrait of a Lady.*" *AL,* XLVII (1975), 377–395.

3008 PAGE, Philip. "The Curious Narration of *The Bostonians.*" *AL,* XLVI (1974), 374–383.

3009 PEARCE, Howard D. "Henry James's Pastoral Fallacy." *PMLA,* XC (1975), 834–847.

3010 PEARCE, Howard D. "Witchcraft Imagery and Allusion in James's *Bostonians.*" *SNNTS,* VI (1974), 236–247.

3011 REYNOLDS, Larry J. "Henry James's New Christopher Newman." *SNNTS,* V (1973), 457–468.

3012 SCHNEIDER, Daniel J. "The Divided Self in the Fiction of Henry James." *PMLA,* XC (1975), 447–460.

3013 SCHNEIDER, Daniel J. "The Theme of Freedom in James's *The Tragic Muse.*" *ConnR,* VII (1974), 5–15.

3014 SEBOUHIAN, George. "The Transcendental Imagination of Merton Densher." *MLS,* V (1975), 35–45.

3015 SHELDEN, Pamela J. "Jamesian Gothicism: The Haunted Castle of the Mind." *SLitI,* VII (1974), 121–134.

3016 TINTNER, Adeline R. "James's Monologue for Ruth Draper and *The Tragic Muse:* A Parody of the 'Usurping Consciousness'." *SELit,* English Number, 1974, pp. 149–154.

3017 TOMLINSON, T. B. "An American Strength: James's *The Ambassadors.*" *CR,* XVII (1974), 38–58.

3018 WARD, Susan P. "Painting and Europe in *The American.*" *AL,* XLVI (1975), 566–573.

3019 WILSON, James D. "The Gospel according to Christopher Newman." *SAF,* III (1975), 83–88.

Melville, Herman

3020 BRANCH, Watson G., ed. *Melville: The Critical Heritage.* London: Routledge & K. Paul, 1974.

3021 FLIBBERT, Joseph. *Melville and the Art of Burlesque.* Amsterdam: Rodopi, 1974.

3022 GREJDA, Edward S. *The Common Continent of Men: Racial Equality in the Writings of Herman Melville.* Port Washington, N.Y.: Kennikat, 1974.

3023 MILLER, Edwin Haviland. *Melville.* New York: Braziller, 1975.

3024 MOORE, Maxine. *That Lonely Game: Melville, Mardi, and the Almanac.* University of Missouri Studies 63. Columbia: Univ. of Missouri Press, 1975.

3025 SEALTS, Merton M., Jr. *The Early Lives of Melville: Nineteenth-Century Biographical Sketches and Their Authors.* Madison: Univ. of Wisconsin Press, 1974.

3026 SWEENEY, Gerard M. *Melville's Use of Classical Mythology.* Amsterdam: Rodopi, 1975.

3027 ABRAMS, Robert E. "*Typee* and *Omoo:* Herman Melville and the Ungraspable Phantom of Identity." *ArQ,* XXXI (1975), 33–50.

3028 ADLER, Joyce. "Melville's *Benito Cereno:* Slavery and Violence in the Americas." *Science & Society,* XXXVIII (1974), 19–48.

3029 ALTSCHULER, Glenn C. "Whose Foot on Whose Throat? A Re-examination of Melville's *Benito Cereno.*" *CLAJ,* XVIII (1975), 383–392.

3030 AUSBAND, Stephen C. "The Whale and the Machine: An Approach to *Moby-Dick.*" *AL,* XLVII (1975), 197–211.

3031 BARBOUR, James. "The Composition of *Moby-Dick.*" *AL,* XLVII (1975), 343–360.

3032 BARBOUR, James. "The *Town-Ho's* Story: Melville's Original Whale." *ESQ,* XXI (1975), 111–115.

3033 BECK, Horace P. "Melville as a Folklife Recorder in *Moby-Dick.*" *KFQ,* XVIII (1973), 75–88.

3034 BERGSTROM, Robert F. "The Topmost Grief: Rejection of Ahab's Faith." *ELWIU,* II (1975), 171–180.

3035 BLAIR, John G. "Puns and Equivocation in Melville's *The Confidence Man.*" *ATQ,* XXII (1974), 91–95.

3036 COOK, Richard M. "The Grotesque and Melville's *Mardi.*" *ESQ,* XXI (1975), 103–110.

3037 EBERWEIN, Robert T. "The Impure Fiction of *Billy Budd.*" *SNNTS,* VI (1974), 318–326.

3038 FLECK, Richard F. "Stone Imagery in Melville's *Pierre.*" *RS,* XLII (1974), 127–130.

3039 HANDS, Charles B. "The Comic Entrance to *Moby-Dick.*" *CollL,* II (1975), 182–191.

3040 HENDRICKSON, John. "*Billy Budd:* Affirmation of Absurdity." *ReAL,* III (1969), 30–37.

3041 HERBERT, T. Walter, Jr. "Homosexuality and Spiritual Aspiration in *Moby-Dick.*" *CRevAS,* VI (1975), 50–58.

3042 IDOL, John L., Jr. "Ahab and the 'Siamese Connection'." *SCB,* XXXIV (1974), 156–159.

3043 JOSWICK, Thomas P. "*Typee:* The Quest for Origin." *Criticism,* XVII (1975), 335–354.

3044 KELLNER, R. Scott. "Sex, Toads, and Scorpions: A Study of the Psychological Themes in Melville's *Pierre.*" *ArQ,* XXXI (1975), 5–20.

3045 MCCARTHY, Paul. "Elements of Anatomy in Melville's Fiction." *SNNTS,* VI (1974), 38–61.

3046 MCDONALD, Walter R. "Ishmael: The Function of a Comic Mask." *CEA,* XXXVII (1975), 8–11.

3047 MCELROY, John H. "Cannibalism in Melville's *Benito Cereno.*" *ELWIU,* I (1974), 206–218.

3048 MCHANEY, Thomas L. "The *Confidence-Man* and Satan's Disguises in *Paradise Lost.*" *NCF,* XXX (1975), 200–206.

3049 MAROVITZ, Sanford E. "Old Man Ahab." See **2943,** pp. 139–161.

3050 MELDRUM, Barbara. "Structure in *Moby-Dick:* The Whale Killings and Ishmael's Quest." *ESQ,* XXI (1975), 162–168.

3051 MILDER, Robert. "Melville's 'Intentions' in *Pierre.*" *SNNTS,* VI (1974), 186–199.

3052 MULQUEEN, James E. "Ishmael's Voyage: The Cycle of Everyman's Faith." *ArQ,* XXXI (1975), 57–68.

3053 NECHAS, James W. "Ambiguity of Word and Whale: The Negative Affix in *Moby-Dick!*" *CollL,* II (1975), 198–225.

3054 OLDSEY, Bernard, ed. "Special Issue: *Moby-Dick.*" *CollL,* II (1975).

3055 QUIRK, Tom. "Saint Paul's Types of the Faithful and Melville's Confidence Man." *NCF,* XXVIII (1974), 472–477.

3056 ROSENBERRY, Edward H. "*Moby-Dick:* Epic Romance." *CollL,* II (1975), 155–170.

3057 ROSENTHAL, Bernard. "Melville's Island." *SSF,* XI (1974), 1–9. [On "Benito Cereno."]

3058 ROSS, Morton L. "*Moby-Dick* as an Education." *SNNTS,* VI (1974), 62–75.

3059 STEIN, Allen F. "Hawthorne's Zenobia and Melville's Urania." *ATQ,* XXVI supp. (1975), 11–18.

3060 STEIN, William Bysshe. "Melville's *The Confidence-Man:* Quicksands of the Word." *ATQ,* XXIV (1974), 38–50.

3061 STELZIG, Eugene L. "Romantic Paradoxes of *Moby-Dick.*" *ATQ,* XXVI supp. (1975), 41–44.

3062 STEN, Christopher W. "The Dialogue of Crisis in *The Confidence-Man:* Melville's 'New Novel'." *SNNTS,* VI (1974), 165–185.

3063 STEN, Christopher W. "Vere's Use of the 'Forms': Means and Ends in *Billy Budd.*" *AL,* XLVII (1975), 37–51.

3064 STONE, Edward. "The Function of the Gams in *Moby-Dick.*" *CollL,* II (1975), 171–181.

3065 STONE, Edward. "The Other Sermon in *Moby-Dick.*" *Costerus,* IV (1972), 215–222.

3066 STONE, Edward. "The Whiteness of the Whale." *CLAJ,* XVIII (1975), 348–363.

3067 STONE, Edward. "Whodunit? *Moby Dick!*" *JPC,* VIII (1974), 280–285.

3068 VAUGHT, Carl G. "Religion as a Quest for Wholeness: Melville's *Moby-Dick.*" *JGE,* XXVI (1974), 9–35.

3069 VITANZA, Victor J. "Melville's *Redburn* and Emerson's 'General Education of the Eye'." *ESQ,* XXI (1975), 40–45.

3070 WADLINGTON, Warwick. *The Confidence Game in American Literature.* Princeton: Princeton Univ. Press, 1975.

3071 WALLACE, Robert K. "*Billy Budd* and the Haymarket Hangings." *AL,* XLVII (1975), 108–113.

3072 WATSON, Charles N., Jr. "Melville's *Israel Potter:* Fathers and Sons." *SNNTS,* VII (1975), 563–568.

3073 WATSON, Charles N., Jr. "Premature Burial in *Arthur Gordon Pym* and *Israel Potter.*" *AL,* XLVII (1975), 105–107.

3074 WELSH, Howard. "The Politics of Race in 'Benito Cereno'." *AL,* XLVI (1975), 556–566.

3075 WILLIAMS, David. "Peeping Tommo: *Typee* as Satire." *CRevAS,* VI (1975), 36–49.

3076 YANNELLA, Donald J. " 'Seeing the Elephant' in *Mardi.*" See **2943**, pp. 105–117.

Norris, Frank

3077 CRISLER, Jesse S., and MCELRATH, Joseph R., Jr. *Frank Norris: A Reference Guide.* Boston: Hall, 1974.

3078 CROW, Charles L. "The Real Vanamee and His Influence on Frank Norris' *The Octopus.*" *WAL,* IX (1974), 131–139.

3079 DAVISON, Richard Allan. "Frank Norris' *The Octopus:* Some Observations on Vanamee, Shelgrim and St. Paul." See **3000**, pp. 181–203.

3080 FRIED, Lewis. "The Golden Brotherhood of *McTeague.*" *ZAA,* XXIII (1975), 36–40.

3081 GRAHAM, D. B. "Art in *McTeague.*" *SAF,* III (1975), 143–155.

3082 GRAHAM, D. B. "Frank Norris's Afternoon of a Faun." *PLL,* X (1974), 307–312.

3083 JOHNSON, Lee Ann. "Western Literary Realism: The California Tales of Norris and Austin." *ALR,* VII (1974), 278–280.

Poe, Edgar Allan

3084 HARP, Richard L. "A Note on the Harmony of Style and Theme in Poe's *Narrative of Arthur Gordon Pym.*" *CEA,* XXXVI (1974), 8–11.

3085 MOTTRAM, Eric. "Poe's *Pym* and the American Social Imagination." See **2943**, 25–53.

3086 RICHARD, Claude. "L'Ecriture d'Arthur Gordon Pym." *DeltaES,* I (1975), 95–124.

3087 RIDGELY, Joseph V. "Tragical-Mythical-Satirical-Hoaxical: Problems of Genre in *Pym.*" *ATQ,* XXIV (1974), 4–9.

3088 VITANZA, Victor J. "Edgar Allan Poe's *The Narrative of Arthur Gordon Pym:* An Anatomy of Perverseness." *EA,* XXVII (1974), 26–37.

3089 WATSON, Charles N., Jr. "Premature Burial in *Arthur Gordon Pym* and *Israel Potter.*" See **3073**.

Simms, William Gilmore

3090 MEATS, Stephen E., ed. *Joscelyn: A Tale of the Revolution.* The Writings of William Gilmore Simms: Centennial Edition 16. Text established by Keen Butterworth. Columbia: Univ. of South Carolina Press, 1975.

3091 *The Revolutionary War Novels.* With introduction and explanatory notes. 8 vols. Spartanburg, S.C.: The Reprint Company, 1976. [The seven Revolutionary Romances plus *Joscelyn,* reprinted from the Author's Revised Edition, with historical annotation.]

3092 COOK, George A. "Porgy Reexamined." *TAIUS* (Texas A&I), V (1972), 65–71.

3093 HOLMAN, C. Hugh. "Simms's Changing View of Loyalists During the Revolution." *MissQ,* XXIX (1976), 501–513.

3094 WEIDMAN, Bette S. "White Men's Red Man: A Penitential Reading of Four American Novels." See **2842**.

Stowe, Harriet Beecher

3095 HILDRETH, Margaret Holbrook. *Harriet Beecher Stowe: A Bibliography.* Hamden, Conn.: Shoe String Press, 1976.

3096 KIRKHAM, E. Bruce. *The Building of Uncle Tom's Cabin.* Knoxville: Univ. of Tenn. Press, 1977.

3097 ADAMS, John R. "Structure and Theme in the Novels of Harriet Beecher Stowe." *ATQ,* XXIV (1974), 50–55.

3098 BRANDSTADTER, Evan. "Uncle Tom and Archy Moore: The Antislavery Novel as Ideological Symbol." *AQ,* XXVI (1974), 160–175.

3099 EAKIN, Paul John. *The New England Girl: Cultural Ideals in Hawthorne, Stowe, Howells, and James.* See **2921**.

3100 HOVET, Theodore R. "Christian Revolution: Harriet Beecher Stowe's Response to Slavery and the Civil War." *NEQ,* XLVII (1974), 535–549.

3101 MCCONNELL, Frank D. "Uncle Tom & the Avant-Garde." *MR,* XVI (1975), 743–745.

3102 MILLER, Randall M. "Mrs. Stowe's Negro: George Harris' Negritude in *Uncle Tom's Cabin."* *CLQ,* X (1974), 521–526.

Wharton, Edith

3103 LAWSON, Richard H. *Edith Wharton and German Literature.* (SGAK 29.) Bonn: Bouvier, 1974.

3104 LEWIS, R. W. B. *Edith Wharton: A Biography.* New York: Harper & Row, 1975.

3105 LINDBERG, Gary H. *Edith Wharton and the Novel of Manners.* Charlottesville: Univ. Press of Virginia, 1975.

3106 WOLFF, Cynthia Griffin. *A Feast of Words: The Triumph of Edith Wharton.* New York: Oxford Univ. Press, 1977.

3107 AMMONS, Elizabeth. "The Business of Marriage in Edith Wharton's *The Custom of the Country."* *Criticism,* XVI (1974), 326–328.

3108 DAHL, Curtis. "Edith Wharton's *The House of Mirth:* Sermon on a Text." *MFS,* XXI (1975), 572–576.

3109 EVANS, Elizabeth. "Musical Allusions in *The Age of Innocence."* *NConL,* IV (1974), 4–7.

3110 MCDOWELL, Margaret B. "Viewing the Custom of Her Country: Edith Wharton's Feminism." *ConL,* XV (1974), 521–538.

3111 POTTER, Rosemary. "The Mistakes of Lily in *The House of Mirth."* *TAIUS* (Texas A&I), IV (1971), 89–93.

3112 ROBINSON, James A. "Psychological Determination in *The Age of Innocence."* *MarkhamR,* V (1975), 1–5.

3113 TINTNER, Adeline R. " 'The Hermit and the Wild Woman': Edith Wharton's 'Fictioning' of Henry James." *JML,* IV (1974), 32–42.

3114 WOLFF, Cynthia Griffin. "Lily Bart and the Beautiful Death." *AL,* XLVI (1974), 16–40.

Lesser American Novelists

Brackenridge, Hugh Henry

3115 HAIMS, Lynn. "Of Indians and Irishmen: A Note on Brackenridge's Use of Sources for Satire in *Modern Chivalry.*" *EAL,* X (1975), 88–92.

Eggleston, Edward

3116 UNDERWOOD, Gary N. "Toward A Reassessment of Edward Eggleston's Literary Dialects." *BRMMLA,* XXVIII (1974), 109–120.

Fuller, Henry B.

3117 SWANSON, Jeffrey. "A Checklist of the Writings of Henry Blake Fuller (1857–1929)." *ALR,* VII (1974), 211–243.

3118 SWANSON, Jeffrey. " 'Flesh, Fish or Fowl': Henry Blake Fuller's Attitudes Toward Realism and Romanticism." *ALR,* VII (1974), 195–210.

Holmes, Oliver Wendell

3119 GALLAGHER, Kathleen. "The Art of Snake Handling: *Lamia, Elsie Venner,* and 'Rappaccini's Daughter'." *SAF,* III (1975), 51–64.

3120 GARNER, Stanton. "Elsie Venner: Holmes's Deadly 'Book of Life'." *HLQ,* XXXVII (1974), 283–298.

3121 MARTIN, John Stephen. "The Novels of Oliver Wendell Holmes: A Re-Interpretation." See **3000**, pp. 111–127.

Paulding, James Kirke

3122 O'DONNELL, Thomas F. "*Koningsmarke:* Pauling vs. Scott in 1823." *ATQ,* XXIV (1974), 10–17.

3123 OWENS, Louis D. "James K. Paulding and the Foundations of American Realism." *BNYPL,* LXXIX (1975), 40–50.

INDEX

INDEX

INDEX

INDEX

INDEX

INDEX

INDEX

INDEX

INDEX

INDEX

INDEX

REF.
Z
1231
.F4
1979/24,800

CAMROSE LUTHERAN COLLEGE
Library

INDEX

NOTES

NOTES